Also available at all good book stores

9781785315282

9781785315077

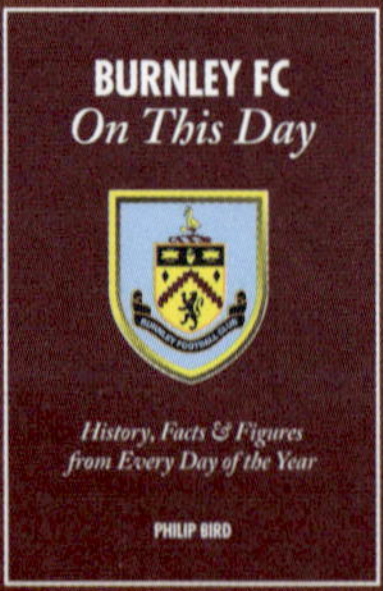

9781785314254

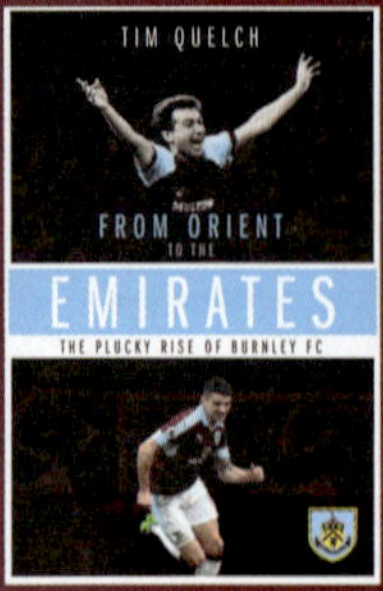

9781785313127

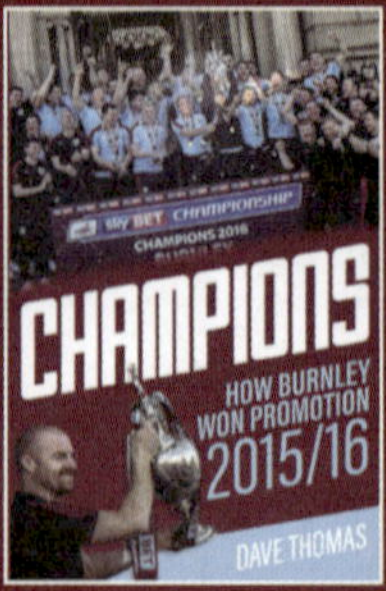

9781785312274

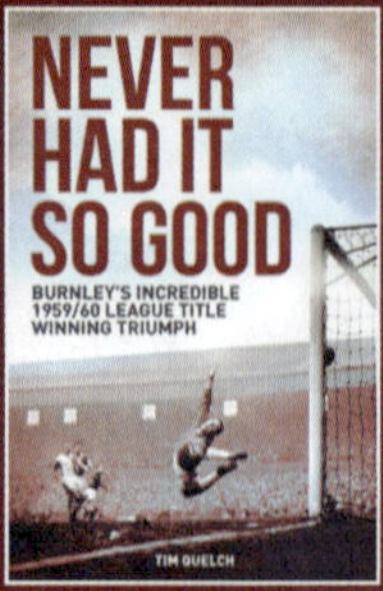

9781909626546

9781909626690

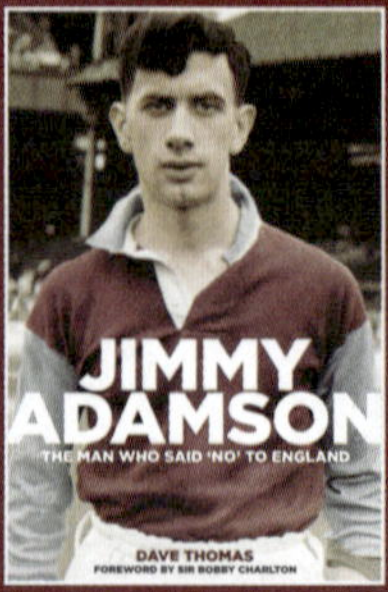

9781785314032

NOT SUCH A BAD LIFE

NOT SUCH A BAD LIFE

BURNLEY, GAZZA, WRIGHTY, WADDLE AND ME

PAUL WELLER

With Dave Thomas

pitch

First published by Pitch Publishing, 2021

Pitch Publishing
A2 Yeoman Gate
Yeoman Way
Worthing
Sussex
BN13 3QZ
www.pitchpublishing.co.uk
info@pitchpublishing.co.uk

A CIP catalogue record is available for this book from the British Library.

ISBN 978-1-78531-768-2

Typesetting and origination by Pitch Publishing

Printed and bound in India by Replika Press Pvt. Ltd.

CONTENTS

Dedicated to my family. My mother who worked so hard for us all. My dad who loved football. My wife Zoe who has put up with life with a footballer. And my two children Flynn and Imogen, growing up so well.

ACKNOWLEDGEMENTS AND THANKS

THE LONDON CLARETS supporters' group produce a wonderful magazine that goes back years. I have dipped into it frequently and thank its contributors: Andrew Firmin, Tim Quelch, Steve Corrigan, Barry Heagin, Igor Wowk, Phil Whalley, Eddie Lea and Julian Booth.

Steve and Jane at Tubbs Restaurant Colne: we met and consumed breakfasts, tea and coffee at Tubbs on an industrial scale. Steve is a Burnley fan; it helps. Great food.

Tony Scholes at the Up the Clarets website.

Author and former club historian Ray Simpson.

Bury author and historian James Bentley.

Dan Barnes at ClaretsTalk.

Robert Smith, for his help in digging up a mountain of old newspapers and articles.

Journalists: Chris Boden, Pete Oliver, Andy Jones and Dany Robson.

For sourcing photographs: Dan Black, Kelvin Stuttard and Adam Riding.

Players: Graham Branch, Gareth Taylor, Jamie Hoyland, Steve Davis, Glen Little, Tony Grant, Dean West, Andy Payton, Peter Swan, Gordon Armstrong and Luke Chadwick.

Former Burnley manager Stan Ternent.

The *Burnley Express* and the *Lancashire Telegraph*.

At Burnley Football Club: Darren Bentley and Adam Riding.

The *Under the Cosh* video interviews with Robbie Blake and Glen Little, viewable on YouTube.

John Gibaut, David Atkinson, Mark Griffiths and Winston Sutcliffe.

Paul and Jane Camillin, Dean Rockett and Graham Hales at Pitch Publishing.

Duncan Olner for the cover design.

PREFACE

From the Crohn's and Colitis UK website:
Crohn's Disease and Ulcerative Colitis are the two main forms of inflammatory bowel disease affecting more than 300,000 people in the UK. Yet they are largely hidden diseases causing stigma and isolation, with many victims suffering in silence and embarrassment. Many people suffer with the condition undiagnosed.

'It takes guts to talk about Colitis and Crohn's.'

'How you doing today?'

'Er fine.'

'Yeh fine.'

'I'm fine.'

'When you have Colitis or Crohn's a lot of the time you look fine.'

'But your body is attacking itself, it's like having a wound on the inside.'

'No one can see it.'

'No one can see what it's doing to you so no one understands how hard it is to get to work every morning.'

'No one can see my pain.'

'No one can see my embarrassment.'

'No one can see my exhaustion.'

'It's just easier to say I'm fine.'

'But actually, I'm struggling today.'

'I feel bad.'

'I'm too tired to do all the things everyone else does.'

'I'm afraid to do all the stuff my mates take for granted.'

'Being open about your condition isn't always easy to do and isn't always fun.'

'It takes guts to talk about Colitis and Crohn's and it can be hard to find the right time or the right words.'

'No one can see it until we talk about it, until we say it.'

'I have Colitis.'

'I have Crohn's.'

From the *Daily Express* Friday, 12 June 2020. Judge lets colostomy man, 30, die.

A man in his 30s who did not want to live with a colostomy bag has died after a judge ruled his life-support could end.

The hospital patient had a history of bowel problems and was ill and sedated after surgery.

Specialists said the man had a 60-70% chance of survival but needed a stoma, an opening in his abdomen with a bag attached for his bodily waste.

He feared it meant he would never find love or a job.

Bosses at the Hospital Foundation Trust asked the Court of Protection to decide what was best.

Mr Justice Hayden said, 'He made a calculation that life in these circumstances is not what he wanted.

'This is not a case about choosing to die; it is about an adult's capacity to shape and control the end of his life.'

Make no mistake, Colitis and Crohn's are serious.

FOREWORD

IN MY BOOK *Stan the Man*, I probably only mentioned Paul Weller two or three times, but that doesn't mean I didn't rate him.

In fact, quite the opposite. When I arrived at Burnley in 1998, he was one of maybe three or four decent players that I felt I could build a team around and I could count on. I wanted to achieve things at Turf Moor and identified Paul as one of the players that could help me with that. It took a while to do that but he was one of the players that was there through thick and thin.

He was fiery, dynamic, single-minded and reliable; and on top of that he could play a bit. What I didn't know was that he was in the very early stages of a potentially disastrous illness. So, if I didn't mention him much in *Stan the Man* let me make up for that here.

What I remember him for is his bravery and determination, not only on the field of play but also off it as he lay in a hospital bed, underwent three operations and then battled to recover to a normal life and playing career, after months out of the game. As the saying goes, it takes guts to come back from Colitis. To do that, and get back to sporting excellence, takes some doing.

Some players might have thrown in the towel, maybe drowned their sorrows in drink or suffered deep depression at the prospect of losing their livelihood. But not Paul Weller.

When he returned to fitness – and it was a long battle – then regained his place in the team, he went on to become Supporters' Player of the Year, scooping nearly all of the awards. That is an astonishing feat.

I used to visit him on a Sunday morning in hospital. He doesn't know that I always knew that the minute I left, he'd be on the phone to his pals to say, 'He's gone now, you can come in.'

One particular moment that I remember is the winning goal he scored in an away game at Oxford United in our promotion season. At that point he hadn't regained his first-team place and we were at loggerheads on account of me judging him not fully fit, and him insisting that he was. All he wanted to do was play, so I took him to Oxford and put him on the subs' bench. Being the feisty little so-and-so that he is, he bent my ear several times but it's a manager's job to decide whether or not a player is ready to play. To this day I still don't think he was 100 per cent but gave him his chance late in the game. He was desperate to play and that counts for a lot in my book.

In the dying seconds of the game he scored the winning goal. The crowd that had followed us went mad. So did Paul, along with Ian Wright who had laid on the cross. Wrighty always said the cross was inch-perfect. He was actually aiming for big Steve Davis who was thundering in behind Paul. Such is football.

Ian Wright at Turf Moor playing for Burnley. Paul has a few tales to tell about Ian and there are others about Chris Waddle and Gazza.

Ian was a livewire and the players loved him. He was worse than hyperactive. To keep fit he began to ride a bike from where he lived with Mitchell Thomas at Harle Syke, down to Gawthorpe where we trained. Trouble was, he had to ride it back after training. Mitch, by now back in the house in his car would get a phone call from Satch [Wright]. 'Mitch, I'm lost, come and find me.' But he wasn't lost, he was just knackered. Mitch would go and find him. He would ride the bike home and Ian would drive back in the car.

The first game he played, I drove down to the ground and parked up. There in the car park, was a huge Bentley Corniche with the registration 1 IW. I just looked at it disbelieving. 'OK gaffer,' he shouted out. 'You can't come in that,' I shouted back incredulous and wide-eyed. 'You can buy a whole street here for that.'

So next he turns up in a Ferrari, and it was one of those models where you can see the engine visible at the back. I used to wind him up. 'Can't you afford a car with an engine cover?'

Gazza [Paul Gascoigne] was even more hyper. He was one of the best players this country has ever produced. Again, the lads loved him despite never knowing what he would get up to next. Good trainer as well and he sometimes had the lads open-mouthed with his skills. A goalkeeper just an inch shorter would never have saved the two stupendous free kicks of his against Coventry in the last game of the season when just one more goal would have got us into the play-offs.

My manager style was, shall we say, aggressive and confrontational, but Paul was never afraid to stand up to me if he felt aggrieved. He left the club at the same time as me and I hadn't got round to extending his contract since I didn't expect to be leaving. If I hadn't left the club, his contract would have been renewed. 'If' – the biggest word in football. The new manager didn't want him.

Paul has filled this book with stories of the club and the players. Then there is the account of when he was ill and the long road back.

But, a word of caution. Many of the stories involve me and some of them are tall tales. Footballers love to exaggerate. Some of them are embroidered a wee bit especially after a few beers or a glass of wine. I gave most of the players hell. Glen Little was one and Glen is a born storyteller. He could make a living at it. I could write a book myself about him and Robbie Blake. Many's the time my head was spinning listening to Glen. Many a time he and his Mrs and his two kids would visit me at home. Those kids always ate me out of every biscuit in the house.

Paul's co-author Dave Thomas told me he spoke to a dozen players for this book and all of them had their fond memories and tales. Glen and Robbie could write their own books. Chris Waddle, Ian Wright and Gazza already have.

But, despite me treating them mercilessly, Dave also tells me that all of them spoke of me with warmth, affection and with a smile on their face. They always knew I wanted them to be the best, and for Burnley to be the best.

Paul ends his book with his 'best team'. He had many a go at me and me at him, but he made me 'best manager'.

Thanks Paul.

Stan Ternent
September 2020

INTRODUCTION

UNLESS YOU live in north-west Lancashire you won't know the name, Paul Weller. I was a footballer and most people won't know that either.

But people in Burnley and thereabouts should do. I played over 250 games for Burnley, but was never a star, was never a celebrity. I never had an extrovert bright red suit, bleached hair and a cane. If I'd ever turned up like that I'd have been thrown in the bath. Back then the fashion crime was wearing a shell suit. But they were cheap.

I never had a Bentley, or a garage with at least three sports cars in it, or a haircut that cost me three figures. But I did have a personalised number plate. I never had a huge gated mansion in leafy Cheshire with six bedrooms and *Hello* magazine features, or a trophy room.

I wasn't particularly tall so never headed spectacular goals like Peter Crouch; to start with I was a tricky winger with a decent turn of speed, but then they went out of fashion. I became a grafting wide midfield player.

It was drilled into you: 'Don't lose the fucking ball.' Where's the glamour in that? Glamour was in short supply at Burnley when I was there.

So, I was never one to do anything dazzling like a Glenn Hoddle. A nippy scuffler I suppose you could say. A worker, a grafter. But I was good at that. And I could pass a ball, short passes especially. I can't have been that bad; I was supporters' player of the year one season.

I was never feted or mobbed on red carpets and never earned huge sums like today's lads. Not that I begrudge them; few, if any, of us oldies are resentful. We did OK, made a living and enjoyed the life while it lasted.

Hmmm: while it lasted. I was disposed of via a phone call by a manager on the eve of my wedding. The eve of my wedding; think about that. It's the cold, callous side of football. Bills to pay, a car to run, a house to furnish. How?

Now I sell cars for a living. I have to. But it's a good business, reliable and respectable, and it's doing OK. There's an old joke about a garage called Floggit and Scarper. That's not us.

Leaving the sport that you love is hard at best, devastating at worst. Harry Redknapp took a group of ex-players, mostly in their 40s, mostly overweight and unfit, some of them well-known for their boozy days, and made a TV programme with them, preparing them for a game against German counterparts. Some of it made for sad viewing. My ex-colleague Andy Payton, who watched, wrote about the memories that returned to him. Andy had some bad times when he finished but came out the other end in one rejuvenated piece. These are his poignant words.

> The absolute joy of being part of a team of young men who would do anything for each other both on and off the pitch. The banter, the togetherness, training, games, injuries, wins, losses, ups and downs. Harry reminded me of Stan 'the man' Ternent, the gaffer who looked after us all, who put us straight and guided us to promotion. In Paul Merson I saw a lot of myself who really struggled to come to terms with life without my football, my reason to be on the planet to score

> goals for Burnley Football Club. Yes, life does go on but never will we see those days like we did when we were playing the beautiful game. They were the best days of our lives.

They were the best days of our lives. Amen to that. The players whose lives take a turn for the worse when they leave the game are the ones who can't let go. I was OK; I had a mentality that simply said, 'right let's get on with it, what's next, don't mope. Just do it.'

I'm one of the legions of players who didn't have millions to fall back on. Mind you, half of them today lose what they have on dodgy deals and worthless investments. Or half of it goes when they divorce and maybe the rest on gambling. Repossessing footballers' cars is an industry. It's sad.

Some of them can't adjust to a life without football. After Burnley I went to Rochdale for a few games, the arse-end of the football world back then. I couldn't hack it. Mind whirring; what the hell do I do next? It's horrible getting older.

Perhaps if there is anything I do resent, it's just the bad luck that I had when I developed Colitis when I was in my early 20s. I was doing OK, Harry Redknapp fancied me for West Ham. And with Burnley forever cash-strapped I've always assumed it was a move that would have gone through. Maybe then I might have become a bigger player in a bigger team for a bigger wage, saved some money in the bank for a rainy day, and a bigger car and all the trimmings. I'd have been forever blowing bubbles. But I still wouldn't have had a gaudy, fancy suit or a daft haircut. That was never me.

When Harry Wilson, a full-back, left Burnley for Brighton, it was Brian Clough that signed him. The story goes that Harry wore a check suit so garish that Clough took one look and allegedly said, 'Don't ever come in that fucking suit again.' I would have been perfect for Clough. Harry came into my life when I joined Burnley and he was a coach. I'll tell you later what we called him.

Colitis came first, the diagnosis hit me like a hammer. What was going to happen? The consultant said I'd be able to play with a colostomy bag. You've got to be joking. It was certainly goodbye West Ham. Crohn's came later, after I left football. A double whammy if you like. I was in my mid-30s when that arrived. Bloody hell, hadn't I had enough? I could have just buckled but didn't, it's not in my nature. Get up, get on with it, sort it, beat it. What's that Chumbawamba song? Something about Tubthumping. I get knocked down; I get up again.

How could I get around the Colitis once it took over? I was a footballer for God's sake. How could it happen to me? Could I get over it? You go through all the stages: shock, hurt, resentment, anger, throw in a little bit of depression. You look at doctors, consultants, the manager, team-mates, and family. And cry a bit. Team-mates come in and say all the right things: they'll fight it with you, you'll come back stronger; just platitudes; but inside they're just bloody glad it's not them. They can get on with their lives and the game. You can't.

'Poor sod' they might say as they exit the ward and then forget about you. And you wonder what you're gonna do.

The Colitis could have finished me well before the Crohn's but it didn't. I wanted to get back; the pleasure of playing, the banter of the dressing room, the smell of the liniment, the joy of a win, the roar of the crowd. All gone, all finished, all over and done. Or so you think at the time.

But giving in never entered my head, and two years later I was well and truly back. Sometimes I wonder how I did it. More often than not I don't know how I did it. Got over the angst, got over the problems, came to terms with it; fought all the debilitating effects, got back on my feet and at last back on the grass. The NHS was superb. The laughs on the ward were better than medicine. But God, it was a long road. What great support I got from manager

Stan Ternent; I'll tell you some cracking stories about Stan ... and Ian Wright ... and Paul Gascoigne ... and Chris Waddle. There'll be a lot about Stan, a hard man, an 'in yer face' man, but deep down a good heart.

For the record, this isn't a book that starts with where I was born and which school I went to, and then plods its way through the years; it actually starts with Stan Ternent, a larger-than-life character with whom I had many a tussle, but the man who saw me through all the hassle of the Colitis times.

Taking everything into consideration – the illness, the time out of the game, the injuries and niggles, all the trials and tribulations you encounter, good days and bad, the way it all ended – there were still all the good times and the good days that outweighed all that. So much so that it has to be said. It wasn't such a bad life.

I've written this book with Dave Thomas. A few of his recollections might just slip in every now and then. He's written a few Burnley books; he lives in Leeds and I live in Clitheroe. But my car business, W18, is in Colne so that's where we met at a place called Tubbs, a restaurant down the hill from the town centre. We've lost count of the number of coffees and teas we have consumed. Dave thinks they do the best scrambled eggs on toast in the business. He's eaten so many he's egg-bound. He thinks they must have some secret recipe or ingredient handed down from father to son, but Steve says no. Steve and Jane have looked after us for a year nearly; thanks both of you.

Chapter 1

ALMOST THE BEST DAY OF MY LIFE

'It was brilliant to see Paul Weller coming on as substitute against Scunthorpe. His courage and determination provide an example to us all. I hadn't realised just how serious his operation had been until I read a piece about him in the local rag. I will spare you the details. Suffice it to say this illness is a pig. It often greatly inconveniences people living quite sedentary lives. To have overcome this disability and to have returned to life as a professional sportsman is an incredible achievement. I'm rooting for you Paul along with everyone else.'

A BURNLEY FAN, Tim Quelch, wrote that in a fanzine way back in October 1999. There have been a few best days but this one was up there with them. I'd been out for an age with this ghastly illness and for this game I was back. It was the culmination of a long, hard slog, days of hopelessness, feelings of worthlessness, feelings of why me? They were days of frustration and despondency. Black days, angry days, days of just feeling utterly fed up. But full-scale depression, no, that was not in my nature. If it was, I'd have never made it back into the game.

So, it was only Scunthorpe, not exactly Manchester United; there's precious little glamour in Scunthorpe and at the end of 90 minutes it was a game we lost. The ground half empty, supporters wrapping collars and scarves round themselves with drizzly rain spreading over a misty Turf Moor. Scunthorpe fans in a reasonable number and the game on TV. The TV cameras didn't come that often to Turf Moor, so this game was 'a quid a kid' to try and swell the numbers. On the bench I was sat next to Lenny Johnrose; I think of him today as he battles with Motor Neurone Disease and he's not even 50. Here's me, now, today, back up on my feet and running and there's Lenny; when we began this book, he could still walk, but by the time we finished it, a year later, he was in a wheelchair. My problems are nothing. Today I can even turn out for the Vintage Clarets every now and then when we play charity games, some of them in support of the stricken Lenny. He can still joke about it on Twitter, that he is going for the record for how many different ways you can fall over.

In the grand scheme of things football isn't that important if you see it against the backdrop of people's lives, problems, health and real tragedy. I loved playing, but at the end of the day it was just a job and a livelihood, same as anybody else. In the week that I sat there itching to get on the pitch again, there had been the Paddington train crash disaster. It was actually at Ladbroke Grove, but is often labelled as Paddington, and 31 people died. Something like that puts your own problems in some kind of perspective. Mind you, 1999 was also the year of President Clinton and Monica Lewinsky, forever to be known as Zippergate – funny that. The manager then was Stan Ternent. We'll mention him a lot. This account of him comes from Dave's book *No Nay Never Volume Two*:

> If Jimmy Mullen began the process by which Burnley moved away from the lower reaches of the Football League in Division Four, then it was Stan Ternent who, in 2000, continued that process. He had taken a drifting club, inherited a mixed assortment of players, and eventually taken the club to promotion from Division Two to Division One, later to be renamed and repackaged as the Championship. During that process for every three steps forward there had been two steps back and many, many unhappy experiences. Players had been publicly sacked. Two home games saw 11 goals go in the home net. He was jeered, abused and insulted on several occasions as he did his sorting and stuck to his intentions. Bit by stubborn bit however, things came right as he brought in his own players and turned things round.
>
> The two seasons after the promotion were heady days. The club twice missed the play-offs by just one place. In one of those seasons, the number of points gained would have earned a top-six place in any other season. All of us will remember the finger-tip saves made by Coventry 'keeper Hedman from Gazza's two free kicks to deny us a play-off place. Those saves denied us a top-six place by just one goal. From then on it was pretty much slowly downhill for Stan and the side.

But I was a part of those two good seasons when success was so close and it was down to all the support I got from Stan Ternent. After that, it was always a struggle with little or no money at his disposal. But he worked miracles and kept the club in the Championship. The more it became a struggle, however, the more support lessened. When the novelty of a Championship place has worn off, when there are no more seventh places, fans vote with their feet. The career of Stan Ternent is told in his book *Stan the Man*. The snapshot is this:

He came to Burnley in the 60s from the north-east, sent by legendary scout, Jack Hixon. Six years later, unable to command a first-team place, Harry Potts sold him to Carlisle United and his travels, as player, manager or coach, took him to Sunderland, Blackpool, Hull, Bradford, Chelsea, Crystal Palace, Bury, Gillingham, Derby County and Huddersfield. He had tremendous success at Bury on a shoestring but his adopted roots remained in Burnley. He belongs to that small group of managers who brought post-war success to Turf Moor, the others being Cliff Britton, Harry Potts, Jimmy Adamson, Brian Miller, Jimmy Mullen, Owen Coyle, and Sean Dyche. Just a handful of names in a 70-year period. They will be remembered whilst others are forgotten.

He remained at Burnley until 2003/04 when it was decided he had taken the club as far as he could. But with better finances who knows what he might have achieved? It was the collapse of the ITV Digital agreement with the Football League that resulted in problems. When that TV deal imploded Burnley had to make major adjustments and changes. Suddenly a major source of income was gone. Players had been signed, wages agreed, policies decided all on the strength of money assumed to be coming in from ITV. He could no longer sign the better players he wanted. Through much of his final season (and mine for that matter) the team hovered worryingly above the relegation zone and towards the end of the season things looked truly ominous. He stated that to keep Burnley in the Championship would be his greatest achievement. He kept them there. He is in a position to say he left the club in a better place than when he found it. There are plenty of people who will say that where Burnley are now, begins with Stan.

Like so many players who came to the club as a boy in the 60s, he went through the Gawthorpe training ground system, stayed in homely lodgings, married Kath a Burnley girl, developed a real affection for the town and came to identify with it. His management years at Burnley were a labour of love. When the end came for him, he was in tears. It was a day of sunshine and a home defeat to Sunderland. At the final whistle he walked round the perimeter festooned with scarves and received a long and emotional standing ovation. We were watching the end of something special and saying goodbye to a man who had helped us all achieve something. And today I sell him cars.

Tony Grant was a great admirer. 'We had a falling-out once but he was right and I was wrong. You could go to Stan with anything on the pitch or off it, he was approachable and would listen. He cared, he wanted to play football the right way and this was evident every time we were on the training pitch. He would blow his top more when we won than lost. I think it was psychological, a tool he would use. He liked to see players play with what he would call 'a chuckle in their boots, or a smile'.

In an interview with Dan Barnes Tony added, 'Everyone had their ups and downs with Stan because he wore his heart on his sleeve. He would be quick to put an arm round you and quick to tell you off, but deep down was a really good fella. Away from football he is a guy you'd like to class as a friend, someone you respect. There was a lot of love between the players and Stan.'

Gareth Taylor is another who remembers Stan fondly. 'You have to take your hat off to Stan really; he would drive you nuts on a daily basis really, and you'd think you'd had enough. He could be like a bear with a sore head every single day, but he commanded respect. You couldn't help but love the fella. He knew how to manage people, usually with an iron fist, but I got used to that. You had to have the skin of a rhinoceros to survive. Telling you one week you were brilliant and the following week that you were useless. I don't think you'll see the likes of Stan again.'

Goalkeeper Brian Jensen, a Ternent signing, was well aware of how volatile Stan could be but on a Monday morning any dressing-down was always forgotten. But he remembers he was the victim of a memorable Stan put-down one day. Jensen lived in Congleton at the time, an hour's drive from Burnley on a good day. Stan would much have preferred him to live closer. 'Congleton,' he humphed one day, 'a three-day camel ride from Burnley.'

Robbie Blake has a fund of memories of Stan and was on the receiving end of his outbursts many times. Funny how it was the two flair players, Robbie and Glen, that seemed to get the most batterings. Robbie tells a few stories on the *Under the Cosh* podcast on YouTube.

'My start was an absolute disaster but after the hernia op it took off. But while Stan was nailing you, he always had your back. Madman he might have been but as the full package, he was the best,' Blake recalled. 'You never knew what to expect. He was unique. Anything could happen on any day.

'There was a pre-season when he arrived down at Gawthorpe. "I've been watching the World Cup," he said. "I've been watching Brazil. That's the way forward; we just keep the ball. If you keep the ball, they can't get it. Just keep that ball moving."

'So off we go and start playing. This is great, we thought. Deano inside to Skip, Skip to Cox, Cox to Branchy, Branchy a Cruyff turn, back to Cox, Cox to Skip, Skip to Deano, Deano is just about to play it and there's a loud "WHOA STOP… WHAT ARE YOU DOING? JUST GET THAT BALL FORWARD!"

'We stop and Skip asks "But, I thought we were going to play like Brazil?"

'"I've changed me mind," Stan humphed. "I saw the first coupla passes from you lot, and thought, no, just get the ball fucking forward into their half."' Add a few more expletives into all this and you get the picture.

Robbie Blake continues: 'There's a Tuesday game. I was living in Harrogate and had a few red wines when I got back. Probably had too much. Come the morning I'm thinking I'll stay at home, not feeling too great. Stay in bed. So, I phone Soz, that's Ian Liversedge the physio, and tell him, "Soz I'm not coming in, I don't feel well. Don't feel great at all." "OK", says Soz, "I'll tell the boss." I stay in bed. Suddenly at 12 and I'm laid in bed still and there's a buzz on the intercom. There's a little camera and I can see who's there. Oh, fucking hell it's fucking Stan at the door. There's that moment of shock, surprise, what the fuck do I do? Right, yeh, just ignore it, hide behind the sofa, he'll go away. But then there's the sound of someone scrambling up the drainpipe and Stan's voice.

'"Soz, ged up there, ged up that drainpipe, make sure you ged up there, I know he's in."

'So, there's Soz up the drainpipe leaning over trying to knock on the window. Years later it's hilarious thinking about it. At the time it was terrifying. He'd driven all the way from Burnley to Harrogate to check up on me.'

Dave Thomas told this story to Stan Ternent to confirm whether this actually happened. 'Absolute rubbish,' Stan said. 'No way did we climb up a drainpipe. We found a bloke with a ladder and we climbed up that.'

'Stan was gold, a madman. "You trying to run my club for me?" was one of his favourite lines,' added Blake. 'What made him so good was that he got so many things right. But the batterings from him were always just around the corner. Even if you were winning. We were beating Gillingham 2-0, I'd scored one and made one, but half-time and in he comes and I just knew he was going to go for me. He's gonna punch me, I'm thinking, as he sets into me and I'm saying "but Stan I made one and scored one". His arm is pulled back and he swipes me but in so doing he knocks the teapot off the top of the nearby fridge. Mick Docherty is standing in the nearby doorway, tea everywhere and all over Mick, all over his face. It was always me and Glen that got the bollockings without fail.

Poor Mick now had a bright red, tea-stained face and was wiping himself down.'

Luke Chadwick was at Burnley on loan for just one season but he has fond memories of Stan Ternent. When Sir Alex Ferguson explained to Luke where he was heading, he told him what a character Stan was.

'But he made you feel wanted,' Luke added, 'and had a great sense of humour. Stan was good for me and I loved Robbie Blake and Glen Little. I loved the journeys back from away games with beers and fish and chips on the way. But not the factory run, that was a training run round Padiham. One story I always tell is about the night we landed back at Turf Moor to collect our cars after a pre-season in the Isle of Man. It was late, we were all tired, and most of the cars were blocked in. Suddenly Glen's loud car horn starts blasting away and this was late at night. There are houses around with folks fast asleep. Stan was tired and weary and certainly had the 'ump. He marches over to Glen's car. Glen winds the window down to ask "what's wrong gaffer?" Stan is trying to welly him through the car window, gives up on that and starts whacking the car with his bag. I still smile about that and always think of Basil Fawlty thwacking his car with the tree branch.'

* * *

Stan must have been in despair after the poor result against Scunthorpe. Me coming on made no difference, there was to be no fairy-tale equaliser. The Scunthorpe goalkeeper drove fans mad with his time-wasting, the Scunthorpe fans rubbed it in with their chanting. Burnley couldn't have played worse if they tried and here was I, back after the draining illness, desperate to do well. A few boos rang round the ground at the final whistle. In the away area the Scunthorpe fans sang their heads off at this unexpected bonus 2-1 win. It rained as we came off on what was supposed to be my big day. I'd been out for months. The word dismal was and still is inadequate. I should have been coming off and heading for the dressing room on cloud nine. This was what I'd worked for, for so long, getting back on the pitch but you can't feel elation after a defeat when your team-mates sit slumped on the chairs and the moans begin about where the game went wrong and you wait for the manager to have a go. All of this was on Sunday, 10 October 1999. None of us knew of course that the final game of the season, again against Scunthorpe, would see the score reversed and Burnley promoted. None of us knew that one of the club's biggest ever signings would take place in February before the end of the season. Our mouths dropped when the news broke that Ian Wright was on his way.

The rumours had been going around the dressing room but it was still a jaw-dropper when it was confirmed. Ian Wright had signed for Burnley on a free transfer from Celtic. He wasn't the first big name – we'd already had Chris Waddle – but Wright, just his name gave the place a lift. We were his fourth club that season; he'd gone from West Ham, to Nottingham Forest, then Celtic and now he was at Burnley. Mitchell Thomas knew him already; Stan knew him from way back at Crystal Palace. Wrighty had once said he didn't want to drop down the leagues and end his career on a low. Burnley weren't exactly 'low', certainly had a big history, and he saw an opportunity to help a club that was on the fringe of doing well and maybe provide the push that at least got them into the play-offs. Stan certainly thought so.

The club confirmed the signing in mid-February and it emerged that Mitchell Thomas had been the go-between. At first it was all kept very quiet, in fact it stayed under the radar for a surprisingly long while.

'We managed to keep it quiet, which in Burnley should have got me awarded a VC,' said Stan Ternent.

Wrighty had been having a hard time at Celtic. 'Come down here and play,' Stan told him. Things had been bad enough for him to consider packing the game in altogether.

'Promotion is what Burnley want,' said Wright, 'and I just hope I can make a contribution. I've known Stan since I turned professional and he's been on at me for years to sign for him so I've finally given in. If Burnley can get into the play-offs it means I could finish off my career with a play-off final.'

None of us knew it but we'd do better than that. We'd end the season with automatic promotion. It was something that for certain never entered my head, months before, lying in a hospital bed for weeks on end wondering if I'd ever get back on the pitch again.

To put it mildly the town went mad and the club shop went into overdrive. The next home game was against Wigan. The stands quickly sold out. T-shirts and giant hands flew out of the shop. The shop manager was run off his feet. A normally quiet Tuesday was manic. Sky TV descended on the club. The whole town had the Ian Wright bug, Burnley was back on the map. The queue at the ticket office was all the way down Harry Potts Way. Fans were interviewed. We were famous for 15 minutes. People stood in the rain to see him. He had his own TV chat show at the time, *Friday Night's All Wright,* and he was given time off to keep his media commitments. He was probably the first and only Burnley player to appear on the Richard and Judy *This Morning* programme.

The buzz we got at his first training session was huge. He was just brilliant to be around and so much fun. We were constantly laughing. The smile on his face was infectious, he was constantly grinning, constantly happy. This guy was a winner. His personality bubbled. His grin was infectious. The place was a joy to be at. Every day something was different, a fancy car or even a motorbike. He lifted the place.

It became clear very quickly that he was a team man. Any ego was hard to find. He knew all the top TV stars but there was no Charlie Big Time although he did always joke about was the north really like this, he'd only seen it before on *Coronation Street* and it was like going back in time. He moved in with his mate Mitchell Thomas in the little house that Mitch had. We called them the Odd Couple. Privacy, soon, was hard to find. Whenever they went out to the corner shop, they were surrounded. It became another joke that Wrighty was always cold up here in the frozen north. If it was a culture shock for me coming up to Burnley from Brighton it was an even bigger one for him. The cars he drove cost more than an entire terraced street.

And then it was the Wigan game and was there ever such an anti-climax? On the Friday before the game 1,000 Ian Wright scarves had been sold, 500 foam hands, 600 T-shirts and 300 No 33 shirts. Come matchday and the hysteria was palpable, more TV cameras, a gorgeous day, excellent pitch, the faraway hills looking green and resplendent from the Upper Longside Stand, and a full house. Except of course for the away end. This was Wigan, don't forget, and their end was a third empty. Chairman Kilby and the accountants probably looked at those empty seats and humphed. Rodney Marsh was watching from the Sky Sports studio and you could get 10-1 on Ian Wright OBE being sent off or 5-2 on not scoring. Out they came, Wright receiving a tumultuous reception. Alas, nobody scored, the first half was a bore-fest with a few dubious challenges on the new man. A run from the halfway line that took him past five players woke up the spectators. Burnley dominated the second half; Wright shot straight at the keeper and later also chipped him, leaving him clawing at thin air, but the ball missed the target.

So, 20,000 spectators left disappointed with a 0-0 draw. The match sponsors made him man of the match. Maybe the pace was gone and the electric movement and speed off the mark, but what was still there was the touch, the movements and skill of an international-class footballer.

It actually took him a few games to score and he was fretting about it, but when the goal came it was one of those last-minute goals that wins a point. Away at Gillingham, the night freezing cold and losing 2-1, Wrighty came on after 70 minutes. With 86 minutes gone, we were resigned to defeat against a side that were strong and cussed. Mitchell Thomas sent over a long looping cross more in hope than anything and before you could blink Wrighty was on to it, controlled the ball and lashed it into the roof of the net. It was sudden, deadly, blink and you missed it, and the goalkeeper's attempt to save was simply not worth the effort. It was a reminder of what a talent this bloke was and then he was buried, mobbed by the whole team.

More points were accumulated, but there was still no indication of a top-two finish and automatic promotion. Racist abuse was hurled at Wrighty on occasions and at Colchester it was appalling. Stan Ternent was livid. The 2-1 win seemed unimportant. Ian too was seething, but also hurt that it had been so vicious, even in the car park after the game where it was up close and personal. Stan had let him drive to Colchester from his London home; Lord knows what he thought as he drove back.

Stan banned the players' outing to Cheltenham races, wanting all of us to concentrate fully on the league. Nevertheless, some of the lads went down. Who should they bump into but the chairman in one of the bars? 'Guess who I met at Cheltenham,' said the chairman to Stan. Life makes you laugh out loud sometimes. Stan fined them. They weren't laughing then.

With eight games still to play we were seven points away from a top-two promotion place. Then the legend scored another crucial last-minute goal against Notts County who had equalised to make the score 1-1. Draws were no good. Steve Davis thumped the ball forward as everyone was expecting the final whistle but there was Wrighty to collect the ball and smash it home from 25 yards. There was complete mayhem; this might well have been goal of the season.

I'd been out of the team but if there was a game that signalled that Burnley could do something special it came away at Oxford with me brought back to the subs' bench. This was a big surprise; I thought I was yesterday's man. Stan and I had had yet more differences and blow-ups with me arguing that I was fit to play. I got the hump and went on the transfer list for a while. Losing 1-0, Stan made changes. I was one of them. It was a dream game for me, crossing the ball for big Steve Davis to head home from the edge of the box. One point was better than none but it was to get even better. Wrighty had come on as well at the same time as me and the game wound down with all of the away support assuming that this would be a 1-1 draw. Three minutes of extra time was held up on the board and we pressured strongly. Ian Wright chased a lost-cause ball on its way out. He caught it. He wanted the win and banged it over and I was on the end of it and headed it in. The noise from the away end was deafening. There was barely time to kick off again and the final whistle went just a few seconds later. Me: grinning from ear to ear. I had been lying in a hospital bed having had a major operation, not once but three times, at one point looking at my intestines lying on top of my stomach, wondering if I would ever play again. Looking back, you see some games as defining. This was one of them. And something to tell the grandchildren one day; I scored the goal from Ian Wright's cross.

Four of the next five games were victories. The last of them was away at Scunthorpe and the 2-1 win was enough to secure second place and automatic promotion. Everyone knows what the situation was that day. Gillingham, if they won at Wrexham, would get the second automatic slot. I wasn't even on the bench but shared the joy as much as anyone as the win secured promotion because Gillingham lost. Funny how things panned out. Scunthorpe were managed by ex-Burnley player Brian Laws, who later returned to manage the club. Wrexham were managed by former Burnley player Brian Flynn. It was forever a mystery why he never returned to take up a post at Burnley. Supporters always maintained it was a mystery why Laws was ever appointed after Owen Coyle had upped sticks and left the club in mid-season.

The celebrations after the win at Scunthorpe were just mind-blowing, for both the players and fans. A huge crowd had watched at Turf Moor on a giant screen. The dressing room at Scunthorpe was on pins until the result from Wrexham finally came. And then all hell was let loose as a crate of champagne arrived. The pitch was invaded at both grounds. Stan was in tears and hoped the players didn't see them. Nobody can put a true value on this result and the promotion. You could say it kick-started the slow, steady progress towards the Premier League that came several years later. I doubt Stan has ever had the recognition he deserves but it was his triumph. Nor was there any real recognition from the media on the day. It was Gillingham who were expected to go up and the press said that Burnley had sneaked in. The journey back took place in a haze. Cars and coaches passed us on the M62 waving and scarf-flying. Up outside of Burnley on the way to the moors is a pub called the Kettledrum. The coach pulled up there and we piled in with what seemed like hundreds of supporters all crammed like sardines in a tin. People still talk about it. Stan had blurted out on the radio that we were heading to his local pub, 'the Drum', for a pint. It seemed like everyone who was listening made their way there as well. In the evening many of the players headed for the clubs and bars in the town. The story goes that Wrighty, the inspiration for much of what had happened, was barred from one club because he was wearing trainers.

The procession around the town, the civic greeting at the Town Hall, the acclaim from the crowds as the bus drove round the streets were all the things that footballers remember and work for. Next season it would be the Championship. But before that we had a trip to Portugal as one of the rewards. It didn't get off to the best of starts when the plane had to turn around after take-off and return to Manchester; a problem with doors or something. Wrighty had been asleep and as we exited the plane, he thought this was Portugal and was aghast at how cold it was. We all wanted him to stay on for the next season but it wasn't to be. He had made his mark and left an indelible impression. He had made 17 appearances and scored crucial goals. His smile and enthusiasm never left him. He learned to love Burnley and the fans. In Stan Ternent's book there was one paragraph that was quite telling.

> There is no doubt that Wrighty was a better person for having lived in Burnley. When he arrived, he imagined locals lived like Oliver Twist. He was right in one instance. There weren't too many Bentley Continentals in Burnley. There are not too many millionaires. But people here are proud of their football team and Wrighty understood that he was privileged to be part of it.

He was one of three what you might call galacticos I played with. The other two were Chris Waddle and Paul Gascoigne. The first was impossible to understand and relate to. The second was just a sad case by the time he arrived at Turf Moor.

But I was elated. I was back on the field. We'd won promotion. I'd played a part in that. There were some great fixtures to look forward to. I was settled again and part of things. I couldn't help but look back on how and where it all started and the things that I'd been through to get to this stage. I had never had it easy, that was for sure.

I am forever in Stan's debt. He could be brutal with his players but you knew where you stood with him. So did the directors. I can remember him laying into three of the directors sitting at the front of the coach on one away trip. Barry Kilby and Clive Holt were two of them and I forget the other. I sat and watched, thinking 'How can they just sit there and take all this. How can he speak to them this way?' This was the chairman he was berating. If it had been me sat there, I'd have ordered him off the coach. In fact, it was usually Stan that ordered people off the coach, once for the daftest thing. It was his coach Ronnie Jepson who used to make the teas and coffees on the bus and Stan got so irate at the number of times Ronnie asked him did he want a tea, Stan flipped and ordered him off the coach. Quite funny really.

Suffering with Colitis like I did, I saw the caring side of the man. That, plus the fact that he has had so little recognition for what he did for Burnley is why this book begins with him. He took a club that was left in the dumps after Chris Waddle, with players who were just not up to it, with results that were patchy to say the least, and got it promoted to the Championship. He joined the club when it had stayed in Division One by the skin of its teeth on the very last day. It was in a mess and he sorted it out, got it promoted in 2000 and kept it up there. You could say he set Burnley on the road to where they are now, as we write, in the Premier League. But you won't find his portrait on the walls of the stand, or many pictures of him inside the club; there isn't a stand or a room named in his honour. Yet he still lives in the town as he has done since he first joined the club as a player in the 60s. It was always his dream to manage the club; how he would have loved to have got it into the Premier League. Twice he came close to the play-offs. When he finally left in 2004, after a horrendously tough season at a club without a penny to its name, he walked round the pitch after the final home game in tears with a Burnley scarf round his neck. That's how much it meant to him. Burnley Football Club is in his bones.

Stan knew at that moment he was leaving, but I didn't know that I too was on my way out. But I'd find out soon enough from the new manager Steve Cotterill when he arrived. The way I left was quite pitiless, and that's part of this story.

My experiences have been nothing in comparison with those of many others. There's a list of Burnley players who have suffered far worse than me; Marvin Sordell with racism and bullying, Lenny Johnrose now in a wheelchair with Motor Neurone Disease, Gary Parkinson with Locked-in Syndrome. There are others who have had drinking problems, some with marital problems, there are others who have had gambling problems. Willie Irvine and Clarke Carlisle both tried to take their own lives. Football, tough on players, is filled with their stories. Mine is just one of them.

Chapter 2

BEGINNINGS

WE VISIT Brighton and Worthing a couple of times a year. Sometimes I might go down on my own. The sunshine of the south coast versus the grey clouds of the north and Burnley. That's the image and some of the time it's apt enough. My mother and father were still there on the occasions I went down but dad eventually succumbed to dementia and lived in a care home. Now it's just mum. My father died at Christmas, 2019, whilst we were working on this book. How cruel is dementia. It's like he had crossed over a bridge and we couldn't reach him. I looked at him and one minute I could have wept at the state he was in, then next I felt angry that it just went on and on and you think there should be some kind way of ending it. My mum sat with him day after day crying. It was heart-breaking. When he passed away it was a merciful release from a dreadful illness.

Early life was complex and with my family tree it's a wonder I am sane and normal. It impresses me every day. To say it was complicated is an understatement. Until I was 16, I was Paul McDonald, not Weller, living with my stepfather until he departed the house when I was 11. I was in fact the result of an affair my mum had with a married chap but when stepdad left, real dad arrived. One bloke moved out and another bloke moved in. Still, it worked out OK. I took his name, Weller, when I was 16. It was my real dad that resided in the care home oblivious to the world, to mum, to me and all the rest of us, asleep 90 per cent of the time and when awake just staring ahead.

The funny thing was the name change took some getting used to. After a week at Burnley when the team sheet went up for what would have been my first game for one of the younger teams, I looked for the name McDonald. It wasn't there.

'I'm not bloody playing,' I muttered. And then realised Weller was my name now, and there it was.

Brighton is where I was brought up for the first 11 years. On 6 March 1975, I arrived, a tiny scrap of a thing and I was still a scrap of a thing when I was 16 and Brighton and Hove Albion had decided I wasn't up to much. I played some trial games with them but never really got anywhere. It was disappointing that Brighton didn't want me but not unexpected because at that time they seemed to have blinkers on when they picked out any youngsters. There was a good local team called Bevendean Barcelona from which Brighton took a lot of players without ever much looking beyond, at other boys' teams. I could have joined Bevendean but preferred to stay with the lads I knew in the team I was already in.

I never had any interest in Brighton Football Club as a spectator. Maybe if I'd had a bit more money, I might have been tempted to watch them but instead I was a Spurs fan and still am. I spent many weekends at my Nan's where Uncle Mike lived. I played football with him non-stop when I went there and he was a big Spurs fan so of course I followed Spurs with him, although we never had the money to get to a game. We'd watch on *Match of the Day* and I sat glued to the likes of Glenn Hoddle, Ricky Villa and Ossie Ardiles. Hoddle was my hero: what a player, what vision, control and those beautiful long passes he made – outstanding. Then there was Gazza, who lit the place up and lo and behold years later he came to Burnley and we were team-mates. I wish I could write that it was a dream come true for me, but it wasn't; it was a forgettable episode. Tony Parkes was one of the goalkeepers at Spurs and he and I met later when he was brought up to Burnley by Chris Waddle. He was one of the nicest blokes you could meet and believe me they're not all like that in football.

Brian Clough had just been and gone from Brighton in a blaze of chaos before moving to Nottingham Forest and we all know what miracles he achieved there. In 1979, after Clough left, Alan Mullery took them to promotion to the First Division, which before the Premier League was the top division. It was a good time to be a Brighton supporter but I wasn't bothered and then in 1983 they were relegated with Jimmy Melia as manager. But it was also the season they reached the FA Cup Final against Manchester United and with the score at 2-2 and a winning goal in the final minutes of extra time looking a certainty, Gordon Smith's shot was saved.

'And Smith must score,' said TV commentator Peter Jones. But he didn't and United went on to win the replay 4-0.

After that relegation there were a few years of misery and gloom with relegation to Division Three in 1987. Yet, the next year they bounced straight back. They remained a struggling club though, crippled by increasing debts. Maybe it was a good thing that they had no interest in me; life took a different direction, the north beckoned, but not just yet. If is a big word. If Brighton had taken me on, how different life might have been.

In those early days mum worked at two jobs every day to make ends meet, and pay for the two-bed flat we had overlooking the beach. Well not quite directly overlooking the beach but we could see it and the sea and the green, where we played, over the tops of the newsagents and the shops on the other side of the road. I was on that green every night playing football.

I was never in. Football, football, football, that was all that mattered. Street football, park football, on-the-green football. Small I might have been but it never phased me against bigger lads. Street football is where you learn just as many skills as any academy today. You dribble and beat player after player, you hog the ball and try to go from one end to the other. Skills and ball control come out of all that. If you are on your own you kick a ball against a wall and control it when it comes back, over and over again. The great Jimmy McIlroy used to say just the same. Today, just where is the street football? Jumpers for goalposts. You might laugh, but it was where so many stars were born.

'Shove him in goal,' they'd say when picking sides, because I was so small, the runt, and it was assumed that I'd be useless anywhere else. But then they realised I could play a bit, so some other loser was put in goal. If not playing, I was out on my bike, doing two paper rounds. The bike was also useful for finding places to play football and back in those days down there you could leave it propped up somewhere and it would never get stolen. Try doing that now.

One paper round in the morning and one every evening; who does paper rounds these days? How many kids actually know what a paper round is? It was a great way to earn some money and with that money it was me that bought my first football boots. Proud of them I was. I'd paid for them; I'd earned the money. They hadn't come on a birthday or under a Christmas tree. I'd worked for them. They'd come from my own efforts. I saw mum working all hours of the day supporting me, and my brothers and sisters. If I have a work ethic it comes from that. Being able to stand on my own two feet comes from that. If there's something that needs doing you do it. If there's a problem you solve it. You get on with life. Make no mistake, my childhood was great. We never wanted for anything.

How many kids today do what I did all those years ago, out playing football every minute of the day? They just don't do it. They're on their iPads or phones.

So, what do you do in Brighton when you're 11 when you're not playing football? The question never arose. I was always playing football. The ball was under my arm if I went over to the green, or rode off somewhere to find a game.

My actual dad came into my life when I was 11 and married my mum some years later when I was 16. We moved to Worthing where they opened a greengrocer's shop and moved into a proper house, which certainly made life and sleeping arrangements easier. The shop was called Pixies, don't ask me why. It still is.

It was goodbye to Hove Park Colts as well – a club I had joined when I was only eight. A few of us had been playing on the park one day and a lone bloke who'd been watching us asked did we want to play for him. Today you'd run a mile and race home and tell your mum that a man had approached you in the park. It's drilled into you. Today no sane man would do that anyway, such is the fear of being branded a paedophile. Anyway, that's what happened and we said yes and joined Hove Park Colts. I started with the Under-9s and then went up to the Under-11s.

The move to Worthing meant changing schools and also a switch to Worthing Dynamos. At school I played for the Under-14s team that was a year above my age. There was a football trip to America; how mum and dad found the money to pay for it I've no idea. It wasn't cheap for the two weeks in Florida over in Tampa and Clearwater with trips to Disneyworld and SeaWorld. There are vague memories of playing a few games but it was a time when football wasn't that big in America.

Don't forget I was still small and skinny. Living in a greengrocer's shop surrounded by food didn't make the slightest difference. But the old adage is true; playing against bigger and older lads toughens you up, although nothing like the 'toughening up' we were subjected to as apprentices and youths at Burnley with the likes of Terry Pashley and Harry Wilson. Those tales come later. They collared me when I was 16. Let's just say for now I was lucky I could still walk when I was 17, the kickings I got.

From Worthing Dynamos, I moved up through the Worthing FC younger teams into the first team, which played in the Diadora league, once I'd left school. Something like £15 a game went into my back pocket. Nice. They were managed by a guy called John Murray who had been a player at Burnley and in the late 60s he had been in a side of young kids that won something like seven games on the spin, a side that had players like Mick Docherty, Steve Kindon and Dave Thomas. For a short while they were the sensation of the First Division but it didn't last and John eventually moved on from Burnley, ending up in Worthing. If life is about coincidences then it was this that had me heading to Burnley for a trial after just a few games. The manager there was Frank Casper who had also been in the same team as John Murray at Burnley; hence the connection. Serendipity.

'Where's Burnley?' I thought, not having a clue about anywhere north of London. For good measure back then in the very early 90s, Burnley was a grim and dilapidated place. I was a 16-year-old scrap of a lad heading north into the unknown, quite literally to an alien land of strange accents, mill chimneys, dereliction, cobbled streets and terraced houses. Mum and dad brought me up by car on a long, seemingly endless journey, from the sunny south to the frozen north. I looked through the car windows and wondered where the hell I was and what I was coming to.

So, up I came for the trial, played a game against Bury, scored a goal, got a dead leg, came off after about 80 minutes thinking well that's that then, but stayed for a week getting treatment from the legendary, shiny-headed Jimmy Holland. To test your fitness, he'd send you to run to the corner flag and back; if you could do that you were fit. There's a story that one player's fitness years earlier was tested by having him run up and down the stairs. He passed. One of the directors commented years later that since when did we play football on the stairs. The club used an old hotel in Nelson called the Hawthorns to put players up. Two other players were in there, Mike Conroy and Mark Yates. Today it's a shell of a wreck, perfect for development or maybe by the time this book comes out, it will have been snapped up.

At the end of the week, despite having been unable to play another game or even to train, they still wanted me. I went back down home to Worthing, having been invited back up again to sign; but found that Frank Casper had left and there was a new manager, Jimmy Mullen. I blinked. Bewildering was an understatement.

I was in digs now near the infamous Stoops Estate and was there six months, perfectly at ease. Then there was a move to Padiham, which doesn't mean village of the Irish, and there were yet more terraced rows and old mills. I moved around various places perfectly happy, well treated despite the horror stories you hear about mean-spirited landladies half-starving you. I stayed with a teacher, a nurse, a retired lady and then a policeman. Some apprentices in digs have endless escapades, adventures and amorous evenings with the landlady. Not me, maybe it was because I still looked about 14 and they thought I was too young. Maybe it was because I was just too tired.

Today's youth players have it made; not for them the chores that we used to do. You read of some youth lads at the top clubs already on £1,000 a week and more. I was on £27.50 and saved money on bus fares by using my bike to get to Turf Moor where we had jobs to do before getting the minibus to the training ground at Gawthorpe. There were more jobs to do there before we could train. We cleaned boots until they shone, the laces immaculate, God forbid you got polish on them. We got kit ready, ran baths, swept and cleaned the terraces where there were hundreds of steps, sometimes helped the groundsman. If it stood still, we had to paint it. You learned about respect, discipline and responsibility. We were just slaves with football boots on, expert cleaners. Another old football saying, 'Sloppy off the pitch, sloppy on the pitch.' It made you appreciate the football even more. And, we were getting paid, not a lot, but we actually got paid. If you found some loose change or even better a fiver on the floor as you swept the terraces, you were made up.

One particular job of mine was cleaning the medical room for Jimmy Holland but it was Harry Wilson who oversaw things and ran his finger over the ledges, skirting boards and shelves to see they were spotless. Even the pipes that ran around high up near the ceiling, he'd even run his finger over those. Dear Harry, Harry the Bastard we called him. He called it tough love. Miss one speck of dust and you did it all over again. On matchday there was one job we always had to do and that was put the whisky bottle and two glasses in an ice bucket for Jimmy Mullen. In the second year I had to clean Mullen's boots and in all the time I was there I can't remember ever getting one tip from him or any of the players whose boots I cleaned. Mullen was superstitious, always had to wear the same boots and the same jumper; one boot had a hole so big where the little toe was you could put your hand in it. But they had to be cleaned so he could wear them. He was hard work. After the 1994 Wembley play-off win, he was so smashed in the evening he fell out of the hotel fire door and couldn't get back in. He and Frank Teasdale, the chairman, were two of the most enthusiastic drinkers I've ever come across.

On the days we went to college for an afternoon on a Thursday we'd meet up with the Blackburn apprentice lads, then flying high, and had to listen to them telling us of the £50 tips they were getting from the top players at Blackburn. They were happy days as an apprentice though; we all got on, there was a good mix between us and the first team players. I never saw any abuse or real bullying or poor treatment from them. It wasn't like that at every club; at some of them the apprentices' lives were made miserable through ritual humiliations and put-downs. They were good to us even though they were tight with their money. I was in awe of some of them and loved watching the two wingers, Steve Harper who could dribble for fun and then Ted McMinn, a real fans' favourite.

Today Gawthorpe is a Category One Elite Player Performance Centre. What a grand name. They aimed at Category One for a while, which in its simplest terms means better facilities and competitive games against other Premier clubs. In my day we were bellowed at by Terry and Harry on those muddy pitches; now the club employs over 30 youth team and under-23 staff on training pitches like bowling greens. Today the coaches talk about growth maturation screening, peak height velocity, bespoke accreditation pathways, performance management application, productivity analysis, benchmark data and bio-banding. You need a dictionary. Some might say that all this jargon and fancy-speak is just bollocks. What the hell is bio-bonding?

The Stoops riots were an eye-opener. I thought it was bonfire night, but no, it was cars on fire. From the genteel charm of Worthing to full-scale riots in one of Burnley's poorest estates. I was already wide-eyed at rows and rows of terraced houses and a shabby town centre; there was no regeneration in Burnley yet, in fact it was a decade away and you could still find cobbled streets that you could buy for next to nothing. There had been riots in several parts of the UK and in Burnley they lasted five nights on two of the poorest estates. Barricades made of pallets were set up and burned, petrol bombs were thrown at a police van, children and teenagers ran wild. There were police complaints that parents were even encouraging their children. On the worst evening 100 police were pelted with bottles and other missiles for four hours and 17 people were arrested. Welcome to Burnley.

I started as a central midfielder but was moved to the right. All this was when Burnley were still in the Fourth Division but it was the season when a terrifically exciting side won promotion at long last. It was a good time to join, with players like Roger Eli, John Francis and John Deary. Roger Eli always had a car boot filled with clothing gear to sell; hideously bright shell suits his speciality … Goalkeeper Nicky Walker was part of the Walkers shortbread biscuit family; his car boot was filled with boxes of biscuits. He went on to play twice for Scotland and after football became a director of the family firm. If you saw someone walking down the street in Burnley wearing a ghastly shell suit and eating shortbread biscuits, it was a fair bet they played for Burnley. After football Roger went on to set up a huge stationery business; selling was in his blood. Selling a shirt out of his car boot, or a printer in later life, gave him as much of a thrill as scoring a goal. I get the same feeling when I sell a car.

I was there at York on the night they clinched promotion at the end of season 91/92 and the crowd went wild. They'd been stuck in the basement for seven seasons and this was a joyous promotion, sweet relief after years of drudgery. It was hard to get in the side though because Mullen had so many players with many of them cluttering up the reserves. He had to put players in that side to try and sell them. Young lads like me didn't get a game at all at that level. Not until some of these dead-weights were shipped out did we get any more chances, but it wasn't long before there was a contract issue. I was offered £150 a week but others my age were offered more. I might have looked about 15 but I had my head screwed on and thought, 'I'm not having that.' It was as if the club thought I should sign for a low wage out of gratitude because they'd kept me on. Or perhaps they thought that because I still looked about 15, I was just a soft touch.

So, I dug my heels in, but the chairman was not best pleased and wasn't having a non-contract player featuring in the team when contracted players were sitting in the stands. It was after I'd played a League Cup game that the chairman, via manager Jimmy Mullen said, no more. It went on for about a month but in the end, I got an extra £25 a week. In the space of three years Jimmy Mullen won two promotions, one of them decided at Wembley in a memorable play-off final. All looked set for more progress and me getting more games but it just didn't happen. Mullen bought striker after striker but none succeeded and following awful abuse from the fans he left. Chairman Frank Teasdale thought Jimmy Mullen was the bee's knees and they were big drinking buddies but Adrian Heath, signed by Mullen, said something quite illuminating to one of the other directors, 'We went up in spite of Jimmy Mullen.' He was far from everybody's favourite.

Temporary manager Clive Middlemass gave me a game against Shrewsbury and I scored my first goal for Burnley. It was memorable only because it was at the end of the ground where there was no stand and no fans. They were building a new one. I must be the only player in league football ever to have celebrated such a momentous moment, a first league goal, with not a fan in sight, and jigging around a rusting JCB that was parked there.

Middlemass was only temporary and Adrian Heath took over. He was still a class player. He put a lot of faith in us younger players; as well as me there was Chris Brass and Paul Smith. He saw me as a sort of Ray Houghton player: small but all over the pitch, energetic, busy, shuttling the ball up and down and getting stuck in everywhere. Plus, chipping in with a few goals. Looking back, I guess I was one of his favourites, he stuck by me if I had a bad spell. Maybe it was because he was small like me; his nickname was Inchy. It was an exciting team to play in, top scorers in the division but when Heath left to join Everton, in came Chris Waddle.

Let us just say for now that the fun stopped and puzzled bewilderment followed. Suddenly I was not a midfielder. I was now a wing-back. Just like that.

Chapter 3

PLAYING AND LOSING

I'D GOT myself into the world where I wanted to be. Living the dream is one expression. But half the time you are living the disappointments. Great when you win but so often soul-destroying when you lose. You have to be able to cope with losing, and learn from it. Moping after a defeat is no good, although of course you do. That's OK as long as at some stage you snap out of it. That's why footballers like to play the next game quickly after a defeat, get it out of the system, just get on with things.

There's a book called *It's Burnley Not Barcelona*. There's a picture on the front cover that has me in it. Happy days. Playing. And you can't beat it. It's about one particular season, 2002/03 and I guess that was when the struggles at Burnley began after the near misses with the top six the previous seasons. There's an introduction in the book that we've adapted for this, because it sums up what the game is so often about. Defeat. Exhaustion. Disappointment. Weariness. Head in hands stuff and wondering what it's all about. The desire to just blank things out. Even more so when you are sharing the plane home from a game with supporters. It was an away game at Norwich, not a particularly important game, a run of the mill game you might say but the description of it is a picture of how we feel when we've lost. Getting supporters on to the plane helped pay for it at a time when the club was struggling money-wise.

Norwich Airport: supporters have funded the plane journey. It's early evening in the departure lounge at the airport and we've lost again, this time 2-0. Wins these days are few and far between. Players' faces look subdued, drawn and worn out as we sit in our grey club suits. Some players stand around and talk quietly. Exuberance is hard to find. Others sit, legs outstretched, bruised and scarred, ankles swollen and red, lost in their private world. No one likes to lose, especially in a game where we've all run, chased, tackled, equalled Norwich in everything, except the one thing where it matters, putting the ball in the net and scoring. Just three shots on target. We've had our chances and missed them. Norwich have had theirs and scored from them. It's been a routine home win in a game that could have gone either way but which sod's law decrees inevitably and predictably goes to the home team. Burnley have given everything but in the great universal scheme of things, Norwich have been the team chosen to win and get the points.

We look drained and pale, all of us. It's been a hot day. Our supporters sitting close to the pitch have seen the sweat pour off us, the stained shirts, felt the bone-jarring fierceness of a 50:50 challenge, seen the pain when a foot goes in high on an ankle, seen the grimaces and grunts when a ball hits us hard and seen the agony when an elbow clatters a player and goes in the face. Robbie Blake whacked so hard he's sent spinning head over heels and lands yards away. All of us have had seven bells knocked out of us. Lee Briscoe is lucky not to be going home in an ambulance, lucky not to have had his leg broken by a late tackle unspotted by the referee. Dean West sits quietly lost in his own thoughts with one foot in a slipper. Blisters. He has run half a marathon. Steve Davis stares blankly ahead with a faraway look in his eyes. What's he thinking? Losing hurts and when you've lost, travelling home with a planeload of supporters, it's the last thing you want.

Manager Stan Ternent stands with his back leaning against a wall. Supporters file past him and commiserate. 'Ah well that's the way it goes', he says in his north-eastern voice. Stan is there with the coaching staff but says little. His face too, is impassive, resigned and tired. What's he thinking? Missed chances maybe, the run of the ball, endless injuries, no referee's decisions going his way. No luck at all today. No little stroke of luck that makes all the difference between winning and losing: the luck that turns a game. It's coming to the end of the season as well. He has decisions to make, who to retain, who to release. Who'd be a manager?

The run of results since March has not been good. Knocked out of the cup ignominiously by Watford. A few players might be thinking of what might have been, for tomorrow is semi-final day, Watford versus Southampton. It could have been Burnley versus Southampton but the defeat at Watford was another sickener. The newspapers are full of the semi-final news just to rub things in. On top of all that these are uncertain times for some players: anxious, nervous times when a contract may or may not be offered. Players have families, mortgages, bills just like anyone else. Nobody here is on mega-money. Football is a fragile, fleeting life and today players up and down the land will be wondering about the future. None of them know, do they, whether it's a new contract offer, a serious injury, or a bad long illness and I know all about that. What's the manager thinking? Some players will find out soon enough. Maybe some have had the hint already. For those released the world will be full of footballers seeking new clubs. Only a few will succeed and if you're the wrong side of 34 or 35 what chance have you got? For some, it's the end of the line.

If a football season is a journey then these last few miles have been one long, rough ride. Since the win at Stoke in early March there has been just one win against Preston a few days ago to lighten the gloom and clinch another season in the Championship. For that we are grateful. That is success. Survival is all.

The supporters on the plane have no complaints; we've played well today and given everything but saying 'well done' or 'bad luck' to someone who has run himself into the ground to the point of exhaustion for no reward, is inadequate. We deserved something today but as ever the gods of football gave us a referee called, of all things, Conn. Conned again. Yet again, the gods have been unkind as they so often are to Burnley. A win today would have been the icing on the cake and I don't doubt for a minute that every player is disappointed that we can't go back smiling and celebrating.

I'm looking at the tired faces around me, but some of them are beginning to thaw out a little, to cheer up, to smile a little and chat. But I'm sat thinking where's the glamour in this then? No Beckhams or Keanes here. This is the Championship, hard and relentless, bruising and painful. Where's the glamour in the punishment of pre-season training, or training in winter in cold, rain, fog, sleet and the Gawthorpe mud? Where's the glamour of a game when it's freezing at Grimsby and you lose 6-5, or pouring down at Rotherham and you lose, surrounded by scrapyards?

Football: the beautiful game. But where's the beautiful game when you're stretchered off at Norwich, wondering if your leg is broken, your career ended? Where's the beauty being sent off at Gillingham, being stung by hailstones at Stoke? Where's the glamour when you're abused by supporters, unable to show your face if you've lost 6-2 at home or 7-4? And where's the glamour when the end of a career is in sight and the fag-end of the season approaching?

Supporters are looking into the players' eyes trying to see what's behind. Maybe we are thinking about the next pointless exercise, a game we have to play, a long-distance coach journey of six or seven hours down to Portsmouth and then back the same night getting back to Burnley in the early morning. Portsmouth are going up but for us, the season is over. We're expected to be the patsies, the fall guys, the sacrificial lambs on the altar of Portsmouth success. We are the re-arranged fixture list's last gift to Portsmouth and a packed, baying stadium. We don't want to lose but probably will. The script is written. We have to turn up and go through the motions. The season can't end quickly enough.

The bottom line is simply this, I've come to realise. There is very little glamour, or even enjoyment, when, at the season's end, you're just about a middle-of-the-table team from a small, deprived town in Lancashire. But at least there will be no relegation and we can be thankful for that. Another season in the Championship and some kind of financial stability. That's no mean achievement. We are just Burnley. We are not galacticos.

Maybe the most disappointing defeat was the cup game at Watford in that same season, 2002/03. It was back when the FA Cup was still a competition that had some standing. I was on the bench, saw it close up, sat frustrated, annoyed and even baffled, wondering why the two best players we had, Glen Little and Robbie Blake, were sat on the bench next to me. An FA Cup quarter-final, a winnable game, or at least a draw – Watford were nothing much – and then a semi-final when anything can happen. In a quarter-final you can almost feel Wembley. Watford had seen some good times, reached a Cup Final and flirted with the Premiership. Now they were being sued by Gianluca Vialli for his lost income. But they were a club counting the pennies like us and just like us probably thinking, Burnley, nowt to beat. The BBC had the rights to screen the tie, fans came down in coachloads filled with hope; the two clubs had cut a deal to share the TV money, £400,000, a tidy sum, or even half of that for any club on its beam ends.

Garry Nelson once wrote that football was just 22 idiots chasing round after a ball in the freezing cold. Maybe a cup tie is a bit more than that when you get this close to a final. Two very average clubs were in there with a chance of fame and fortune, and for average players the chance of a bit of recognition. There was no real reason to think it was a game that we would lose but you are aware that football is fickle. Luck, run of the ball are crucial. Score a winning goal and you are a hero; drop a clanger and give a goal away, concede a penalty, score an own goal, and you are just a target for criticism and even abuse. You can argue that any footballer is capable of deciding the outcome of a game, but then every footballer is at the mercy of a bad bounce, a deflection, a poor referee's decision. You just don't know what fate will bring until it arrives. You can believe that events are already decided before you take the field. What will be will be. Was this a game where the result was cast before we even took the field? Fans wonder to this day why Stan picked the team he did and left the two best players on the bench, Glen Little and Robbie Blake.

And then you ask what is luck? The bounce of a ball one way or the other, a ball that hits a divot and goes off in another direction, the ball hitting a post and bouncing one way or the other, this way it goes in, bounce the other way and it goes out for a corner, one way it bounces back to a striker who scores, the other way the keeper catches it. Luck: the toss of the coin and which way it lands or the luck of the draw giving you yet another away game. This was the fifth away game in a row for Burnley. Your name comes out of the hat second and you groan.

Watford versus Burnley, a cup quarter-final, the chance of glory. We lost 2-0 and even sitting on the bench it was a horrible feeling, maybe even worse because you're sitting there unable to influence the game. It was a feeling like the one we had when we missed the play-offs by just one goal having only beaten Coventry 1-0 at Turf Moor. Hollow, empty, dejected, flat, wondering what might have been. It was a dreadful game, missing any class or style. 'One of the worst spectacles of football witnessed for a long time', said one newspaper. 'A desperate quarter-final tie, bereft of drama and entertainment or anything resembling class or quality', said another.

The day was bathed in spring sunshine, the ground filled with the yellow of Watford and the claret and blue of Burnley. There was a carnival atmosphere inside and outside the ground. But on the pitch, there was nothing. We didn't deserve to win. We didn't play. We didn't create one single chance and gave their goalkeeper absolutely nothing to do. No goalkeeper will ever have an easier afternoon. At the end of the game the supporters gave the team a standing ovation as they trudged off disconsolately. The fans had roared, cheered, sung and made a thunderous noise for 90 minutes and more. But it just wasn't to be.

If it was to be a game decided by one chance, one player, one moment, it fell to a Watford player, Tommy Smith. In a game today filled with exotic names from Spain, Italy, France and Africa, it was then years ago decided by plain old Tommy Smith. He was in the right place at the right time.

It was a nothing game, 22 players giving each other no time or space, the ball in the air more than on the ground. Spectators got neck-ache. There was a corner that wasn't cleared, flailing legs and feet, the ball bouncing and ricocheting around until it continued to Smith who, falling, poked it home from just a few yards so that it slowly, agonisingly, scruffily trickled past a despairing Marlon Beresford. Smith was just back after four weeks out, following a car crash. Tell me now that these things aren't worked out in advance in a ready-made script. Their second goal was almost an irrelevance, coming direct from a free kick that sailed over the wall, scored by a player who was in the side because someone else was injured and who had already been told he would not be retained. And another twist of fate; we failed to score for the first time in 20 games. Blake and Little sat on the bench kicking their heels, two players capable of taking any game by the scruff of the neck.

Watford were then drawn to play Southampton. For us it was over, no more cameras, no more limelight, no more spotlights. But what can you do? Shrug it off but carry on thinking what might have happened if Robbie Blake, Glen Little and me had started and played that day? I think Blakey and Glen eventually came on, certainly one of them came on, but it was all too late and almost futile.

The memories of most defeats fade away as you simply get on with the next game. The memories of some defeats linger; this was one. Big centre-half and skipper Steve Davis was gutted to miss the game and still thinks what a chance was missed to get to the semi-finals. TalkSPORT radio was switched on when we travelled home in the coach and one of the pundits was having a real go at us. Stan thunders 'get me the TalkSPORT number' and phones them up and gives them hell over the radio. Stan ordered the coach driver to pull in and then proceeded to berate Micky Quinn over the airwaves. When he'd finished, we applauded him. He stuck up for us and said exactly what we were thinking.

Some games are emotional experiences. Not the winning, not the losing, just the whole thing when there's some special meaning or you know there are after-effects. Burnley 1 Sunderland 2, the final game of 2003/04 was just such a one. We knew it was Stan Ternent's last game as manager, he knew it was his last game and over 18,000 people in the ground knew. He'd been told by the chairman that it was time for change, round about the time of the Rotherham game, a ground surrounded by scrapyards back then, rusting derelict hulks of old engines and machinery and all matter of any old iron. It was a horrible ground, although funnily enough it was a ground where I always enjoyed playing, despite the freezing cold dressing rooms. The surroundings matched the manner of the defeat when we played like something that was just broken down and clapped out.

It was a nightmare of a game, a defeat that you want to get away from as fast as you can and hope you don't bump into any supporters. It was woeful, with players bickering and arguing on the pitch in front of the supporters, 'A disgrace,' said Stan publicly. When players argue and berate each other on the pitch it is demoralising. Opposition players love it. Brian Jensen in goal, who could be superb on his day, and was a star of the 2009 promotion season to the Premier League, had a horror of a game. It ended up 3-0 at this dump of a ground. There are days of utter depression both during and after a game and this was one of them. It was only Walsall losing that day that meant the place in the division was safe. Stan always said that keeping Burnley up that season, with all the money problems, was his greatest achievement. In later years he described it as the eighth wonder of the world.

Why on earth would I write about Barnsley? Here's why. Some grounds are graveyards. Barnsley is one; once upon a time a win here for Burnley was as rare as hens' teeth. Barnsley 1 Burnley 0 in December of the season after promotion was typical, one of the games we can look back at and point to as being where lost points cost us a play-off place. There is something bleak about the location of that stadium to start with. The very name Barnsley conjures up images of factories, wasteland, slag heaps, old mines, coal dust, terraced houses, brass bands, Michael Parkinson, football tales, and smoke. There was nothing pretty about the place back in 2000. Where there's muck there's brass, the old saying goes. But there's not much brass at Barnsley FC these days. And who on earth is Tiverton Preedy? Only the bloke in 1887, the Reverend Preedy, who founded the club.

There is the tale that when the main stand had swing doors, one player's habit was to open them with a head butt. The last time he did that was when he discovered that some joker had reversed the swing and the poor unfortunate knocked himself out. But they were 'ard back in those days. Another player during a game broke his collar and shoulder bones … and played on.

An astonishing 5,500 fans, filled with Christmas turkey and pud from the day before, had followed us there with high hopes against a middle-of-the-road side having a modest season and with no manager. They were there for the taking, or so we and the supporters thought. Unfortunately, football has a habit of providing banana-skin moments and this game did exactly that.

A frantic start, Burnley on top, we were aggressive and determined, Barnsley offering little, from us and the fans a bit of passion. They had Stuart Ripley who used to play for Blackburn. Abuse and ribaldry abounded and followed him all around the pitch. We had most of the game but couldn't score. Fans are cruel especially when they write match reports in magazines like the London Clarets produce six times a year. In this one it was poor Ronnie Jepson who came in for merciless criticism.

'He was once a cult, but that now looks like a spelling mistake,' wrote the scribe in this match report.

A 0-0 draw then looked on the cards as the end of the game ticked closer. To get a point would have helped us make the top six. But no. Another Burnley free kick came to nowt. More seconds ticked by. Groans all round, a Burnley mix-up when two players got in each other's way. The defence froze. This was now the 89th minute. All it took then was a tap into an empty net to ruin the day, to ruin Christmas, to eventually ruin the top-six place in May. Barnsley fans woke up and there was a murmur of support, they being as surprised as we were horrified at this scoreline. The ghost of Reverend Preedy rejoiced. The game finished two minutes later.

Stan T was incandescent. There's a Robin Hood film in which Alan Rickman plays the Sheriff of Nottingham and utters the immortal line with narrowed eyes and curled lips, 'And call off Christmas.' Stan was much the same with a legendary rant that has gone into the history books.

'It's not often I have a go at them. But I am now and I've told them in the dressing room. The gloves are off, let's get on with it. They might feel a little bit like Billy Big Time, but we'll see. Our holiday period ended at quarter to five. I'm going to put this right for the Burnley fans because they deserve better than this. Those players are having a laugh. I'm stuck with them but they're having a jolly. That's not good enough. I'm angry and I've told them. It's not good enough and I'll sort something out. There'll be no time off until I get better performances than that. When I saw Paul Weller going to the line and whizzing balls across, and I see one striker and no midfield players, that tells me they've either eaten too much turkey or too much plum duff or they don't have the desire. But I'll sort it.'

When Stan went off on one, he was unique. But nice of him to mention me in a kindly sort of way.

Grimsby: another place that conjures up horrible images. It crops up again in a later chapter when a defeat left its indelible mark; but a defeat there at the end of the 2001/2002 season left Burnley a mountain to climb in the very last game that would decide if there was to be a top-six place or not.

The situation was simple enough. If Burnley beat Grimsby and then Coventry in the last game of the season, and Norwich lost, then there would be a play-off place. Beat Grimsby? We were so poor in the first half, they just scored at will, almost. Stan shuffled players around and the one goal we scored late in the second half was not enough in the 3-1 defeat. A second goal would have got us into the play-offs. There were enough chances to do that but only the one went in. Grimsby, meanwhile, were relegation candidates. We couldn't have chosen better opponents, and still managed to lose.

One fan wrote that analysing how we missed the play-offs that season would be an exquisite method of self-torture, but why look further than the one result at Grimsby with such an abject performance? Woeful defending at one end and missed chances at the other. Another fan who took a taxi to the game related that the taxi driver had warned them that Grimsby had this pacey guy called Boulding, a semi-professional tennis player of all things. He had jet heels, said the taxi driver, who sounded quite eloquent. And Boulding did indeed have pace and tore Burnley apart in the first half. Was this the only game in which he was ever a star? No idea, but he starred against us that day, for sure, and for all I know was never heard of again. Our goalkeeper Nik the Greek copped it from fans that day but all of us were responsible.

The Sunderland game that saw Stan leave the club two years later was an irrelevance in terms of the result. Sure, it would have been nice to win but we didn't. If it was supposed to be a day that celebrated another season of survival and another in the Championship to follow, then any kind of celebration never happened. There was a gloom, a stillness, a quiet air of let's get this over with. For him it was the end of the road. For us it was the uncertainty of what happens now. A new manager, a new broom, unknown territory. What would it mean for us? It would be bad news for me, but I'd no idea about that at the time, and I was looking forward to getting married. Glen Little would be leaving as well, but with a move lined up and a bit of certainty, he already knew that and so did the crowd.

It's a results game and they'd been going wrong for Stan. Fans were split, those who wanted change and those who thought he was irreplaceable. With fans he could be rude, brusque and intimidating; maybe that was because he was actually quite reserved, defensive, arrogant said some, but was it simply that he felt ill at ease with fans? If you are top of the table, nobody cares; if you are struggling all your faults are magnified. But all were agreed, his heart and soul were in the club and the town where he lived.

Burnley took the lead through Glen Little, captain for the day in his final game. We'd already hit the crossbar but then Sunderland, already in the play-off group, equalised. We knew they'd have been happy with the draw but scoring against them seemed to annoy them and wake them up. Their winner was against the run of play, a header that rebounded off the crossbar was struck home. It stayed at 2-1; the whistle went and an era, a short one to be sure, just six years, was over. Stan walked round the pitch once it had been cleared and tears rolled down his face. The mask was dropped, another Stan emerged, a heartbroken Stan, distraught at leaving the club. Overwhelmed as well, overwhelmed by the applause and the appreciation that rolled down from the terraces. Someone had handed him a scarf which he used to wipe away the tears and maybe even to mask them. Glen Little, too, was emotional and came over to me with a tear in his eye.

I'm glad it was a game in which I played, even though it was a defeat, so that I was there up close and personal to what was going on. The recovery I had made from the long draining illness I'd had was aided and supported by this man that was now exiting the field for the last time. Stan was tough, hard as nails, took no prisoners, brutal on occasions, his confrontations with some players memorable. But I won't forget the part he played in getting me back on the grass.

Zoe on her 40th birthday

Mum with Imogen and Flynn

Our shop when I was growing up. It's still there. Don't ask why it's called Pixies.

From this little angel face aged about seven on the left to number 18 in the Burnley first team years later. As a kid I was always playing against lads older than me. They soon found out I could give as good as I got. Burnley picture courtesy of Burnley Football Club.

A little bit of hero worship later on when I was an established player. My love of cars served me well. I sell them now.

Dad and me. Dad was a great support in the early days.

In action against Wolves. A perfectly good goal scored against Wolves in one game that was disallowed cost us a top six place. Picture courtesy of Burnley Football Club.

Hove Park Colts Under-9s. There's me, seven years old I think in this one, middle of front row.

And 20 years later. Picture courtesy of Burnley Football Club.

The gaffer Stan Ternent sends instructions. Picture courtesy Burnley Football Club.

Wrighty made his mark at the club and will be forever remembered. Lenny Johnrose on the right. Picture courtesy Burnley Express

I loved the big games. Playing against the big players, Gianfranco Zola was one. A Will-o'-the-Wisp player, one minute there, one minute gone. Sharp mind and fast feet, a great combination that made him such a wonderful player. Picture courtesy of Burnley Football Club.

Who'd have thought, Gazza in a Burnley shirt. We never knew what he was going to do next. If only one or both of his free kicks against Coventry had gone in, in the final minutes of that final game of the season, we would have got the extra goal that would have seen us in the play-offs. In the game against Wolves he didn't do too well. In the coach heading south just days later we actually overtook the Wolves coach. 'Fuck me, that's the first time all this week I've passed a Wolves player,' he said. Picture courtesy of Burnley Express

One hundred games for Burnley and chairman Barry Kilby presented me with the special award. My mum probably has it now. It was mum who made all the scrapbooks and kept them. I owe her a lot. Picture courtesy of Burnley Football Club.

Chapter 4

GLEN LITTLE

I WANT to give Glen Little a chapter of his own. He's one of my great friends in the game.

It was with Glen that I part-owned a greyhound, one of those things that footballers do with time on their hands. Players have more money now and have moved up in the world with racehorses. Some of the current players at Burnley have formed a small syndicate and bought one. We, on the other hand, could only afford a greyhound.

I seem to think our dog actually won a few races. It was a pal of mine that suggested sharing one, so six of us ended up in part-ownership. We ran it at the Belle Vue track in Manchester and it was called Coole Date. It was never anything expensive even though we paid a trainer to look after it. I was never a real gambler but it was always fun going to any of the race events. The first time it won we actually missed it because we were at a sportsman's dinner.

We weren't the first at the club to go into this. Way back, 60 years ago maybe, two players, Harold Mather and Arthur Woodruff, owned a greyhound. They kept it under the Cricket Field Stand and they and the other players fed it scraps and titbits. Food was scarce, this was a time of rationing. The story goes it never won a race.

Harold and Arthur trained it by running it along the canal and it was here they realised why it never won. It was always behind them. They weren't the fastest players in the world but the dog couldn't even keep up with them.

The Premier League: Spurs had just beaten Burnley 5-0 at White Hart Lane in a display that was breathtaking at times. I'd been there to do a radio commentary with mixed feelings, pleasure at seeing my favourite team play so well, disappointment because the club that raised me were so poor. The game featured a goal by Son that saw him collect the ball just outside the Burnley box, and then race away to score at the other end in a matter of seconds. It was quite simply sensational from his point of view, but a comedy from the Burnley point of view as he left so many of them in his wake with not one of them committing the necessary professional foul to block him or bring him down. But Glen Little was reminded by that goal of one that he scored in his non-league days.

'I've just seen Son turn into Glen Little,' he tweeted.

Glen had scored a goal for Wealdstone that took him past player after player and then he capped it by chipping the goalkeeper. If Son's goal was made by pure pace, Glen's was made of deft skill and technical ball control. And he was 38 at the time.

Glen had watched the Son goal and thought the same as the rest of us. Bring him down, bring him down, and had seen all the opportunities to commit the foul. Son's goal was the result of him being faster than anyone else opposing him. An athlete's goal. That's what the top players are these days, athletes who can run with a ball. As for Glen, athlete is the last word you'd use to describe him. He was never the fastest player on a pitch. But as for skill, that was a different matter.

His story is almost a typical footballer story; a hero at one club, at Burnley in fact for quite a few years, but then a career winds down, he clings on to playing as long as he can in non-league football, still leaving trails of defenders, but on leaving football, life is never the same again and the problems begin. It happens to so many players. Adjustment for many is hard. Leaving the game behind can be cruel and disheartening. If you are Peter Crouch you have a media and writing career ahead to relish but for so many others the trail of devastation it leaves is a long one. Add to that the fact that when we played, the financial rewards were not that great. None of us who played back at Burnley then amassed huge fortunes, enough to see us comfortable for the rest of our lives. The really top Premier League players were, of course, on a good number, but we certainly weren't. No cushions to fall back on, that was for sure.

He's a bit like me in that not very many people outside of Burnley have ever heard of him. But he was one of the best players I ever played with and his skills were mesmerising. He filled a dressing room with his noise and his personality. He still fills a room with non-stop chatter. Team-mate Mitchell Thomas said he was the life and soul of every party and he could talk under water. Mitch was good at summing up his mates. He used to call me Mr Angry because I was so easy to wind up in training. If Glen stays up here with us for a couple of nights my ears are numb and the silence afterwards is deafening. Players come and go at clubs; strong attachments are few if they move to a different end of the country. But Glen I've kept in touch with.

Players get a lot of grumbles from disgruntled supporters when things are going badly and things had been going badly at Burnley for some time. But Glen was one of those players who was rarely, if ever, criticised by fans. It was managers he drove to distraction. He played for three managers at Burnley and saw near relegations and then the joy of a promotion. He was there in all of the years that we were poor and in the years when the club had no money. It was fitting that he scored the winning goal in the game that secured promotion. Before him the great entertainer had been Ted

McMinn and there were similarities between them. Both were the least likely players you would expect to be a winger: tall, gangly, even ungainly and both ugly, although Glen was the leader on that score.

Glen's own description of himself was simply, 'a 6ft 3in winger who wasn't quick, unheard of. And always looked knackered after just five minutes.'

Being entertainers, they could over-elaborate and tie themselves in knots but both could do things with a ball that we ordinary players couldn't. Football is filled with hard-working grafters but it's the special ones that spectators want to see. Glen was in that category and had supporters on the edge of their seats when he was in full flow. The dullest game could come to life when there was a bit of Glen magic to lighten the gloom. Dribbling his way through and past three or four opponents was not uncommon.

He had many 'best moments', but one that sticks in the memory was at home to Bristol Rovers. He'd had many good games before then and there were plenty more to come but this one was so utterly special. We were down to ten men, Andy Payton had been sent off, and we were hanging on to keep the score at 0-0. Bristol were good, playing for promotion but then Glen took over. Some say he scored the greatest goal they had ever seen that day.

A knockdown fell at Glen's feet when he was stood some distance away from the goal. He shrugged off one man, beat a second and veered into the box. Both the players he had got past had managed to get back into position between him and the goal so he dribbled round them and beat them again. A third defender attempted to stop him but Glen just went past him as if he wasn't there. With three players behind him he had just the goalkeeper to beat and this he did, floating the ball over him and into the net. The crowd erupted and we swarmed all over him. Describing a goal like this you say things like mazy dribble, jinking run, ball glued to his feet, turning on a sixpence, waltzing through the defence. Well, he did all of that. All elbows, knobbly knees, gangly arms, tickling and controlling the ball with both feet, almost impossible to knock off the ball, so clumsy-looking but so deft and balanced. The chip over the keeper was controlled, exact, perfect and precise. If you stood Son and Glen next to each other they'd be chalk and cheese. Son, when he did his national service in his home country, was awarded outstanding recruit. Glen would probably be the one in the guardhouse peeling spuds.

His moment of magic turned a draw into a win; a moment of football genius lit up the ground and the crowd, and us as well. It was in the season when we won automatic promotion and following it came a run of good results so you have to look back and think how significant was that win, and how significant was that goal. When we played Bristol Rovers it was Rovers that were up at the top end of the table. They ended up with nothing.

Glen told journalist Andy Jones that the Bristol goal is number one in his top ten. When Andy Payton had been sent off, he says that Burnley just, 'stayed in the game. We had hardly been over the halfway line but I got myself forward late on. Graham Branch hit a long diagonal and Andy Cooke flicked it on. I knew I had no support so I needed to hang on to it but then chop, chop, chop and all of a sudden, I'm in the box. I chopped again and I was through and I didn't even have to look at the goal, I just instinctively put it in. I was very comfortable on the ball in tight spaces.'

Goal number two on his list was in the game against Scunthorpe when Burnley won promotion. With the score at 1-1 and just 17 minutes remaining the ball fell to Little on the edge of the box. He struck it beautifully.

'If you watch, Andy Payton ducks out of the way. If he hadn't it would probably have taken his head off. It was a special moment and a special day that we had been working for all season.'

Genius is impossible to predict of course and there were times when he frustrated. In his last couple of seasons people only occasionally saw what he was capable of and his final months were so unsatisfactory for him and the fans. He was loaned out to Bolton because Burnley were skint. He eventually went to Reading to save the club a few more quid. It wasn't the same without him, his noise, his bubbly effervescence, his constant chatter. By the end it was clear he was going to Reading on a permanent. He was playing for us but thinking about Reading and that was natural enough. The move made a lot of sense; he was heading nearer to where he came from. He was a south London lad, with all the credentials, London accent, bit of a barrow boy, Manchester United supporter. He could live in some nice posh place not far from where he grew up and be within easy distance of the Reading training ground. That was at the end of the 2002/03 season with Reading a club with prospects, and Burnley a struggling club counting the pennies.

He was an obscure signing when he joined under Adrian Heath. How he arrived was funny enough. He was in Ireland with Glentoran and knew that Notts County were interested. He was fuming when he saw that they had turned down a big bid for him and was ready for a real set-to when the manager asked to see him. Instead, to his surprise, he was told that he was going to Burnley.

He and his dad got the atlas out and found that Burnley was near Manchester which suited Glen because he was a United fan. Over he came for a week's trial to see what Burnley was like and took part in a training session with Adrian Heath. Glen took the proverbial piss (his word) and nutmegged him. Heath as good as signed him on the spot. Clive Middlemass who was then scouting said he thought he'd found the next Chris Waddle. Well that was funny, thinks Glen to this day; Waddle when he arrived, initially clearly didn't rate him at all.

'But one thing I did hear from someone,' Glen told journo Andy Jones, 'was it was felt I could only play as a sub for the last 20 minutes when the game had opened up because I was an impact player. I could understand that but then I wasn't even sub most of the time, or I wasn't getting on at all, so that didn't really add up. It didn't bother me, though. I was a big fan of Waddle. I always played my own game but I took some bits off Waddle in terms of his confidence and composure on the ball. I tried to get that into my game and have that bit of arrogance. We actually got on well. We never had a row, there was no showdown. He just didn't pick me. I was a young player and I didn't cause a fuss. I just kept my head down. I was never bitter towards him. People probably think that me and him never got on but I never had a problem with Chris. I enjoyed playing for him when I got the chance.'

We'd never heard of him and since he came from an Irish club, we thought he was Irish – until he opened his mouth. He cost £100,000 – a tidy sum for those days – but went into the reserves and only made an occasional first-team appearance. Heath could spot good players and one of the good things about him was that he would give young players a chance.

Heath couldn't believe his luck when he got the chance to bring him to Turf Moor. In a recent interview he said, 'I remember Glen coming on trial with us and the weather was that bad, it was snowing at the time and we couldn't get outside to train. We went into the gym behind the Longside and I couldn't believe what I saw the first two days. I called him in and said, "What's happened? You're either on drugs, up for murder, or on the run. Someone with your talent shouldn't be coming on trial from an Irish club." We took him in and within a very short period of time I remember ringing Peter Reid and other people I knew working at Premier clubs and saying I had a player who ought to be in the Premier League. He was a real talent, you only had to watch him play.'

Then along came Waddle and froze Glen out with his assistant Glenn Roeder famously saying that Glen wasn't fit to lace Waddle's boots. There were stories that Notts County asked to take him on loan at this time but they were told, 'No, he'll cost you £20,000,' at which they ran away. There were other stories that Stockport County wanted him.

In fact, Stan Ternent wanted to sign him for Bury, then in the Championship, whilst Burnley were in League One. He wasn't getting any game-time with Chris Waddle so Stan was quick to spot this.

'Harry Wilson turns up at my door and tells me to come with him and see Stan. He takes me to Stan's house and there was this bloke in a chair smoking and I had no idea who it was. Then his wife comes in and offers me a cuppa tea. Very nice, I think, and I have no idea who she is. When Stan started talking about me being the missing piece of the jigsaw, it clicks and I realise this is Stan Ternent from Bury. Tells me he'll get me out of Burnley. And then I never heard from him again, until the day he came in as Burnley manager.'

Ultimately Waddle had no choice but to pick him when we were staring relegation in the face and that was the season when only the win over Plymouth Argyle in the very last game of the season made Burnley safe in the Championship. Looking back, Glen thinks that Waddle only brought him into the side midway through that season as a desperate, last resort when they were marooned at the bottom. If it was a last throw of the dice, Waddle was lucky; he rolled a six.

'At that stage even the kit man could have got a game before me. I felt I was being stitched up when I got that game against Watford at last.'

Waddle left after that one season; you'd be hard pushed to find a player or a fan who was sorry.

Two seasons later, Burnley were pushing for promotion to the Championship with Stan Ternent. Andy Jones, writing for *The*

Athletic, went to see Glen and had long talks with him. There was certainly a love-hate relationship between Little and Stan Ternent. It was the 'tough old northerner' dealing with the 'young, cocky southerner'. A recipe for friction if ever there was one. But Little has retained great respect for Ternent to this day and if he is visiting up north will always go and see him.

When Ternent arrived, Glen was one of the players earmarked by him that he could use to build the foundations for the club. A few games into the season and Stockport offered £400,000 for him. Ternent said no. A few months earlier they could have had him for £50,000.

'Stan's one of a kind. We got on great. We had our run-ins at times, there was no doubt about that. I felt I was a scapegoat and he was always on at me but the more experienced players always told me that he was on at me because he cared. He would get stuck into you. The teacups and the drinks bottles would be flying, tea would be dripping down from the ceiling, pens from the tactics board would be thrown across the dressing room. He would be in your face, punches thrown. But I was always mentally tough. You had to be tough and thick-skinned because you were going to be called some stuff, but with me it was always, "Right I'll show you."

'With him it was a roller coaster ride. We had a love-hate relationship: he loved to hate me,' said Little, laughing. 'I thought the things that went on were just normal. I'd had a tough upbringing at Palace, seen fights and bust-ups, and I get to Burnley and with Stan I just think, well this is normal.

'We had pre-season training down at Exeter and I was one of the players caught coming back late; he was waiting for us. "Be back by midnight," we'd been told, but it was well after that when I got in. Three players were told to get the train back home the next day, they were finished at the club. One was Lee Howey. But he used to stay at my house on a Friday night before a game which I didn't mind. I discovered he was a decent cook and I needed someone to cook and he did a lovely pasta. He could'a stayed every night for me but he was part of the clear-out.

'Stan ran the club like a family. He was involved with everything. There was a time when I went up for a header against Norwich and ended up in hospital with concussion. I went home and on the Sunday morning I woke up and could hear voices downstairs in the kitchen. And I walked down and standing there, in my kitchen, it's him, having a coffee with my missus.

'I was pleased when Robbie Blake arrived because in the dressing room, he took some of the same flak that I got. I'd sit there and see Stan going for him and I'd grin and think yeh, it's you not me getting the treatment.'

At Christmas in 2001/02 we were actually top of the division. Everything looked good but Manchester City made a bid for Glen, £3m it was said. Riding high, Burnley turned it down. At that point Burnley didn't need the money but soon they would when a deal with ITV for the screening of live Championship games fell apart. Like many other clubs, on the strength of this deal Burnley had spent money and were paying (for them) decent wages. Everything went belly-up with Burnley in a financial mess. Somebody had forgotten to check the small print in this contract so that ITV were able to wriggle off the hook. Glen was on a long-term and decent contract and overnight he was expensive and unaffordable. You can blame ITV Digital as much as you want for the problems it caused so many clubs. Secure income turned out to be anything but, and clubs including Burnley had been spending money on the strength of a worthless contract. The lessons learned from that still influence the Burnley board of directors. Once bitten twice shy.

The impact affected the remainder of Stan Ternent's Burnley reign with huge negativity. He offloaded Glen for a short while to Bolton Wanderers, then a Premier League side. It saved some wage money and in return in came two of their reserve players. Just months earlier they could have got £3m for him from Manchester City, if reports were to be believed. Now they had to get rid on the cheap. He got little chance to do anything much at Bolton; five minutes here, five minutes there, occasional late appearances as a sub. He told Andy Jones:

'It would have been nice to have given Premier football a go, but if you only come on for a minute here or a minute there, what chance have you got? When I went there, big players like Youri Djorkaeff and Jay Jay Okocha weren't playing well so I thought I would get a chance. But they are players who even if they are not playing well, they play every week. How do you leave them out to play Glen Little?'

On his return and in the season when it was a near miracle that we stayed up, he wasn't quite the same. Supporters began to forget the dazzling performances he was once capable of. In any case there are always supporters who are intolerant of players who try things but sometimes get them wrong, when a dribble results in loss of the ball. And that happens with flair players. But you need them. A team of workers and grafters would soon have a stadium half empty. But then a team of geniuses would probably be relegated. You need a mix of both. But the genius needs understanding. Celebrate the five out of ten times he does beat his man and get the cross over, rather than grumble at the five out of ten times the attempt fails. Even when he did have an off day, his value was that defenders were kept preoccupied wondering what he was going to do. He was so often the player the opposition feared.

If receiving awards is a measure of success then he won precious few, one to be precise, at one of the supporters' player of the year evenings. It was awarded by the London Clarets. Even today they grumble (with a laugh) that they never got it back.

There are so many great moments to recall, so many spins, and turns, and attempts to beat the same defender two or three times. So often he would look like he was losing the ball but then emerge the other side of the defender with the ball at his feet. There were other favourite moments. There's a description of one of his goals in the London Clarets' magazine, written by Andrew Firmin, when he played a huge role in a 4-1 win away at Stoke City. It was another season when relegation seemed certain at one stage.

> It was one of those slow-motion goals. Little ran from the touchline to the heart of the goal. As he approached the goalkeeper, he tried a shot, but it bounced off the goalkeeper's legs straight back to him. He exercised instant control and demonstrating that Hamiltonian ability to seemingly take the ball straight through people, he ran on. The goalkeeper was beaten. He took several more touches; should he score now? Too easy. He ran on, beat someone else. In the end, after 20 or so touches and with no one else in the ground left to beat, and with the goal right before him, he thought he might as well score. It was a mad and brilliant goal and that is the nature of genius.

For an encore he scored a second in this game, capping a masterful performance with a last-minute curler. Having collected a header that came to him he skinned a defender unlucky enough to be in the way before striking the ball past the goalkeeper and inside the far post. He stood in front of the Burnley fans; hand cupped to his ear. The Burnley fans were by now rapturously singing 'Bye Bye Delilah,' waving to the now disappearing home fans as they exited the stadium.

Some fans saw him as a luxury player but he brought excitement and the thrill of seeing someone do something that most people can't. You saw him score a goal like that, and indeed others, and you stood in wonderment because you know it was something you'd never manage.

Then there was the unforgettable game against Spurs in the Carling Cup as it was back then. Glen's night was described in *It's Burnley Not Barcelona.*

> We won, on a magnificent, magnificent, glorious night. A feeble first half-hour was transformed when sub Glen Little came on in an early reshuffle that changed the game. If this wasn't his best ever game in a Burnley shirt, or in his lifetime, then I haven't seen it. His impact was immediate, electric, mesmeric and quite simply stunning. Playing so badly, gifting them a goal, all we can suppose is that this was part of some master-plan. First lull Spurs into complacency and then bring on the secret weapon, Glen Little. The second half belonged to Blakey, as fans called him, and Robbie Blake. Blakey and Blake sound like a pair of comedians. They were. Glen's other name was Bendyman, for the things he seemed able to do with that rubbery body of his. In short, they ran amok and simply destroyed Spurs. Weller was transformed as soon as Bendyman came on. They all were.
>
> In just a handful of games in a career, a player can rise to sublime heights and is untouchable and unplayable. For Glen this was one of those nights. The man gave a masterclass in wing play from the moment he came on. Time and time again he ran past Spurs players as if they weren't there and those watching on Sky saw something special. He weaved his way through tight clusters, or jinked his way out of impossible positions. His legs would go one way, his body the other. He tied himself in seemingly impossible clumsy knots, all waving arms, long legs, large nose and knobbly knees, but

> still emerged with the ball glued to his feet. All that plus Blake's link play, a joy to watch.
>
> 'We couldn't handle him,' said a glum Glenn Hoddle, no slouch himself at recognising talent.

'I'll miss the place,' he said, when he left after something like 300 games. There were talks to remain but he felt he'd had a good stay and it was time to move on. He played alongside Ian Wright and Paul Gascoigne at Turf Moor.

'He was a noisy bloke,' he said of Ian Wright, 'and there was lots of banter, but to be fair he wasn't around a lot, with his TV shows and celebrity lifestyle. Funnily enough he never really played that well and his first few games were a bit of a nightmare so the gaffer made a brave decision to drop him to the bench. That was a masterstroke because from then on, he came on as a sub and his contributions were always important.

'Gazza seemed to be OK in training but that was when there was no pressure. But it was incredible to see the state he got into before a game. He was such an insecure person and for someone who was once the greatest player England had, it was a sad, sad sight. You wanted to shake him up and tell him everything was going to be fine. But so much had gone on in his life and it had all caught up with him.'

After several seasons, Glen's time was up at Burnley. Steve Coppell came to watch a game and Steve was one of Glen's heroes. 'Do you fancy playing for Steve next season?' Stan Ternent asked him. How could Glen say no? They were a Premier side but ironically were relegated the next season. Next it was to Portsmouth for a season with Harry Redknapp and the UEFA Cup. 'A no-brainer,' said Glen when he found out that Harry was keen.

Today Glen lives in Moreton-in-Marsh with his mother, looking after her since she had a stroke. His father died four years ago from lung cancer. It was a family that was close and supportive during his career, travelling with him and taking him everywhere in his boyhood period, starting at Crystal Palace when he was nine. At Palace on work experience, he hero-worshipped Ian Wright who was there at the time. The players kidded him and gave him Ian Wright's kit, 'Ere see that kit, take that old kit over there in the corner.' It was a joke so when Wright caught him with it, he went mad.

'"What you doin' with my kit" … he used to bully the fuck outta me, I used to 'ide if I saw 'im comin'.'

As a lad Glen played every day of the week just about, and his mum would drive him everywhere. When he was at Burnley, they would get to a game maybe every couple of months. To this day he is grateful to his family.

His huge stock of football memories makes him a great raconteur and after-dinner speaker. He has a fund of stories that he tells in his London, Wimbledon to be exact, patter. Not quite cockney but almost. He's a natural and needs to be on the dinner circuit. If you're an agent reading this, sign him up. He has endless tales such as:

'One of the best things Chris Waddle did was signing Andy Payton. One of the best finishers I ever met. On his first day we was in two groups and he was over on the far side and then he walked over to us with his kind of bouncy walk, so I walked over to him with the same kind of walk.

'"You taking the piss?" he said.

'"Yeh."

'"Oh, that's alright then."

'Much later when Stan was manager, there was a morning when Payts didn't turn up. We'd heard he was in a bit of trouble for taking a golf club, a driver, and causing a fair bit of damage with it somewhere and the police had taken him in, but, we thought, they'll probably let him go because they'll all be Burnley fans. So, we all asks Stan … "where's Payts today … we hear he's smashed a place up with a driver." Stan eyed us.

'"No, load of rubbish," he said after a minute. "It was a five-iron."

'Gazza was an idol of mine when I was a kid so that when he came to Burnley, they hoped he'd have the same impact as when Wrighty came. But he just wasn't the player we knew and loved. There was a game against Wolves, a top-of-the-table game at Turf Moor, sell-out and I was sub. After 15 minutes you knew he was lost and was losing the ball to people who years earlier wouldn't have been fit to lace his boots. He really should have been taken off but I reckon Stan was thinking, how can I drag him off after just 15 minutes. At half-time we were 3-0 down. Gazza comes in and just goes straight in the shower. He must have known how bad he was and took himself off. I went on and we pulled it back to 3-2, battered 'em, even with a man sent off, but couldn't get the third.

'After that game we went straight down to Portsmouth ready for the next game on a Monday I think it was. Gazza is at the front with Stan, and Gazza is drinking red wine. Who do we pass on the motorway but the Wolves coach. So, Gazza waves to them all, laughing, and to us, grinning, turns around.

'"Fuck me," he says. "That's the first time I've passed a Wolves player this week."

'We were all in hysterics. We all loved 'im.

'We met again when I was at Reading in the dressing room. I was with my lad. Who's the first person I see but Gazza and he comes over, hugs me and my lad, tells my lad how proud he is of me now that I'm playing for Reading. "We were at Barnsley together," he says to my lad. I look at my lad and he looks at me and I think naw, leave it … he don't remember.

'Mitchell Thomas lived with me for a while but never paid me any rent, and so did Mark Ford. But that was so he could be my driver after I got a six-month driving ban. What happened was that we had a couple of days off so I decided to go home for a quick visit. I'm on the M6 and get pulled over; 11 o'clock at night, no traffic, I'm doing 85 and get pulled over. Ah well, three points, and get on my way again. But bloody hell I'm the only car on the road. Next up I'm down on the M40 and get pulled up again.

'Aw no. This time it's West Midlands police and out gets a cop who thinks he's a real comedian. Thinks he's Jasper Carrot. And, he has a broad Brummie accent.

'"Scuse me sir, do you know you're speeding?"

'I get out the car and he sees my Burnley top. "Footballer, are we?"

'"Well yeh, I play for Burnley."

'"Oh right, Burnley eh, that's Chris Waddle isn't it. You got any points on yer licence?"

'"Well yeh, funny you should mention that, I got stopped just earlier on the M6 and got three points."

'"Aw right. Burnley eh. They not doin' so well, are they?"

'I'm thinking now, this might be alright, bit of banter, bit of football chat, he might be impressed by me being a footballer. I might just get away with this.

'No, I didn't.

'"Well sir, you got six points now." And then he laughed. "And that's more than Burnley have got so far all this season."'

Chapter 5

BULLYING AND BUST-UPS

YOU'LL OFTEN hear it, 'It never did me any harm ... it toughened me up ... it was part of the life.'

We were talking about things for this book in our usual meeting place, Tubbs in Colne just around the corner from the car salerooms where I work. It's a wonder Dave doesn't weigh twice what he is now. He wrote a book with Roger Eli in the café in a garden centre where they met every week. He wrote a book with Paul Fletcher, meeting in various cafes in Hebden Bridge. We meet in Colne just up the road from Burnley. A book can take six months of meetings and sit-down talks. That's an awful lot of bacon sandwiches or scrambled eggs on toast.

Anyway, on this particular morning the news had just broken that Steve Stone the Under-23s coach at Burnley was under investigation. At that point no reasons were given but both of us said straight away, 'Bullying I bet.' The day after in the press that was the reason given, although he hadn't been suspended, merely asked to stay away from the ground while investigations took place. You wondered if it was outright bullying and emotional abuse, clear and obvious, incontestable; or was some young lad simply over-sensitive and couldn't take the rigour and demands any more that were once quite standard. If your head isn't right it's easy to feel victimised and abused. Had the accusations come direct from the lad himself or his parents? If it was the latter that wouldn't be the first time. Speculation was rife.

Football is a tough environment, it's competitive, you're out to get that first-team spot at the expense of others who are your age. Coaches push and push, demand and demand, and sometimes it goes over the edge. There are lads who can take it and lads that can't. The good coach, the sensitive coach, knows when to back off certain young lads and by the same token will know the lads he can push even more. The problems come when a coach lacks sensitivity and awareness. There are boundaries these days. Once upon a time there weren't.

We had a coach at Burnley, Harry Wilson, we called 'the bastard'. And he really was one with us. With today's cotton-wool approach, I think maybe he'd be out the door faster than you can say 'bully'. I was still an apprentice in one of the younger teams and walking out for a game. 'The bastard' comes up behind me and kicks me as hard as he can while I'm just not expecting it, and lands his boot right up my backside. It was a deliberate and violent kick, nothing playful about it, nothing gentle or delicate, it was a full-on, hard as he could kick. God it hurt. It was agony, horrible, almost sadistic. In real pain I swung round to see who it was and it was him.

'What the fuck did you do that for?' I blurted out, almost crying with the pain. I was mad as hell and ready to swing at him. He laughed.

'That's made you mad, hasn't it,' he responded at me. 'Now, stay mad, go out there and do the same to them.'

In training, playing five-a-side in the gym, it was no holds barred with all the encouragement you can imagine to be tough with each other. I was still small and skinny and it was decided I was a prime candidate to be toughened up. So, whenever I had the ball in a corner the other lads were instructed to pile in on me, corner me, and kick the hell out of me. The toughening-up process. We just saw it as normal. I'm able to say, it never did me any harm. It didn't do me any emotional damage. It didn't scar me for life. But we're not all the same and some lads couldn't take it.

Tony Grant who I played with for three seasons makes some interesting comments. His apprenticeship was at Everton and like mine started when he was just 16. He remembers it as being one of the happiest and funniest periods of his life but it was tough. You could get a slaughtering if you didn't put 100% in but it was normal back then. It was never seen as bullying nor does he accept suggestions that it was. Demands were made and you were expected to meet them. It simply made Tony work harder. Coaches told you the truth then with no sugar coating. If you didn't progress with the basics you were told in no uncertain terms. Today, coaches have to skirt round the truth, back then you got it, full on, in your face, no holds barred. Some lads just couldn't handle that.

We'd just learned that Steve Stone was back from his 'suspension' – not a suspension in fact, he'd been asked to stay away while investigations took place. But whatever he had, or hadn't done, was now closed, said manager Sean Dyche. He wasn't back with the Under-23s though, but supervising the players out on loan. Speculation I know, but had he merely been giving some of the lads some aggressive home truths of the kind that we accepted 30 years ago, but which are now seen as too forceful?

Today, the biggest word is welfare, the welfare of the youths in their formative years. There was none of that 25 years ago. It was sink or swim, kick or be kicked; you were subjected to verbal abuse every day of the week and Harry the Bastard could certainly dish it out. It was the way things were. Today clubs can have a safeguarding officer, a welfare officer and an education officer. Do bullying accusations therefore come to the surface because there are so many avenues to turn to if a player is feeling victimised and singled out for criticism?

Dressing rooms can be brutal places with their own pecking orders. They are not as bad now as once they were; today different times, different codes of practice, different awarenesses. And yet, there is still the need to stretch young players, but how far can you stretch a lad before it becomes uncomfortable, before it can be seen as bullying? Coaches will make the point that you have to find out how far a kid can go, what are his tolerance levels, how much can he take, what is his mental strength, can he survive at the top if he gets there, what level of pressure can he withstand, can he cope with the first team dressing room? The manager wants the tough lads; the Premier League is no place for shrinking violets. Attitude is a key word but how do you measure it? Not with a questionnaire, that's for sure.

Coaches and managers have to make judgements about how mentally strong a player is. That's how they made judgements about me, by watching me penned in a corner of the gym being given a kicking. I must have passed.

And where does criticism come into all this? How harsh can a coach be? In my time criticism was frequently in the form of screaming at you, harshness was endemic. Being told to 'fuck off' was a frequent occurrence. Or 'you're fucking useless'. We were singled out regularly. But back then it was all part of the 'manning up' process. But culture has changed and if that happens today a parent can come in and accuse a coach of goading, victimising, and verbally and emotionally abusing their son. The accusation of bullying soon follows. And bullying is an emotive word. Look at what happened at Aston Villa with coach Kevin MacDonald, or Cardiff City and coach Craig Bellamy. Whatever they were doing, standard stuff 30 years ago, was deemed unacceptable in today's game.

There's this wonderful book by an ex-player called Mick Rathbone, *The Smell of Football.* If you want to know about how young players can be terrified by senior pros who ritually humiliate them, continually put them down, and destroy any confidence that a young lad might have, then this is the book to read. It starts with his time at Birmingham City in the 70s. It was so bad he hated going in the senior dressing room, he hated any appearances in the first team when he was a teenager. He dreaded matchdays and prayed that he would be in the reserves and not the first team. I can honestly say I never saw anything like this at Burnley, in fact it was much the opposite, even to the extent of getting £20 for accepting a 'dare'. Peter Swan was the best at this.

'Shorts down son and sit in that bucket of ice for two minutes. £20 if you can do it for two minutes.' Which apprentice is not going to earn an easy £20? Easy? My God it was freezing, agonising on the old crown jewels. But £20. Funnily enough, today to aid recovery you immerse yourself in a tank of freezing icy water and you don't get a £20 bonus for doing it. You could say we invented this, but with buckets of ice years ago at Burnley.

Graham Branch was a team-mate at Burnley. His experiences were much the same although he didn't enter the game until he was 19.

'I entered professional football at 19 straight out of the West Cheshire League playing for Heswall. Most of the senior players treated me fine but two in particular treated me terribly with daily abuse to my face in training in front of everybody. Most of it was really nasty stuff. One of them tried it on a bit too much one day and I threatened to knock his head off. Surprisingly he never spoke to me that way again and nor did the other nasty one either.

'Ray Mathias was my first coach and I have total respect for this man but the manager for a year treated me so badly until the PFA got involved, after I had refused to sign the contract he offered.

For a whole year he had me running to the training ground, about four miles, along 60mph roads. He ran me every day until the PFA told him he couldn't do that. He wouldn't let me leave until 5pm when everyone else had gone home and then slagged me off in the newspapers. From there it was to Tranmere and a manager who was a pure bully. You were criticised if you didn't do things right or do it their way. Stresses were constant and had a terrible effect on me personally to the point where I used to feign injuries, especially to avoid going to away games overnight.'

I played for Stan Ternent. His wife Kath said he was a man's man and that was true enough. If there is such a thing as an alpha male, then that was Stan. He made demands and had expectations of you that stretched you to the limit. But his demands sometimes bordered on the brutal. But: you would tell yourself, he's just trying to make me better, and when my serious illness arrived it was then that his genuine concern for the welfare of players surfaced.

There was a reserve game at Stoke and other than me and David May, it was a team filled with kids. We got the run-around and lost. Stan of course was furious afterwards and singled me and David out for the hairdryer treatment.

'I'll pay you up and you can fuck off,' he bellowed at us and we actually had no idea if we had been sacked or not. Was he kidding? Was it just a knee-jerk reaction that he'd forget five minutes later, or did he really mean it? We had no idea. Whatever: we went in for training the next day and what followed was one of those classic training ground bust-ups that are both funny and serious at the same time.

Training. Gawthorpe. I'm in possession of the ball and David May whacks me hard. I'm on the floor painfully winded and in agony, holding my ribs. I could hardly breathe. Stan took exception, maybe he was out for David May that day, maybe he was in grumpy mode; who knows? Anyway, he marches over to David and takes a swing at him but it didn't really connect. In fact, from where I was on the floor looking up at them, it looked hilarious. I couldn't help but laugh despite still being in agony and struggling to breathe. It all ended up with Stan being dragged off the pitch by Arthur Gnohere, and David May full of apologies to me; there was nothing personal in his challenge, and both of us were still wondering if we had been sacked and should we come in the next day.

The next day and still we didn't know if we had been sacked or not. In fact, we hadn't been, and when the next team sheet went up, I was down to play and David May was named captain. Football, eh?

Andy Payton was not bothered much about the bust-up. What bothered him more was that someone let the story out. There was a mole and who was it? Training ground fights happen all the time, said Andy. He'd seen the lot, managers hitting players, players hitting managers and players fighting amongst themselves even after a win. Football is a highly charged game, tempers spill over so it's inevitable you will get a clash of personalities or disagreements over something like a slightly late tackle. Andy could recall that his old Hull City team-mate, Billy Whitehurst, was in some sort of fight every week. But the unwritten rule was that what happens on the training ground, stays on the training ground, and that meant not running to the local journalist with a story to tell. There should be solidarity in the dressing room but sadly in this case someone had let the cat out of the bag. It was the talk of the pubs before the next game, said Andy, and no player could possibly be pleased to see the incident plastered all over the back pages. Instead of talking about the local derby coming up against Preston, they were talking about a behind-closed-doors incident that was best forgotten. Christmas was just around the corner, OK the club was only five points above the bottom three, but the top six were only nine ahead. There was still everything to play for and supporters needed to see optimism and confidence, not tittle-tattle from someone who had broken the basic rule of keeping things private.

Stan would defend his players in public. He might give them a rollicking in private but harsh words were behind closed doors. But someone on this occasion had done the dirty on him. He was fair though, he picked on everybody if he needed to, the skipper Big Steve Davis, Kevin Ball, Glen Little or me, all of us. Physio Ian Liversedge had a signal he'd give us when Stan was coming into the changing room. A thumbs up meant good mood, he's OK today, you can have a laugh. A thumbs down meant bad mood, watch out, mind how you go. Some days you just had to be on your best behaviour or you'd be on the receiving end.

Years later you look back and laugh and one of the funniest bust-ups involved Stan with physio Ian, aka Soz. Robbie Blake tells the story on *Under the Cosh* on YouTube, where four footballers sit round a table with a beer or a glass of wine and tell tall tales. Look it up and have a listen.

Gordon Armstrong was another one on the receiving end one day at Gawthorpe, when he said something to the gaffer that resulted in him being told to clear off. So, he left the pitch along with Ronnie Jepson and as they got to the far side and were almost at the bridge over the river, they heard Cliff Roberts the chief scout, puffing and panting behind them trying to catch up. Cliff was 60 at the time, maybe more, not entirely fit and he was wheezing and trying to get the words out after he'd been running after them all the way across the field. Stan had clearly sent him after them. 'Wait lads, wait,' he croaked.

Armstrong remembers, 'We were smiling at the sight of Cliff panting and out of breath and assumed he'd run all that way after us to tell us to get back to training. But no. Cliff had a different message. "And Stan says to tell you, fuck off and don't come back."'

Glen Little certainly has his own fund of bust-up stories. Glen is a born story-teller.

'When Stan came in, it was a poor start to the season and in the last minute at Gillingham they scored the winner. I was on the line and the ball hits my hand and goes in. Now if it was a southern game, I'd get someone to drive my car down, I'd be on the bus, and then be able to get home for the rest of the weekend. You'd ask Stan first and he'd be OK but this time he'd said only if we win. And we didn't and there's my car in Gillingham and I had to drive it all the way back to Burnley. But that wasn't the worst bit. I knew what was coming in the dressing room. Of course, he'd single me out, the scapegoat, and true enough he was looking for me and he kicks the nearest bin but he breaks his toe. It was concrete.'

'Not true at all,' said Stan when Dave asked him about the story. 'It was a metal bin bolted to the floor.'

Glen continues: 'At Bournemouth we lost 5-0, got a real chasing. In we go to the dressing room at full time expecting the worst. But no, he seemed calm. Hmm, we thought, maybe he realises that what he's doing just isn't working so what's the point of bollocking us yet again. All he says is, "Listen, you're gonna get in that shower, you're gonna get on that coach, and we're gonna get back to Burnley."

'OK, we're not happy that we lost 5-0, but this is alright then, we thought. Stop for fish and chips, then stop at the off licence, we know it's gonna be a long, long drive, before we get home. The first couple of hours were OK, all was quiet, and then … Stan gets up and comes down the coach. And starts picking on us, hammering us, tells us we've got a blind centre-half and a centre-half that's colour blind, no wonder we're letting five fucking goals in. "Get yer mother on the phone," he tells John O'Kane. "No don't ring my mother," pleads John.

'We get to Warwick services where goalkeeper Paul Crichton is gonna get off. He's let five goals in but I call out to him down the coach as he gets off, "GOOD DEBUT CRICHTS." Not the best thing to shout probably.

'And that's when the Budweiser bottle hits me on the back of the head. "And you Blakey, I shoulda sold you while I had the chance," he yells at me. Maybe it was an accident and he was just waving it about.

'Nobody can believe it. I've been hit with a beer bottle. But I just think it could have been worse. It could have been a wine bottle. They're bigger.

'We get back to Burnley and by next day the rumours are flying around; it's a small town and news travels. The next weekend it's Stoke and I go up for a header and the centre-half gives me a cut and this needs five stitches. The bottle story is now that I've been hit by a bottle and needed five stitches. Amazingly nothing ever come out of it. The bottle thing is in his book.

'Something like this just seemed normal, part of things at Burnley, all part and parcel of playing for Stan. He was always on at me yet I knew he was also my biggest supporter. Gareth Ainsworth was sold for £2m and he tells me if he's sold for £2m then I'm worth £4m. He insisted with the chairman I got a big pay rise when I wasn't sold to Manchester City. I was there with the wife as we sat with him and the chairman. "Get it done," said Stan.

'But it wasn't just players. The directors got it as well. Before travelling overnight to a game, he wanted us to do some moves on the Turf Moor pitch on the Friday morning because Gawthorpe was such a mess. We get out on to the pitch and it was rock hard and icy. He'd asked for the undersoil heating to be put on for us. It wasn't. On the coach he tore into the director responsible. "But Stan, Stan, it costs £300 an hour to switch it on." It didn't matter, he got both barrels.

'We'd just got a promotion and were doing well early season. We were having a five-a-side session in the gym and it was near the end, I was tired, we were losing, the session dragging on and on, and I let someone go past me. I thought session's over, we'll be off any minute. Time to go.

'But a voice calls out, angry, "Whoa whoa, stop, stop, stop, stop, what the … you just let 'im run past yer. What you doin?"

'"Well," I answered him. "Stan, we been doin' this now for two hours, I'm knackered."

'"Knackered?" he says, "Knackered …" and he sends me out the gym.

'So, I go out through the doors but it's raining and blowing a gale at 100mph like it does in Burnley, the doors fly in the wind and crash open. And Stan thinks it's me that's slammed them. I'm halfway across the car park soaked and cold in the rain and wind and John Mullin comes running after me. "Glen, Glen, he wants you back in, you gotta come back." So, as I'm walking back in and all of a sudden, he comes out the door and he's fuming. And I think oh no, I know what's comin' 'ere and he 'its me with a right 'ook. But I've put my arms up and block it with my right hand. He grabs me and now we're falling back in through the doors and two players grab him and try and pull him off. And while they're doin' that he's trying to kick me. I'm larfin, couldn't help it, as he calls me all the names under the sun.

'"You fuckin' get out the other door." He thinks I'd kicked the first door when I went out.

'After that, some of the other players came over to me. I'm sat in the dressing room, and they told me to go and see him and just say sorry, which I was happy to do, I'm not that bothered, I'm easy-going. "Come on Glen go, and have a word with him, he's sat up in the laundry." So, I do.

'"Gaffer one o' them things, let's get on with it, everything's alright."

'Next comes a few words with Ronnie Jepson, he tells me he thinks there is no way back and I think well someone will 'ave me, plenty of takers. At the end of it I'm not bothered. I go home and two hours later there's a call from the *News of the World*, would I like to make a statement, we've heard that Stan's hit you. It's clear that someone had seen him hit me. I just said, "Nah, no comment."'

Stan himself tells the story rather differently with a shorter version. 'One morning during training he'd got the hump with a refereeing decision I'd made and it was ruining the session. I told him to get out. He booted open the emergency exit door which slammed back against a brick wall and crashed loudly. A dozen people in the car park turned to stare. I told his mates to get him back in but he refused. I wasn't having my authority flouted in front of witnesses and barged outside, caught him by the arm and clipped him round the head. "Get back in there," I told him. He did.'

Back to Glen's version: 'The next day, after we all had a walk, he gets us into a meeting and the gaffer says "you alright Glen?" That's the nearest to an apology you'd ever get, and I say "yeh". But word had obviously got back to him that he's been seen hitting me and there's no doubt about it, he could have been sacked.

'"But," he says, "if I find out who grassed …", and again, he said, "You alright Blakey?" That was another nearest to an apology you're gonna get.

'What we found out later was that some woman from the office was sitting in her car and saw it all. The rumour was she'd told one of the directors. And from that, word had got round.'

* * *

Only once did I get the better of Stan. I was either on the transfer list or we'd had one of our bust-ups. Bust-ups were usually when I thought I should be in the team, and wasn't. He'd sent me to train with the kids so I wasn't best pleased. Small I may be but I'm a cussed little sod. Anyway, I see him staring over at me and it's one of those times when you think, oh he's talking about me. So, he's staring with a grim face at me and I think, right, I'll just stare back at him. I stop playing, stand still, and stare back. Steve Davis said it was like watching two gunslingers waiting to see who was going to draw first, except in our case it was who would back down and stop staring. I don't know how long it went on for, it feels like an age in the middle of it and you're thinking should I start playing again, should I give in, and meanwhile the game the kids are playing in is carrying on around you. Anyway, just when I'm thinking this is silly, it was Stan who stopped and turned around and walked away. Victory to me. But I reckon it was the only time I ever got the better of him in anything and it was something so silly.

Both Robbie Blake and Glen Little had their rows with him and one thing that irked them both was the way in which on some days Ronnie Jepson and Sam Ellis would give us a tick for every time we won the ball back in a practice game. 'Course, I always got plenty of ticks, that was my game. Ten ticks and you were teacher's pet. But where this system went wrong was that they expected the flair players to be ball-winners as well. And two of the best were Robbie and Glen, but definitely not at ball-winning. So when, at the end of a training game, they had no ticks or just one, they were pulled up and criticised. It infuriated them, especially Robbie, and Robbie was no shrinking violet when it came to sticking up for himself. He'd eff and swear and take them apart, eyes blazing and face red with anger.

'Not my fucking job to win the ball. Why don't you give ticks for every time I beat a man? Why don't you give ticks for every cross I get over? Why don't you give ticks for every accurate pass I make? Why don't you give ticks for every goal I score?' All this was shouted at the two of them as he stood scowling at them.

The problem was however, we suspected that this tick system was used in team selection so that the ball-winners got in the team, but lose the ball too often, and you didn't. It counted against the flair players and the match-winners who were prone to committing the awful sin of losing the ball. I can only guess, and I may be wrong, it was the reason why Glen and Robbie were on the bench sometimes instead of playing.

There are a few players who will say Stan was a bully, but that was football in those days. He wanted the best for the team, and for you. He wanted you at your peak. That's what he was there for. He loved Burnley Football Club and would have done anything for it. He wanted to get the best out of you and that's all he was doing. And it was all at a time when irate managers were quite common. There was nothing unusual about it. There are YouTube videos of Neil Warnock berating his teams that are not for the faint-hearted.

But we did find a good way eventually to defuse the gaffer's anger, and when he gave up smoking there were times when you needed a tin hat. His son Dan had a lovely little daughter, Olivia, and she was the apple of Grandpop Stan's eye. She could do no wrong and when she was a toddler around Stan he melted like butter. We noticed this on the occasions that Dan brought her down to Gawthorpe. We had a simple ruse. If we knew Stan was having one of those bad mood days, we would give Dan a ring and tell him to get Olivia down sharpish. It never failed.

Woe betide anyone who ate the tuna sandwiches on the coach. There were always sandwiches and flasks of soup for the journeys we had to make. Pea and ham soup was a regular delicacy, and piles of sandwiches. Footballers are a hungry lot and the sandwiches soon went and one day he came up the coach aisle and we knew he was fuming, but had no idea what about.

'Who's eaten all the fucking tuna?' he growled.

Nor did you behave all laughing and jolly after a defeat on the coach. If the manager was glum and morose whether it was Stan, Jimmy Mullen or whoever, you didn't want to be caught laughing and joking. The irrepressible Glen Little usually tried to break the ice at some stage, he couldn't help it. But we'd tell him, 'not now, not now'.

Apparently, Mitchell Thomas used to call me 'Mr Angry'. Said I was so easy to wind up in training. I never knew that. But yes, I could fly off the handle, and David Beckham was not the first to aim a boot at his manager. There was the time I threw mine at Stan Ternent. I'd missed some pre-season training because of an injured foot and pre-season training and build-up of fitness is so important, more than supporters probably realise. Miss some and you play catch-up. I joined training unfit, was on the bench for the first game not fully fit, was picked for the team a couple of games later and was still not fully fit. There is no hiding place in midfield, no way can you take a breather, take 30 seconds to get your breath back, and I felt it. I came off that pitch exhausted and Stan collared me, accused me of being unfit – well of course I was not fully fit – and he carried on grumbling that I'd been running around like an idiot. I have a short fuse, was incensed, effed and blinded at him, picked up my boots and hurled them at him. They missed him and flew across the room. Beckham's boots got in the news. Mine didn't. But he was never one to hold a grudge with me and I was in the team again the next week. The importance of pre-season fitness is massive, miss some and adrenalin might get you through a couple of games but then it all wears off.

There was another occasion which showed you just have to stand up for yourself. Some players can't and just take it. Again, it involved coach Harry Wilson and was a game at Port Vale when Mullen was manager. It was also a first game for Jamie Hoyland, now a great pal of mine and who taught me a lot. Jamie had just signed on loan, wasn't up to full fitness, and to his great surprise was told he could play the first 45 minutes. At half-time he was close to collapse but then they said 'leave your boots on, you can play another 20 minutes'. You could hear him groan from 20 yards away. But it was me that Harry Wilson went for, telling me at half-time I was this and that, and unfit and useless. 'Course I was, I'd missed some pre-season training because I'd been smacked in the eye with a ball. Young and skinny as I might have been, I wasn't having any of it and went back at him. No way was I going to sit there and take it. Jamie says that was when he first realised, I was a gutsy little so and so, well able to take care of myself.

If Harry Wilson was my bête noir, then for Jamie it was Tony Book, his coach when Jamie was just a young lad at Manchester City. And yet Jamie is like me and will say, 'Well it didn't do me any harm.' But then both of us are strong characters. Back then this kind of treatment was designed to sort out the wheat from the chaff, to see who had the mental strength that was needed. Jamie is now a top chief scout for Everton and travels all over Europe. He has thrived.

Sometimes a good coach had no need to be a bully or destructive. Such a one was John Ward, coach for Adrian Heath at Burnley. Jamie was there when David Eyres, another great player, once simply refused to do what Ward asked on the training pitch. He was a top pro, a senior pro, had been round the block many times but objected to a routine Ward wanted him to do.

'I'm not doing that,' said Eyres.

'Then go off, get changed,' said Ward, just very quietly and calmly.

A stunned Eyres walked off and trudged to the changing rooms on the far side of the field. He apologised later. You don't always need to rant and rave to get a point across.

The Alex Ferguson hairdryer treatment is famed in football. We might laugh at the mention of it. This tongue-in-cheek description of a full-on Fergie explosion at a player has entered legend. Players who suffered it might look back and laugh at it and see it almost as a badge of honour. And what about the boot he kicked at David Beckham that hit him on the head? Where do these things come on a one-to-ten scale of bullying? Have they ever been described as bullying? Maybe not, but you can bet your house that if any coach kicked or threw a boot at a player today, he'd be hauled over the coals, suspended maybe.

Would a supermarket manager try the hairdryer treatment on some hapless young lad who'd made a mess of stacking shelves? Probably not. A bit of a gentle reprimand maybe, but a full-on Fergie, no. Only in football.

Bullying apprentices was once standard practice, accepted as part of the toughening-up process. Senior players had apprentices cleaning boots and doing odd jobs, and woe betide the apprentice who got a smear of polish on the laces or missed a bit of mud still stuck to the sole. Aggression was part of the culture, with too often a one-size-fits-all approach to any bunch of young lads learning their trade. Individual sensitivities and needs were frequently unacknowledged.

Chapter 6

MANAGERS COME AND GO, MULLEN AND HEATH

AS EVER, we were in Tubbs going over things. It was the day after the bust-up between Raheem Sterling and Joe Gomez at the England training camp prior to the game against Montenegro. At the weekend in the game between Liverpool and Manchester City there had been a bit of aggro between them. At the England camp, Sterling carried on in the canteen grabbing Gomez and sending crockery flying. A storm amongst the teacups you might say. At Anfield, Gomez had shoved Sterling away just as I did Dennis Wise in a game at Millwall years ago. Wise, the artful dodger, conveniently fell backwards and landed on the grass. It looked like I'd landed a killer blow but it was just a routine shove. Not even handbags. I was sent off. Gomez was not.

We were also bemoaning all the VAR offside decisions, the decisions that were based on a player nudging ahead of the defender by a toe or a knee, and in one incident, by an armpit. Decisions that were taking an age to reach, with players and crowds standing waiting, getting more and more exasperated by the time taken. The answer is simple; it needs clear daylight between attacker and defender to decide if a player is offside or not. That's not rocket science and so simple instead of these magnifying-glass examinations to reach a conclusion. And what of Glen Little with that rather large nose of his. How ridiculous it would have been to have heard that a goal had been deemed offside because of Glen's nose. Offside by a nose, not as daft as it sounds, the day will come.

* * *

Frank Casper came into my 16-year-old life and went very quickly, within a week. Frank always says it was him that signed me. Jimmy Mullen says it was Jimmy Mullen. Anyway, on 25 November 1991, and with my parents, secretary Albert Maddox and director Basil Dearing (I'd never met anybody called Basil before but I'd heard of one in *Fawlty Towers*), I signed on as a trainee. It was £29.50 a week for three months and then up to £35 a week. Plus, there was £10 for every first team appearance or as a sub. There was a £50-a-week lodgings allowance. A £5,000 signing-on fee like some kids get today? Er no, this was bottom division Burnley. I never saw anything like that kind of money when I arrived. There are many stories of parents getting washing machines and fridges. Mine didn't.

Frank Casper always used to say, 'look smart, play smart'. Harry Wilson used to say it as well so maybe he picked it up from Casper. 'Tuck your shirts in and pull your socks up,' Harry Wilson would order us and woe betide you if you didn't.

Who'd be a manager? They're a breed apart. To be successful or even just survive for more than a couple of years, you have to be stubborn, thick-skinned, single-minded and know what you want. You also have to have the players on your side. That's whether you are a gentleman like Arsene Wenger or Roy Hodgson, unorthodox like Brian Clough, or ruthless like Alex Ferguson. You work all hours of the day, travel hundreds of miles, watch reserve games miles away on cold wet Tuesday nights, need to handle chairmen and directors, the media, the supporters and then not least of all players, who can range from dedicated professionals to galactico playboys. And on top of all that is all the abuse when things are not going well. Ask Frank Casper or Stan Ternent about that. Ask Jimmy Mullen. He said that being a manager was like living in a goldfish bowl, and when he first arrived as assistant, it was Frank Casper who had told him 'you're joining a big club in a tiny village'. In a tiny village there is no hiding place for either you or your family. It's why so many players and managers choose not to live in the town where they play or manage. The abuse does get through to you. Once I got a house of my own it was in a place called Great Harwood, not a long way away but far enough to be away from things. The estate was a mix of Burnley and Blackburn fans. I kept quiet and once established, never read the papers. It was my mother who made the scrapbooks.

Frank had been a legend of a player at Burnley, had worked his way through all the various stages of management eventually to be sat in the hot seat. Once he sat in it, it was indeed a hot seat with demanding fans thoroughly fed up with being in the Fourth Division. He started his managerial career with an amazing 4-1 League Cup win at my beloved Tottenham of all places. A Fourth Division side winning 4-1 down there; it was unheard of. Centre-forward Billy Hamilton scored twice, today a Burnley legend and hero. Casper ended his managing career after a desperate and abysmal game away at pitiful Scarborough that Burnley lost with Burnley fans abusing him terribly after the game and banging on the dressing room windows in their rage. He'd had enough. Stan Ternent might simply have turned on them and told them to 'fuck off, this is Burnley not Barcelona'.

So, it was Jimmy Mullen his assistant that took over towards the back end of 1991 and kept me on. I was set to be at Burnley until Steve Cotterill arrived in 2004.

As a rule, players tend to be loyal towards the managers who signed them or gave them their chance. I'm no different and despite all his shortcomings and problems, I always say that I owe a debt to Jimmy Mullen. He was far from everyone's cup of tea, certainly not mine; he could treat players badly, Chris Pearce and Roger Eli will attest to that; he could rant and rave and shout at players; you might say he drank too much but he was my first manager and saw something in me that he persevered with.

It was his 67th birthday just as we were writing this section and I thought of him as the man who gave me my first pro contract and my debut. Supporter Steven Brown on Twitter made a telling comment: 'Legend: we can never thank him enough, he made us believe again.' It's hard to knock him, then, but many did, and by the end of his time at Burnley the abuse he was receiving was totally unacceptable.

Funny how just a change of manager can send a club in a different direction, even with the same players. When Frank left and Jimmy took over, the team immediately won nine games in a row. The bunch that took Burnley to promotion in 91/92 was one of the best ever, filled with characters and winners. I was only an apprentice then but loved to watch them. They tore at the opposition, bombed down the flanks, snapped up the chances; Fourth Division they may have been but they played a brand of football far above that. The season started badly but Mullen came in and the wins piled up. It was remarkable. You can't really put your finger on why there should be such a transformation; perhaps it was just that Mullen tweaked things on the wings and just took the brakes off. Whatever, it was a stunning season that people still remember and several of the players still get together.

Don't ever think that every dressing room is a happy place filled with camaraderie. Far from it. There have been well known and very successful teams at Manchester United and Liverpool where several of the players couldn't stand the sight of each other. But I was lucky that I never played in such a dressing room. Sure, there were disagreements and arguments. A dressing room is filled with egos and adrenalin, alpha males and cussed devils. But only very occasionally did two players really not get on at Burnley.

John Deary, who I still know today, said it was one of the best-ever dressing rooms at Burnley, mental at times, a real mad house. But it was a winning dressing room, 23 games won out of the 35 that Mullen was in charge that season. It makes a difference. Mullen was like a breath of fresh air, said one supporter, with an attractive, attacking style, using two wide players and pinging balls into the box for Eli and Conroy. It worked so well.

Make no mistake, Mullen could be volatile but he could also be warm and friendly when he felt like it. The kind of bloke you'd like as a next-door neighbour even. He was never one to hide his emotions; maybe he should have hidden them more, especially on the touchline.

But the side of him that I saw as a young lad, as an apprentice, was not nice at all. We were allowed a week off to go home if we wished at Christmas but you had to knock on his door and ask permission. The unpleasant, bully side came out.

'What do you want to go home for?' he'd bark at you loudly, trying to be as awkward as possible, making you feel thoroughly uncomfortable. 'Well go on then, yeh, just fuck off.' Why was he like this? Who knows?

'Fetch those balls,' he yelled at Roger Eli on one occasion in training, purely for effect, balls that were a mile away. Roger ignored him.

Signing Adrian Heath was a masterstroke and he immediately scored 20 goals in his stunning first season when Mullen brought him in. The biggest disappointment was leading in an FA Cup tie against Premier League side Sheffield United with just ten minutes to go and then conceding twice to draw 2-2. They won the replay 4-2 at Turf Moor.

But Burnley fans are a fickle and demanding lot, or at least they were. In the Premier League for the fourth consecutive season as we write, grumbles seem to be few and far between, with Sean Dyche having as good as 'trained' supporters to realise that miracles are being worked and that being at this level is an amazing achievement. But it wasn't always so, especially in the days of Frank Casper and Jimmy Mullen. At the end of the 92/93 season Mullen and chairman Frank Teasdale had to write a letter to critical supporters in the local paper to calm them down and to assure them there was no lack of ambition at the club. But, it added, finances meant that this was not a club that could attract star players with large price tags. Nearly 30 years later Sean Dyche is saying much the same.

Jimmy's problem with supporters, as well as them being so demanding, was maybe that they saw him sell popular players. Mike Conroy was one whose goals had ensured promotion. He didn't want to leave Turf Moor but was sold to Preston, feeling quite let down by Mullen. He loved the fans and the town and felt it was his second home after Scotland. Steve Harper, one of my favourite players, was another to go. At the same time, though, Mullen was no slouch at buying replacement players. That, however, would result in yet more criticism in his final months when he bought striker after striker, each one failing badly. But that was yet to come and the big grumble of the new season was the team's failure to do well away from home; at Turf Moor they won game after game but away they were almost hopeless. Mullen shouted at them, kept them locked in the dressing room, tore his hair out, publicly criticised them and described it all as ludicrous. It was the abysmal away form that cost automatic promotion, but Burnley still reached the play-offs.

The two semi-final games are part of Burnley legend: the 0-0 draw at Turf Moor, the treatment dished out to Ted McMinn, the assumption by Plymouth fans that with the draw they would then coast to Wembley, then Burnley putting on one of their best ever away performances in the away leg. Remember, this was a season when we could barely buy an away win. Rough treatment, racism, presumption of a win, abuse from home supporters, confidence that Wembley was a formality – all of these were on full display at Plymouth. Burnley won 3-1. Wembley beckoned.

Burnley won the final with 40,000 fans ecstatic at the end. Down to nine men, nevertheless, Stockport County had everyone chewing fingernails by the end. Mullen had done it, or had he? 'We did it despite Jimmy Mullen,' said Adrian Heath. I was there to see it. True or not, two promotions in three seasons looked good on his CV and all these years later still does. Alas, from that point on it all went pear-shaped as what director Clive Holt called 'infectious enthusiasm' turned into a manager who appeared 'to be losing his grip'. The new level was far more challenging and ended in an immediate relegation with a side bedevilled by red cards, just 11 wins out of 46 games, indiscipline and the leakiest defence in the division. New players were bought that never really clicked. It was a real struggle of a season with Jimmy floundering so that by the end the cries of 'MULLEN OUT, MULLEN OUT' rang around the ground.

Director Clive Holt, as eagle-eyed a man as you could wish to meet, knew what the problems were. He could see Jimmy struggling. He could see him wilting under a greater pressure. He knew the story that during a home game Jimmy had disappeared and was found later asleep in a toilet cubicle. Was this the right man to be in charge at this higher level, he asked? Probably not. Poor Jimmy came to a torrid end, abused verbally and physically in a Burnley restaurant with his wife. Chairman Frank Teasdale went to see him at his home and decided it was time to call it a day.

Do I have fond memories of him then? Not really. It seemed I was always arguing about, or holding out, for more money. Not out of greed but out of a sense of fairness and what I was worth; if you see other players getting that bit more, you want the same. There was the time I was on under £200 a week, was offered £200 but wanted £250. It was almost a game, with me saying 'I'll play when I get what I think I'm worth.' Eventually he agreed. But it wasn't over. 'Yes, but I want it backdated to when we first started all this.' He agreed. I'm a stubborn little sod when I want to be. There's talk about what motivates a player, what or who does he play for, himself, his team, his manager, the fans? But of course, money is a motivator especially back then when wages were not great and players had a mortgage to pay and a family to support. For us the win bonus was a big factor and motivator so we played to win. The bonus made a big difference on a winning Saturday to players who were not on megabucks as so many are today in the Premier League, the Championship and even League One at some clubs. Basic wages were very basic.

There were four of us younger players there, coming through the ranks with Mullen, and the press labelled us 'The Young Guns'. Myself, Chris Brass, Paul Smith and Andy Cooke, although he had been bought. All of us were getting good press reviews and plenty of mentions. At one point we were fourth in the table and confidence was growing all the time. Chris Brass and myself had played together for so long it seemed we had such a good understanding and helped each other out all the time. 'If you're good enough you're old enough,' said the manager after we had beaten Carlisle 2-0. 'The older players will need to sit up and take notice of these young lads,' Mullen warned them.

I'm in my 40s now and it all seems an age ago but you see a clipping in a scrapbook and it comes back. I was called a 'starlet' back then. 'A breath of fresh air,' said another report, 'with vast potential.' A starlet, it makes me laugh to think what those great days were like. 'Wonder Weller' was another. I'd just had a good league debut game against Carlisle, had a helping hand in both goals, the report says. Left Carlisle chasing shadows with impressive runs and distinguished passing ability. Chasing shadows: I occasionally play these days for the Vintage Clarets in charity games and my shadow is somewhat larger than it used to be back then.

We had some fun with Jimmy though. There was the time we found him asleep on a matchday in the loo. There was the time he named 12 players for a game. Jamie Hoyland's version of the story is that John Deary looked at him and says, 'Er Boss, you've named 12 players in the team.'

'Oh,' says Mullen, 'have I put you in?'

'Yes,' says Deary.

'OK then,' says Mullen. 'You can be sub.'

Another version is that it was Big John Gayle who was demoted to sub to reduce the numbers. 'Can you play up front on your own?' asked Mullen.

'Er no,' said Gayle.

'OK, you'd better be sub then.'

The matchday whisky bottle was famous. In the bucket with ice and two glasses. Big John Gale saw it for the first time and thought it was for the players and was about to have a nip. 'Er no,' Jamie Hoyland tells him. 'It's not for us, it's for Mullen and Teasdale.'

After one incident we began to call him Jimmy Burnley. He'd locked himself out of a hotel somewhere and was hollering to get back in. 'I'm Jimmy Mullen from Burnley, let me in.'

But he was so confused it became, 'I'm Jimmy Burnley, let me in.'

The name stuck. Footballers are cruel. One sign of weakness, one mistake, and they're on to you.

In all honesty I can't say I knew too much about the abuse he received towards the end. On the field you don't hear it unless there's a lull in play for an injury maybe or a rare occasion when things go really quiet. We ignored his rants and raves from the touchline. Senior pros just shrug it off and I learned such a lot from them, especially in the reserves when you played alongside several of them.

Today it's all about development squads; there are no reserve sides as such. There is no Central League where you come up against gnarled and grizzled pros who've seen it and done it all and from whom you can learn so much. Some of them quite bitter at their fading careers and determined to kick lumps out of young upstarts. That's certainly a learning curve, avoiding serious harm. There used to be a natural progression from 'A' team, to reserves to first team, but today at Burnley it seems so hard for a young lad to step up to the first team because that has gone. If Dwight McNeil got a chance at Burnley, it was only because all the regular wingers were injured. Without that, I suspect he would have gone out on loan. For him it was serendipity, not design. The press lauds him as the next big Burnley sale, £30m maybe.

Adrian Heath was the new hope after caretaker Clive Middlemass. We knew him well; we knew he could play a bit. He was a top player and made all the right noises; he wanted to take Burnley to the top; he thought it was a great club and wanted to reach the Premier League within five years. He remembered the great rapport he had with the fans as a player. I liked him, he brought younger players like me into the team, and in his first season we might well have got to the play-offs but for four defeats near the end of the season.

As a player he became a good mate, took some of us younger players to go and see Everton and at one stage when I was out of contract in the summer, he organised for me to go and train at Stoke City with Lou Macari. We called Stoke the running club because that's all they seemed to do. Meanwhile, Mullen kept phoning and phoning, 'get back here, get back here', and I kept saying no. But boy was I fit and boy could I run. Eventually of course I did go back. All this attention from Heath had a consequence, when he came back as manager.

'Yer dad's back,' said the other players. 'Yer dad's back.'

Fans thought that under Heath things were slowly getting better and there was a newspaper story he wanted to sign Sean Dyche, who is now Burnley manager. His coach was John Ward and some folks thought that when he left that was when results tailed off. Teammates Jamie Hoyland and David Eyres rated him highly. We had a 1-0 defeat at Liverpool in the FA Cup and played so well. Over the season as a whole it was the bottom sides we couldn't beat. One of the big words in football, the dreaded word – 'inconsistent'.

Heath's problem was that as a manager he still wanted to be part of the dressing room, part of the banter and high jinks. You can't do that. He used to wonder why the dressing room went quiet when he came in. Players will always say there has to be a gap between players and manager, you can't stay pals because you once played with him. He wanted to have nights out with the players and people were uncomfortable with that. But for me he was a plus and he was also the manager that brought Glen Little to the club.

Heath wasn't everyone's cup of tea though. Peter Swan was no fan of his. Swanny was a big, big man who could play centre-forward or centre-half equally well. Not a man to tangle with and he didn't suffer fools gladly. Said what he thought and took no nonsense. They used to travel up from Stoke together at one stage and Swanny got tired, he says, of Inchy rabbiting away in the car about life at Everton, who he had played with, all the big games and names, what he had done in football and how one day he would go into management.

'If ever you went into management, I wouldn't want to play for you,' said Swanny. Heath asked why. 'Because you're a pillock,' was the answer. If Peter wasn't driving, to avoid listening, he'd bury his head in a pile of papers he bought. If Peter was driving, he'd give the newspapers to Heath.

When Heath became manager, he told the players he'd like to be called gaffer. Version one of the next story is that Peter politely told him he would not call him gaffer because he had no respect for him. Version two is that Peter grabbed him by the throat in the loo one day and told him in no uncertain terms that he would never call him gaffer. The latter might be one of those fanciful tales that abound in football.

One game I remember is the FA Cup tie we played at Liverpool, if only because I was marking John Barnes and never got near him. I laughed at Chris Brass because he had the job of marking Steve McManaman, a player who was in peak form and was like the elusive pimpernel. Better you than me, I thought, confident that I'd handle Barnes, who by now was a bit overweight and a bit slower. I should have known. Brassy played well but I never got near Barnes. He ran rings round me for 90 minutes. I looked and he was gone. I tackled and the ball had gone. I anticipated where he would be, and he wasn't there.

Jamie Hoyland is adamant to this day that if Heath's coach John Ward had stayed, we would have walked promotion. He always says that when Ward left it was like a balloon bursting. But Ward left for Bristol City and in came Colin Harvey, another Evertonian. Harvey walked in on crutches. As a coach on crutches there is a limit to what you can do.

Director Clive Holt said that Heath was a breath of fresh air when he came in and that was true enough. But then Howard Kendall at Everton came after him again to be assistant manager there and he couldn't turn it down since Everton was always his great love. He came and he went, his time at Burnley a short one, leaving no great impression on the club, but personally I was massively disappointed. In the press he'd called me a 'cocky little so and so'. Maybe I was. Perhaps when you're a bit small like I was you have to be to get anywhere. 'He can do things at this level that other players can't,' he said of me. 'There is a lot more to come from him if he listens and learns.'

Perhaps with Heath I would have done; I took to him and he took to me.

There was one occasion I was truly grateful to him. The boo boys had been at me, a section of the crowd decided I was the reason the team was struggling in a cup game, a replay if I remember, against Walsall. Tell me in what way booing a player makes them play better. It doesn't. If there was any consolation, the game was abandoned at half-time because the floodlights failed. The lads in the dressing room were angry at the abuse but joked it was the groundsman who'd turned the lights off to shut the idiots up. Heath after the game was furious and made it clear in the press how disgusted he was with those fans who were booing. It was atrocious, he said, and nobody deserved that kind of treatment. Booing a team off at half-time, I can understand that. Booing an individual is unforgivable; football is a hard enough game as it is for anyone. Trust me, a player knows when he is having a bad game. I appreciated and respected Adrian Heath even more after that.

But a manager can leave and the course of a career can change. Sometimes for the better and sometimes for the worse. A manager can change a person's life, attitudes, career and direction. A manager can finish a player's career. Steve Cotterill ended mine. But that's a later story.

Years later, Heath revealed that he should have stayed at Burnley, gone with his head and not his heart. His wife, too, to this day reminds him he made a mistake re-joining Everton. The Everton he went back to was not the Everton he remembered. 'I should have stayed, Teasdale was really upset when I left and offered me a new deal and told me we had some good young players, that I should see it through. He was right, I should have done.'

Heath is convinced that the side would have gone on to promotion the following season. 'When I look back, I could have handled the situation better and the bottom line is, I should have stayed. It was a big decision but it was the wrong one.'

Such is football. Full of ifs, maybes and should-haves. Next up, in came Chris Waddle. And where do I start?

Chapter 7

THE YEAR OF THE WADDLE

'HE'S A bright spark with a lot of ability but his attitude needs sorting out. I took one look at him and thought, wonderful but I'm not sure about his mental state. He didn't seem to appreciate the game as much as he should and I don't want people like that. So, I stuck him in the reserves for a couple of matches, just to make him think a bit. Sure enough, he came to see me and asked me what was wrong. I told him and hopefully now he knows what is required.'

That was Chris Waddle on me as a player. Irony. Change a few words and I could have written some of it about him as manager. What on earth did he mean? I still wonder to this day. Communication was never his strong point. There was an occasion when I found out from the media that he had booked me in for a knee operation on the Monday after a game. 'Oh, we hear you have a knee op on Monday,' said the TV guy. I had no idea.

Then there was the time he pinned up a team sheet. It was versus Grimsby, just a list. He announced he'd just picked the best 11 players. I was on the list. None of us knew what position we'd play. We found that out at two o'clock on the day of the game.

Any excitement and anticipation when we heard the news of his arrival lasted about 15 minutes. We'd started the pre-season stuff and when the day came that we were told that Waddle was coming we'd already done a tough, really tough, running morning. Sat in the changing room, the sweat pouring off us, our kits dripping, groaning with exhaustion, sitting there knackered, the news comes that Waddle is arriving to see us all.

In he comes with Glenn Roeder by his side, the sergeant major, that's how he stood, that's how he acted from day one. 'Get your kits back on,' he orders us.

We look at each other in astonishment. On goes our kit again to be told we're having another training session, and more running and more running, and more running. Was he trying to prove something? Was it his way of announcing that he was here and was the boss? The senior pros were fuming. This was crazy. What was the point? We just ran until we dropped, had never experienced anything like it before, or since. It was futile and unnecessary. You just don't do this sort of thing unless you are a sadist or out of touch with what is needed. And maybe that was his problem. From that moment on he had lost us, nobody wanted to play for him. It set the tone for the season.

Me and Glen Little didn't get a look-in during the first pre-season games but then there was a game against Harrogate Town I think, in which both of us played and did really well; each of us scored goals and thought we'd impressed. But no, we weren't in the first side of the season. There was a disastrous start with no goals scored in the first six games and there was no win until the 11th game in October. By Christmas this was a side marooned at the foot of the table. Waddle was not going to be the Messiah. It was just a mess. We'd been the league's highest scorers with Heath; now it was six games and no goals. This is madness, we were thinking. The atmosphere was dreadful, team meetings were stormy, the whinging and moaning was terrible. Players walked out of meetings angry; Paul Barnes was one, announcing, 'I'm not having this anymore.'

At this time, I was still only a young kid and I was thinking that so far, this madness was just normal in football, that football was just a mad, mad world.

How did I cope? I remembered what Adrian Heath always said. 'No matter what's going on, ignore it, play and do your best. There will always be someone watching you.'

Supporters were as bemused by the early results as the players were. On hearing the news that Waddle was the new manager, Burnley folks had been amazed by this stellar appointment. I suppose Adrian Heath was a bit of a 'name' but the name Waddle was on a higher level altogether. He'd played over 650 games and scored 120 goals in his career so far. This really was a big-name appointment. He'd played 62 times for England. It looked a fantastic appointment and people were thinking if Bryan Robson could transform Middlesbrough, why not Chris Waddle at Burnley? If only they could have heard the players cursing him in that dressing room when he'd had us running til we dropped. The phones between us were red hot that night. The air was blue …

Initially however, the word promotion was being bandied about with such a megastar pulling the strings and attracting more big names to the club. But people were soon wondering, players and fans alike, if he was out of his depth and struggling with the responsibilities of management, especially as he was sometimes away with media commitments. It just never worked out and today his name is almost on the same level as John Bond in Burnley.

Gerry Creaney made a difference when he came and scored goals but the board would not sanction the permanent transfer. We struggled again and the more so because Waddle totally ignored Glen Little. He was perplexed at the treatment he received, training away from the first team, not even being spoken to by Waddle for three months. Glen was ready to pack in and go home especially when Sergeant Major Roeder said he was not even fit to lace

Waddle's boots after the fans demanded his inclusion. Glen recalled a strange incident when he was sitting alone in the boot room and in walked Waddle. Was Waddle surprised to see him there? For sure he didn't know what to say and stood there uncomfortably, spoke to him half-heartedly with a cursory 'alright then', and walked out.

There were mixed feelings about the training sessions, with David Eyres saying they were good, although you never came off feeling exhausted except for that crazy first day, but Glen Little saying they were a joke with Waddle often absent and that his team talks on a Friday would last about five minutes. More often than not there was just no game plan. But then even David Eyres began to get a bit dismissive of Waddle, with a dressing room argument on one occasion. Before he knew it, he was sold.

On a matchday, Waddle would sometimes say, 'Just go out and play.' Some of the lads would look and ask him, 'Where?'

By Christmas, Chris Brass and myself were regulars. By January, Burnley were well and truly in bottom place. If there was one thing that rescued the season it was the signing of Andy Payton in an exchange deal with Huddersfield when Paul Barnes went the other way. When he signed, the club were four points adrift at the bottom. Waddle himself played a few games but then another turning point was the return of Glen Little. With directors, as well as ourselves, very frustrated at Waddle's absences, he was actually instructed by the board to pick Glen Little and myself after I had lost my place. On the occasion when he was told to report to the board, he sent Glenn Roeder instead, and that was when he was told to pick us. They'd seen him buy a lad called Mark Ford from Leeds who just never really clicked and they were out of patience. We found out that Waddle was furious.

Fans were angry at Waddle's perceived attitude. He was seen as being far too-laid back and casual. Churchill speeches were not his habit. It was as if he found it difficult to show he cared and that 'it mattered'. There we were scrapping at the bottom for points and in the press, he was saying we should relax more, and he was leaving things to the Sergeant Major. Roeder was even doing some of the press conferences after a game.

With all this as the background, bit by bit, somehow, we clawed our way back to a position where escaping relegation was a possibility. Truth is, the form in the second half of the season was good and had we managed that over a whole season who knows if promotion might not have been the result? It really was a Jekyll and Hyde of a season and safety was assured in the very last game at home to Plymouth Argyle.

Waddle might well have stayed on as manager if he'd felt that the board were behind him. Somewhere he is on record as saying he would have struggled to find a harder board to work with and that he was just banging his head against a brick wall. Presumably the board thought the same of him. Even after the victorious Plymouth game at the end of the season that saved our skins, he maintained there were glum faces in the boardroom. When Stan Ternent took over, he is alleged to have asked Waddle, 'How on earth did you get this team to survive?'

Waddle in fact had been to see Stan who was then manager of Bury and lived in Burnley. This was a few games before the end of the season. Stan knew that Waddle was struggling, or at least the team had been, so when he got a call from Waddle one night, he responded, agreeing to meet him up at his local pub, the Kettledrum. There were just six games left. With too many pub regulars in there doing their best to overhear what was being said, they moved to Stan's house and without being too obvious or patronising, Stan tried to prop him up, the wily old experienced manager who had seen it all, 'advising' the novice, for that in fact was what Waddle was, out of his depth and struggling.

I just didn't get Waddle at all. I didn't get the way he told me to show more hunger and desire. There are two buttons in football, he said, you press one for competitiveness and the other one for creativity. I'm still trying to figure that out.

In the press he was saying, 'Weller is a bright spark with a lot of ability,' but he was telling me my attitude was wrong. He said I was like a car with five gears but I was stuck in fourth, too laid back. Me – too laid-back? If Adrian Heath called me cocky, and Mitchell Thomas called me Mr Angry, I couldn't quite work out how I was too laid-back.

He said I should be playing in a higher division but then kept sticking me in the reserves. Again, in the press, he said I thought that he and Roeder were always picking on me. But that was because I was so frustrating. I was a wonderful talent but my mental state was all wrong. Mental state – what the hell was that? It was only looking at the scrapbooks again that brought all this back.

Waddle is quoted as saying: 'I know he has the ability to go to the very top. If he wants to become a top-class player he can be. It's basically about one word: desire. We keep having a pop at him because I'm trying to help him. He has got to look and learn and drink in the experiences of players like Gordan Cowans and myself. Paul is a very frustrating player; I think it is a mental thing with him. If he can get his head sorted then he has the ability to play in the Premiership because he has got so many attributes as a footballer. He has pace, he can dribble, can cover ground quickly. In short he is a player who can make things happen for himself and his team-mates.'

'Perhaps the players are in awe of me, frightened of me, because of my 62 caps,' he wondered. No, we weren't in awe or frightened. More like baffled by him, much of the time. Or wondering where he had gone when he disappeared for his TV duties. 'A mental thing' – to this day I am puzzled by that.

Jamie Hoyland met up with Dave in Tubbs (where else). They drank the place out of coffee by lunchtime. Jamie remembered the crazy running that Waddle had us doing. 'Utterly pointless,' said Jamie. On pre-season trips we always worked hard and then enjoyed the evenings with a few drinks. Work hard, play hard, was the mantra. Waddle wasn't having that. Away we went and he laid down the law. He said there'll be no drinking, we'd by in bed by this time or that time, this was not a jolly boys' outing. The seniors, remembered Jamie, just looked at each other and raised their eyes.

Jamie has always been proud of the fact (and amused) that Waddle was away so much that the seniors even took a lot of the coaching sessions themselves. There was an attitude of 'we'll bloody show him'. Sometimes after a game we never saw him til Thursday. The seniors set themselves a challenge, because so many of them were in the reserves: let's win this reserve league.

He found it difficult coaching and working with Division One players. He used to tell us in his Geordie accent how he used to play at Marseille, a top side then, with players like Papin. And, Papin was world class, he insisted on telling us. Let him come here then, on a wet and freezing night in February, we'd think.

Mark Winstanley, bless him, good mate, honest as the day is long, was not world class. The day comes that Waddle is telling Mark he wants to receive the ball from him in a certain way when Mark is passing it out from the back. Passing, however, was not really his strong point. We used to call him 'Whoosh' which tells you all you need to know. The word passing was not really in Mark's vocabulary. Waddle's accent was so broad even at the best of times it was hard to decipher what he was saying and, on this occasion, it was even worse.

'I had this signalling system at Marseille,' he began, 'so that when I was facing and receiving the ball, I indicated which side of me I wanted it playing. But I'd disguise it.

'I'd use my left hand to point round my right side, but if Papin saw that he knew to pass it to my left side. I'd use my right hand to point round my left side, but if Papin saw that he knew I wanted him to pass it to my right side … OK let's try it.'

Whoosh did his best. Sadly, with us killing ourselves laughing, the ball went everywhere but where Waddle wanted it: here, there, left when it should have gone right, right when it should have gone left and more often than not, straight over his head. We think it was Waddle that learned a valuable lesson that morning rather than Whoosh. World class players, we were not. None of us was a Papin.

Mark was strong, quick and had a good left foot. Right foot, not good. So, for a laugh some of the players would always pass him the ball so that he had to use his right foot, or get into all sorts of contortions trying to avoid using it. They never did it if there was any danger, but loved doing it.

More often than not though, it was Roeder who took meetings and sessions. But we'd look around while he was sorting us out and Chris would be in the background somewhere doing keepie-uppies. Roeder would say to him, 'That right Chris?' or 'Waddya think Chris?' Chris would just say 'Yeh yeh,' and carry on with the keepie-uppies.

One by one, Waddle seemed to sideline all the senior players but at last he brought Jamie back to be sub at Bristol Rovers. What followed was one of the great BFC stories that is remembered to this day by those who were there. Jamie tells the story.

'So, I'm warming up and Waddle and Roeder are in the dugout. So, I get to the bottom end where the Burnley fans are and suddenly, I hear a voice, "Jamie … Jamie … fetch us a pie will yer …"

'What? I'm thinking, have I heard that right?

'The voice shouts again, louder still. "Jamie … Jamie, fetch us a pie will yer?"

'I look at where the voice is coming from and this Burnley bloke is standing there grinning.

'"What?"

'"Fetch us a pie if you've nowt else to do."

'I'm a bit taken aback of course, but then think, oh well, why not, for a laugh.

'"Give us some money then."

'He lobs a pound over which I grab, turn around and without bothering to think what will Waddle and Roeder think, jog back up to the other end, collar a ball boy, and ask him to get a pie from the pie stall while I continue to jog up and down.

'The ball boy comes back but without a pie. "Sorry they're £1.20," he says.

'Damn it, I think, I'm not going all the way back down the other end to get 20p, so tell the lad to go back and explain to the pie man what the situation is, it's for a player, and can he have one for a pound.

'The lad comes back. It's a Cornish Pastie, not a pie and it's absolutely red hot. Back I go down the touchline juggling the pastie because it's so bloody hot and burning my hands. The ball boy had gloves on. Passing Roeder and Waddle, I see them eyeing me as if to say "what the fuck" but they say nothing either then or after the game. The bloke has his Cornish Pastie, not a pie as requested, hand delivered.

'"Thanks Jamie," he shouts as he and his mates fall about laughing. I declined the other 20 requests to bring more pies down. The only thing I regret is not asking Waddle and Roeder did they want one as well.'

With the final Plymouth game out of the way, the win and safety, would Waddle have stayed if he had felt the board were sympathetic and supportive? In later interviews there were hints that he might well have done. But then maybe he remembered the board meeting when in his absence, two directors, Clive Holt and Bernard Rothwell, savaged Glenn Roeder and laid into him over the lack of Glen Little in the team. Apparently, Waddle rang them the next day with the intention of telling the directors a few home truths, but he received little sympathy.

Years later he thought with maybe two or three more players he might have done better and wished he'd had more money to spend. He remembered long faces in the boardroom after the Plymouth game.

It was a funny year, he went on, but he enjoyed it. He remarked that Burnley is a football-mad town and this is a club with a great history. 'The lads were great,' and the form of the second half was good. He reckoned they were always confident against Plymouth.

'Some fans still give me a bit of stick when I see them but that's part and parcel of football. A lot say they enjoyed the football we played.'

Some fans might have argued with that. 'Chris Waddle, the manager who complained that Burnley fans didn't get behind him,' said one. 'He criticised supporters and players at every turn. While he was in charge our fortunes took a turn for the worse. The best thing that Waddle did was to leave and it didn't take too long for his crop of players to leave the team sheets.'

But, credit him with one thing though. With Glenn Roeder and Gordan Cowans, it was said he was well capable of drinking The Woodman dry, a pub at the top of Todmorden Road on the way out of Burnley.

But, at the end of the day, after all the pressures of management, which he later admitted to, the stresses, the conflicts in dealing with directors, criticism from supporters, maybe he just felt that the warmth of a TV studio and a pundit's comfy chair was the better option. If you read the biography of Chris Waddle you wonder how he ever became, or even wanted to be a manager: he was so shy and reserved as a person in his formative years.

Years later I found out that he called his dog Weller. On Twitter a Burnley fan asked him had he named it after me. Waddle simply replied, 'good footballer'. I suspect it was named after the other Paul Weller from The Jam. But I like to think it was me.

Chapter 8

A GAME TO REMEMBER AND AN ILLNESS BEGINS

YOU CAN win a game and be thoroughly deflated. How can that be? You can walk off, shoulders slumped, body language poor, head empty and thinking 'if only'. Such a game was Burnley 1 Coventry 0, a game at the end of a season when if we had won 2-0, we would have earned a play-off spot.

You can win a game and all you feel is relief and exhaustion. Such a game was Burnley 2 Plymouth Argyle 1 at the end of the Waddle season. It was must-win; lose it and relegation would follow. Even then we had to wait to hear other results that were needed to save us from relegation. When we heard those results at pitch side, that was when this mixture of elation and sweet relief overcame us. It wasn't the only end-of-season game that was huge. There had been one as far back as 1960 when Burnley won the First Division title in the very last game. There was the Orient game in 1987 when Burnley had to win to stay in the league. Another one would come later when in 2000 Burnley won at Scunthorpe to win promotion to the Championship. But now there was this one.

> It is 2 May 1998, and Chris Waddle is saying that things could be on a knife-edge all afternoon. Burnley pubs are packed, mounted police are patrolling the town centre. Outside Yates, the bouncers look big and mean. In other pubs the queues are ten-deep. Outside one pub, topless lads grip their bottled beer. Not many people are shopping in the Charter Walk market centre. The skies are clouding over as if to say this is going to be a grim afternoon. Three clubs are involved in this journey to the bottom, the triangle of doom.

All this is a description by visiting writer John Aizlewood. It costs him 20p to get into the Miners' Club which still has a men-only area. Burnley always was a bit behind the times. Some bits of Burnley have yet to recognise women's lib. Even at midday the queues to the ticket office on Harry Potts Way are 100 yards long. In the shop, Waddle's biography is not doing too well. Who on earth wants to buy it even at the reduced price? Nobody.

The previous week Burnley had been winning 3-1 at Oldham but ended up drawing 3-3. Priceless points squandered. Stories that there were rows in the boardroom abounded. 'Legend Ralph Coates is at the game with hair like Shredded Wheat,' writes Aizlewood. In the middle of a TV interview someone shouts to Coates, 'I hope you've brought your fucking boots.' He thinks Burnley will win, but then he would say that. At two o'clock roads and pavements to Turf Moor are blocked by a shuffling procession of people heading to the ground. So much is at stake and most faces are set grim. The consequences of defeat are unthinkable.

The teams come out to the sound of Van Halen's 'Jump' and Aizlewood is caught up in the tension, excitement and drama. The noise is sustained, deafening, hysterical, Plymouth fans nearly fill the away stand and make it a sea of green and white. They release green and white balloons. The whole thing is akin to mass hysteria. A fifth of Burnley's population is inside the ground. In the concourses the crush is frightening. In the directors' box there is apprehension and tension. Burnley fans are unforgiving and chairman Teasdale is by no means their cup of tea. He is no stranger to abuse and chants of 'Teasdale Out'. Lose and he will be vilified with a renewed intensity.

Who'd be a chairman?

You can see it today on YouTube but I've never watched it. What nobody knew at the time was that my stomach problems had started months earlier. On New Year's Eve I'd noticed something. Blood spots, and these were caused by the build-up of ulcers in the large bowel. It was the first sign of passing blood. Then there was much clearer bleeding when I went to the loo.

What I certainly didn't know at the time was how serious it would become. I told Doctor McDevitt at the club who sent me straight up to Burnley Infirmary. I was given tubes of antibiotics to insert into my rectum and squeeze the stuff in. He was the only person I told but you would presume he informed the manager, Waddle. Waddle never said a word to me or ever made an enquiry. Maybe he hadn't been informed but I would think that unlikely. I was doing this right through the rest of the season, day after day. It was easy enough, not particularly sore or painful.

If stress was the cause, and at this point it had not been identified as Colitis, then there were reasons enough to be anxious. I'd just bought a house and yet was facing the expiration of the contract I had at the end of the season. Plus, here we were at the bottom of the division at that point. Plus, I was bottling up what was going on. Didn't tell anyone else other than the doc. Maybe I should have. And yet I wasn't outwardly worried, I'm not that sort. My attitude was like everything else; 'OK I've got this whatever it is, let's just deal with it.'

And so, I kept on collecting the tubes of antibiotics and inserting and squeezing until it was just something that I did without even thinking. It hadn't stopped me playing. So, what was there to worry about? Just carry on inserting and squeezing, again and again and again, day after day after day. And telling no one. It's why they call it the silent illness.

Waddle, meanwhile, was forever on at me, saying that I frustrated him, that I had to decide did I want to be a lower-league player on a few hundred a week, or did I want to step it up and be a Premiership player on a few thousand a week. Perhaps the illness was subconsciously already affecting me, inasmuch as it was there and no one but me knew. Something was wrong, but as yet without any real detrimental impact. I had no idea how it was going to develop. In the summer, I would.

But nobody was terribly worried so I simply carried on playing through the rest of the season. It didn't affect me too much and I do know that the YouTube clip shows the run I made at pace getting past Plymouth defenders, weaving in and out of more defenders in the penalty area, and smacking a beautifully hit shot. Not beautiful enough though, it hit the crossbar. 'Skipped through four tackles,' said the newspaper. Trust me, on form I could play a bit.

Tim Quelch, a dedicated Burnley supporter, was at the game:

> Heath left and for a short while we were stunned and apprehensive. Then Chris Waddle was appointed. Suddenly all those dormant ambitions sprang rapaciously to life. But we know what happened. Waddle's early signings were hopeless. We were playing catch-up all season. So, we went into the final game of the season needing a win to stay up. The drama was greater because our opponents, Plymouth, also needed a win to stay up. Brentford completed the menage-a-trois.
>
> This was a day for rugged determination. As Mick Jones, Plymouth's manager said, 'It was a bear pit out there.' Of course, it wasn't entirely in Burnley's hands so when word got

around that Bristol Rovers had taken an early lead against relegation rivals Brentford, our vociferous support was turned up a notch or two. Alas it was a false dawn, the goal was ruled out. At least Cooke helped our account by heading Little's superb cross past Sheffield after 12 minutes. I cannot remember greeting a goal as ecstatically since Parkinson's winner at Wembley.

As well as Burnley were playing, they couldn't make this crucial advantage count. We all knew it was coming and sure enough, on the half hour, Plymouth's midfielder Mark Saunders arrived late and unchallenged for a left-wing cross, before heading powerfully down and in.

Burnley were not deterred, though. Weller slithered like an eel through Plymouth's rearguard before smacking the underside of the bar with a blistering drive. Little, too, turned inside his markers and cracked a rising drive against the bar. Cooke headed the rebound goalward but Sheffield made an athletic backward stop to deny him. But, just as the counter assault was losing momentum, Glen Little served Matthew on the right. Matthew immediately whipped in a pacey centre and there was Cooke to thump in his second headed goal.

The second half was about hanging on. There were chances for Burnley on the break but after all the anguish we had endured this year, Burnley weren't about to indulge us. Why should they put away the chances that would allow us to relax a little and focus on events in Bristol? We'd come for a white-knuckle ride and that's what we were given; especially when Winstanley's air shot allowed Earl Jean a simple chance. Jean was only six or seven yards away from goal, he was unmarked in a central position and had only goalkeeper Chris Woods to beat. With just nine minutes

> remaining, this goal would most certainly have saved Plymouth and condemned Burnley. Brentford meanwhile had gone 1-0 down.
>
> It's true what they say. When something critical takes place, like a road crash, events happen in slow motion. We saw Jean size up the opportunity. We saw him draw back his left foot. We watched him make perfect contact. And we watched with horror as the ball propelled goalward. We gasped with relief as Woods clutched the ball to his midriff.
>
> Several minutes later, our worries intensified as news of Brentford's equaliser spread through the ground. But frowns turned quickly into excited smiles when Bristol restored their lead. We urged Burnley forwards knowing that salvation was just minutes away but there was still more pressure to absorb. Plymouth lined up their crosses as we closed our eyes for fear of what might happen. We focussed on the referee, willing, imploring that final whistle. At last we were released. All that anxiety finally combusted. But still it wasn't over as the announcer told us there were still five minutes to play at Bristol.

And then it was all over as the Bristol game ended. Sweet relief. Burnley would stay up. Safety. My scrapbooks say that I 'was eye-catching going forward'. A remarkable recovery over the second half of the season from that position of utter desperation in January had scraped us home. Waddle without a word or a turn to the crowd had run off the field when the game ended faster than Roadrunner. Those with cruel humour said it was the fastest they'd seen him run all season. Plymouth fans were understandably distraught, many in tears. The balloons had long since disappeared along with their hopes. Waddle was on the radio later with those who listened saying he sounded drained, exhausted, wiped out, not saying a word about what the victory meant to anyone connected with it.

Years later director Clive Holt disclosed that he would have been offered the opportunity to stay but on different terms. The players, he said, never knew whether they, or he for that matter, were coming or going with his frequent absences. The board were clear. If he stayed, he would have been pinned down to accepting this was a 365-days-a-year job. Holt left notes for Frank Teasdale to go through with Waddle which he believes were shown to him. Waddle thus accused Holt of being the director who had given him a hard time and wanted him out. Holt's view was straightforward enough; Waddle was a good player and a good media man. But a manager, no, he was not cut out for that.

Co-author Dave remembered where he was on the day. Not at the game but up in wild and windy Northumberland sheltering behind a wall at Vindolanda, the Roman fort on Hadrian's Wall. His mind wasn't on the Roman ruins though, he was fiddling with a tiny transistor radio (who remembers what they are these days) trying to tune in to the sports programme. Reception was hopeless; the Romans invented many things – roads, aqueducts and central heating – but decent radios were not one of them. Windswept and damp, he got as far as hearing that the score was 1-0 to Burnley but then lost all connections. In a nearby garden centre reception was a little better so he heard out the game. Dinner in a local pub tasted all the better that night. It might have been all those years ago but he still remembers it was steak and ale pie; it was all part of the images of the day that have stayed in his mind. His diary says that Stuart Hall reported on the game afterwards as only Stuart Hall can. But that was before his disgrace and exit from public life.

Sitting in Tubbs and reminiscing, Dave makes the comment that winning the final 'decider' game in such a way and escaping from relegation so dramatically, gives the illusion of success. The euphoria is so great that you think you've won a cup final. Past sins and grumbles are forgotten and even forgiven. The real story was somewhat different.

In the dressing room afterwards, it was just such a feeling of pure relief. We had avoided relegation and the feeling it gives is far different to the euphoria of winning promotion. For sure there was mad joy in the dressing room but there was also the knowledge that we had avoided something that has such an impact on your career and life. Relegation impacts everything: wages, contracts, the way fans look at you, going out into the town. Poor sods, other pros will think. It can be a shattering thing and there are real tears. So, whatever went on in the dressing room afterwards, it was mixed with the pure relief of having got such a traumatic season out of the way. And believe me it had been traumatic. Chairman Frank Teasdale came in. In fact, he always came in after a game, put his hand in his pocket and bought drinks for us in the tiny players' bar down the corridor. That night I went out with my pal Andy Cooke and we had the best night ever.

The idea that Chris Waddle disappeared up the tunnel and into the sunset immediately after the Plymouth game is more myth than fact. Many of us went into the club on the Monday after the game to say our goodbyes for the summer, collect a few odds and ends and in my case to see Chris Waddle after he called me in to see me. It was to offer me a new contract. 'I don't think you'll sign it,' he said, 'you're worth more than this.' I didn't sign it. Stan, when he arrived, did think I was worth more. An extra £50. But every little helps as they say, and I signed it.

A few of us headed for Marbella. Waddle was supposed to be with us but didn't show up. We found out why. He had left the club.

With Waddle gone there was a Football in the Community trip to Cyprus. It was just a few of us going to do some coaching on the army bases. Whatever was wrong with my stomach flared up badly. Clearly, the squeezing and inserting of the antibiotics was no longer effective. The lads now knew and were all adamant telling me 'you must get this sorted out' when I told them I was on the loo passing blood. By now the amount of blood was unbelievable. The physio, Nick Worth, identified that these were stomach problems that needed sorting and booked me into Burnley General. So, here was me, illness flaring even worse than ever, out of contract, stalling on a three-year deal, with Waddle gone and a new manager imminent, facing what footballers hate, uncertainty. On top of all that, Dutch clubs and West Ham were allegedly interested in me. Most definitely Harry Redknapp and West Ham were inviting me down to London.

Back to the club doctor then, back to hospital, 19 days I was in there and now it was steroids plus two blood transfusions, as I'd lost so much blood. Steroids do things to you; I put weight on, had spots all over my face, and my face swelled up. It looked like a full moon. I was in a small private room thanks to the club BUPA policy. Privacy is all very well but boredom sets in. Co-author Dave tells me that a small ward of four-to-six patients is about right. There's always something going on, always someone to chat to, always something to laugh at. Nurses coming in and out. Being on your own in a private room is not all it's cracked up to be. Dave says on the one occasion he was in a room for one, the meals people forgot him. He went without lunch and trust me Dave likes his lunch.

I was supposed to be relaxing, in there to de-stress but the press found me and wanted an interview. They wanted to know if I was going to West Ham or Holland. They wanted to know if I was signing a new contract. They wanted to know what was wrong with me and at that point I thought I'd got cancer. And thanks to all this, being connected with other clubs and stalling on a contract, I was being labelled by them and supporters as an ungrateful rebel.

And there I was: in hospital to get rid of stress.

Chris Boden and Pete Oliver were the local hacks, a thankless job in fact. They might even have asked was I feeling any better. The target, I told them, was to be back for pre-season training in July. I should be OK, I added.

The new manager was announced and 'oh shit', was my first reaction. Forgive my language, although when you have developing Colitis it might well be appropriate. It was none other than Stan Ternent. When I was just 19 and he was at Bury he'd wanted to sign me so I had gone to see him and watched a game they played. It was dire. 'This is not for me,' I'd thought and turned him down. Now he was my new boss. Will he remember, I wondered. What will he think? Will he just bomb me out?

There was no place for me on the pre-season tour to the West Country that had been hastily arranged by the new manager. Stan Ternent was disbelieving at the mess he found at the club, from the bottom to the top.

'Indifference and neglect,' he said. 'A club in chaos.

'Physically and mentally, the players lacked everything, he thought. 'Listless and disinterested apart from Little, Weller and Andy Payton.' He took no prisoners. Clearly, he still rated me and saw me as part of his plans, despite the Bury turn-down.

From what I heard, the pre-season tour to the West Country was nothing to write home about, yomping over the moors and staying in dormitories at Exeter University. On the bus Stan told them all to get fit or get out. There were games against Dawlish Town and Elmore. I've no idea where that last place is. After a night out Stan sat up waiting for the latecomers after he had given a deadline for their return. The stragglers returned one by one to receive a bollocking. Stan believed in discipline and focus. A bullshitter he was not.

'Weller has played his last game for Burnley,' wrote Chris Boden, adding that I'd told him I'd had offers from home and abroad but a move to West Ham was on the cards.

'He won't sign for Burnley,' said Stan Ternent, 'and I can only go on what he tells me. We won't increase the contract offer. You don't get big pay rises for finishing fifth bottom of the Second Division.' Classic Stan.

While all that was going on, I thought the medical problems were sorted, 19 days of being bored rigid behind me. Little did I know, they were anything but.

So, off I went to West Ham for a few trial games. Stan Ternent had tried to get a few more quid added to the contract offer but then said 'OK, go down to West Ham'. They'd been on the phone to him. Trouble was I was still fat and still on the steroids and certainly wasn't fit. And I was happy at Burnley. Nevertheless, I went down for a week, played with all their big names, Ferdinand, Lampard, Ruddock, and the rest. I seem to remember Ian Wright was there at that time as well. Played two games at wing-back, did OK. Harry Redknapp said he wanted me to play a third game in centre-midfield but that never happened. It was the last time I spoke to Redknapp. Stan had called me to say 'get back here because West Ham can't afford you'. He told me the move was to be sorted by a tribunal but Burnley wanted £1m. Was he playing games with them and me? I might find out one day. Did he price me out because he wanted me at Burnley?

Anyway, West Ham were not going to pay £1m so back I came, signed the new contract with a bit more money added, and by now was coming off the steroids. But you can't stop with just a click of the fingers, you have to come off gradually, day by day. You know the old joke about steroids; I've put a load of weight on, lost all my good looks, but can now pick up a tractor.

In August back I came and signed the contract. It was just a case of sorting out the right deal. The first three weeks of the season had dragged on and I was nowhere near fit. Even so I was pitched straight in to a League Cup game against Bury. But it was back to square one when the stomach pains returned with a vengeance. What a good job I'd signed that contract. What the club would have done with me once I was really ill, had I been out of contract is anyone's guess. One can't help thinking I would have been left high and dry. Passing blood had not stopped, the steroid pills were now down to four a day from eight. I was trying to carry on playing but after a game at Walsall I just knew I could not carry on. I knew I was well and truly crocked when I saw that even Ronnie Jepson was faster than me.

I saw the club doc at the game and he informed Stan. On the way back on the coach Stan called me down to the front of the bus to talk to him. 'Get it sorted,' he said. 'Come back when you are ready. Take as long as you want.' He said he would just write me off for as long as it took. If there was despondency it was then, but from a manager you couldn't ask for more. If there was a feeling of, here we go again, it was then.

September; medication and rest was diagnosed as the best course of action, so it was back to being inactive and thoroughly fed-up. There were different types of treatment and different pills but the bowel was filled with ulcers. We could have gone on and on trying all the alternatives with no certainty of success.

'Could become cancerous in later life,' said the medical people. Fuck: cancer is not a word you need to hear.

All I could do was wait to see if the tablets had any effect with visits to the hospital for check-ups. They told me the condition could be aggravated by stress so I was told to keep away from the club. It was back to the south coast for a while and just doing nothing.

'Just get yourself sorted,' said Stan Ternent again. 'Take all the time you need.'

At least the stress of being out of contract was off my mind. But from being a fit and healthy footballer, loving the game, the company of fellow pros, playing competitive matches, and enjoying life, now it was the daily grind of boredom, inactivity and just itching to get back. I missed the laughter, the jokes and the banter, even the smells of the dressing room, liniment, sweat, leather, underarm spray. I missed Glen Little and his incessant chatter. I missed everything, the drive to the training ground, getting changed, going out in all weathers, even the mud-bath that was Gawthorpe in the winter. The satisfaction of a good training session, the feeling of fitness, maudlin as it sounds, the warm glow you feel after a shower. And then there was the sheer frustration. The frustration of knowing I had been a part of Stan Ternent's plans but now I wasn't, until I was well again and regained proper fitness.

At least there was that to look forward to – except there was a problem.

'It's more serious than we thought,' said the medical people. 'We need to operate.'

Chapter 9

BEHIND THE SCENES AND A TALE OF COSTA RICAN DRUG MONEY

'A CONFIDENT, funny, good looking, northern bloke with a real swagger about him,' said Ian Wright in his book *A Life in Football*, about Stan Ternent. Maybe the good-looking bit was a tad over the top. Funny, yes, but not in the sense of going around cracking endless jokes like Ken Dodd, but more in his withering put-downs of a poor performance, or his pithy comments. On the outside looking in, you couldn't help but laugh; on the inside on the receiving end you didn't laugh at the time. Confident, yes of course he was, you had to be, to be a manager, especially in charge of a Burnley dressing room with people like Ronnie Jepson and Paul Cook. And with two Bury promotions on his CV, why wouldn't he be confident? There is no doubt he was good for Burnley, the right man at the right club, but five years too late he always maintained and he was probably right.

He had three problems: the bunch of players he inherited was the first and obvious one. Out of shape lumps he called them, listless and disinterested. Graham Branch was one of the first players he signed. Branchy always remembers what he said when he met him at Turf Moor.

'We're shit at the moment,' he said to him. 'But I'll get it sorted.'

In the press he'd said he was going to build a team around the younger players, me, Andy Cooke, Chris Brass, plus Glen Little and Andy Payton. He'd already tried to sign Glen Little for Bury and he'd clearly forgotten, or never mentioned, the fact that I'd turned down a move to Bury …

Straight and to the point. That was Stan Ternent and very honest. And that was why Graham signed for him. His impact was immediate, tightening up on lax discipline. One small example: if we had a problem previously, we'd simply go from Gawthorpe to Turf Moor and see whatever person might sort out any issues we had. That was stopped so that we now had to ask his permission. It was just a small way of saying, 'I'm in charge, you come to me.'

His second problem was the drawn-out change of chairman from Frank Teasdale to Barry Kilby with a background sub-plot that would make a hard-to-believe TV drama.

Third was the ITV Digital fiasco when the TV company pulled the plug on the money they were putting into the game, leaving Burnley high and dry and on the brink of administration.

Frank Teasdale was the chairman who signed the gaffer but, in the background, moves were being made to entice Barry Kilby to join the board and take over. Frank Teasdale often had groups of players up at his house for a drink or to play pool, keen to be one of the lads, except of course when it came to wage negotiations. Those visits stopped, though, when there was damage to one of his paintings.

Businessman Ray Ingleby was also interested in taking control of the club, but Teasdale was fending him and then Kilby off; he had his own preferred candidate, and so a situation dragged on creating uncertainty and factions within the boardroom. We, the players, knew little about this, but of course bits of it filtered to the dressing room although even then you gave it scant attention. We train, we play, we get our wages, and as long as those three things remain unaffected, changes in the boardroom don't really bother players of any club. I have to say, I sat open-mouthed, in Tubbs of course, as Dave told me the full story of how Burnley fan Peter Shackleton tried to buy the club. There were even jokes that South American drug money was involved.

Before Barry Kilby took over there was a bit of a battle between Ingleby and Shackleton for control of the club. Shackleton was Teasdale's preferred choice because he would have retained Teasdale as chairman. As Burnley history books relate, Shackleton's bid came to nothing and faded away as a distant memory. Because of his attachment to Teasdale, Shackleton never had the backing of Burnley's fans, who soon grew weary anyway of his tales and promises.

He had no money of his own but Shackleton always maintained he had huge backers behind him and there were mentions of huge sums of money in the region of £12m that would be available once he took over, with £1m up front. The trouble is no money ever materialised and all the while Teasdale remained supportive of him. This £1m was allegedly already in an English bank account, said local press reports. Once the legal experts had sorted out binding guarantees the rest of Shackleton's £12m would follow. Initially it all seemed very exciting and fans were agog that real money might soon be pouring into the club. One of Shackleton's prominent contacts was a guy called Ian Burns and this was a name that would frequently crop up. Director Clive Holt, however, was always somewhat suspicious. With the mind of a detective he made his own enquiries as to the truth of these promised millions.

He checked Shackleton's home using one of his sales reps who went to establish that there actually was a place with the address Shackleton had given. Having established that, he then did a check on the value of the property. It was decent enough. It was then decided that before discussions could go any further, and before Shackleton's 'people' could examine the club accounts, they must put £1m into an escrow account as an act of good faith. But, Holt recalled, no money ever came. It was always next week, or the week after that. The £1m, when it came, would be theirs to keep anyway, even if the deal fell through. It all seemed too good to be true but Teasdale clung to his belief that all was good. Clive Holt continued to shake his head. He was a hard-headed businessman with a keen eye for dotting the i's and crossing the t's and he knew that proper businessmen do not give away £1m. But after a second promise that the money was coming, Holt shook his head and gave up. Teasdale remained firmly convinced that it was all going to be fine.

Out of the blue came a call from France to Clive Holt to assure him that the Shackleton bid was genuine. The French voice said he was calling from Cannes. Holt wonders to this day was the call from Cannes or Bacup, just up the road from Burnley.

Things dragged on into September of 1998 with assurances being given that the deal was not going to fold. It was the mysterious Ian Burns who contacted the local press to ease any fears that it was all floundering. The saga would end within a week, he said and the delay was only because the huge firm behind the deal and with all the money ready to invest, was engaged in merger talks with another huge company and was currently dealing with that matter. They wished to remain anonymous for the moment, he added. But he could reveal it was a major player in the oil and minerals industry with £750bn in assets and a desire to own a British football club to raise their profile. Frank Teasdale waited patiently, convinced that all this was genuine. Supporters, meanwhile, were beginning to scoff at this fanciful deal and at Shackleton, who on one occasion held a meeting with supporters in a local pub, The Sparrow Hawk. They soon realised that these seemed empty promises, and that Shackleton seemed to know little of what he was talking about. Some were convinced that he too was just a con man.

Ian Burns explained who he was and his role. 'I am simply the guy who made the initial introduction to Peter and am acting as a courtesy spokesman. I am not part of the investors. I can only tell of the difficulties in completing such a large transaction.'

Another name in the Burnley equation was Murray MacDowell, a Canadian stockbroker. 'He is a buyer of shares in the market for the company and was asked to hold funds and make the purchase of Burnley FC when asked,' said Burns. It was MacDowell who told the local press that the investor group portfolio would be provided to the club's bankers and it would show the depth of funding and the source of the finance. Peter Shackleton himself certainly had experience of raising money. This was in connection with the founding and funding of the Derby City Technology College of which he was principal. He would certainly have met financial contacts and big hitters in the finance world whilst raising the money for his Landau Forte College. There were reports in the press that in fact this was how he and MacDowell had first met.

Five years later, according to a report by Brent Mudry in the *Silicone Investor* (not a magazine seen by many Burnley supporters), Wall Street 'Muckster' MacDowell was now in jail charged with brokerage fraud. The article mentioned that he had been involved in aborted bids for a struggling British soccer club in 1998. Detective Inspector Ron Allen of the Royal Canadian Mounted Police was clear in his assertion that MacDowell was part of a group that had been operating for years.

Clive Holt chuckled then, and still does. He had always joked that this mythical takeover money was probably South American drug money. He was closer to the mark than he ever thought. One of the reasons for MacDowell's arrest was in connection with suspected drug importing from Costa Rica.

There are two possibilities in this sorry and time-consuming tale and don't forget that in the background Stan Ternent was waiting for funds, desperate to improve his squad and make progress, with Frank Teasdale still clinging to the idea that £12m was on its way.

One: that Shackleton knew he was dealing with fraudulent people and was willingly going along with them.

Two: he was naïve and simply trusted them as people who could help him with contacts in the investment world. Those who knew Shackleton well describe him as a dedicated Burnley supporter and a highly respected and accomplished professional in the world of education. Did Burns fool him, seeing him as a frontman, almost the patsy, in an audacious scheme to somehow fashion a profit for himself? Or did Shackleton know Burns and approach him, asking about his contacts? It then seems fair to ask would Burns have been doing this on a courtesy basis without asking for any kind of fee?

They had in fact met much earlier, both being residents of Allestree when the local primary school headteacher was looking to raise funds for a nursery and invited members of the community that he knew had business contacts to a meeting. According to Shackleton's daughter, Laura, this is where they met. Burns' company was called KB Securities with offices all over Europe, he said, but this was described by the Serious Fraud Office as simply a paper company with no assets. At one stage Shackleton referred to five Swiss bankers that he was in contact with as backers. Were these bankers known to Burns? Were they fictitious? Were they part of the Burns network? In the reams of newsprint that were produced at the time, all of which led supporters to believe that things were in the pipeline, and raised Teasdale's hopes, there was regular mention of the money being stuck in Switzerland. One piece described Shackleton as being on a 'troubleshooting trip round Europe', saying he was at that moment in Barcelona.

Shackleton described the £12m as being 'small potatoes', and more would follow.

'I am dealing with people who are at an unbelievable height in industry,' he said. 'I am used to dealing with people who have a lot of money.' In this he was not far wrong. The Landau Charitable Foundation and the Forte family were two of them, he added. 'I have wined and dined at the House of Lords and met members of the royal family. I have loose associations with a number of leading football clubs in Europe.' He claimed his backers had investments in some of them.

By now some of the newspaper pieces were bordering on the fanciful. He had been concentrating his efforts, since leaving education, on brokering big money deals. His daughter Laura had no recollections of this. In fact, he had moved into the management of care homes.

There is no evidence or suggestion that Shackleton was ever deliberately fraudulent. None of the available legal documents suggest this. Yet, he was named in Nevada of all places, in criminal investigations, investigations that involved one of the most famous and high-profile victims of the network of schemers and fraudsters – Brazilian football star Romario, captain of the 1994 Brazil World Cup team. Polish investigators collected evidence from a Nevada District Court in the USA and Shackleton's name appeared in those documents because of his association with Burns. Did Shackleton even know this?

As the sorry tale of the Shackleton takeover bid wound down and it became clear, even to Frank Teasdale, that it was coming to nothing, investigations into Burns – who had once been a professional footballer with Everton – continued. Two years later, in April 2000, he was charged with conspiracy to defraud although not in connection with the Burnley FC takeover. After an eight-week trial in 2002 the full scale of his frauds was revealed and in August

2002 he was convicted. As he was ill, the sentencing was delayed but when sentence was eventually passed, he was described as being guilty of 'open and brazen' fraud. In passing sentence, the court took into account that suffering now from a depressive disorder, he was unable to remember any of it, not even to remember the trial. Nevertheless, he was given a three-and-a-half-year prison sentence.

What a story: of intrigue, scheming, fraudsters, and all across two continents, from Nevada to Switzerland, from Burnley to Barcelona. And all because Peter Shackleton met Ian Burns, most likely at a school fundraising function. The Burnley part of it ended in October 1998 when local MP Peter Pike demanded that Shackleton either delivered the goods or called it a day. 'He was making the club look silly.'

The local press wrote at the time, 'The bid seems shrouded in mystery. Why do Shackleton's backers wish to remain anonymous? What is the big secret, too many questions, too few answers?'

Was Shackleton genuine, or just a fantasist; gullible or complicit?

Burnley supporter Robert Lambert knew Shackleton well. They were at school together in Ilkley, played Sunday football together and from 1970 onwards Lambert went to Turf Moor with him. After teacher training in Hendon, Shackleton taught in Colne near Burnley, was ambitious, says Lambert and then became head of a school in Warrington. Lambert went to his wedding in 1975 and years later attended his funeral; he was adamant that Shackleton was devoted to Burnley and testified that he genuinely believed in the takeover, in what was happening, and was eager to confide in close friends such as Lambert.

In January 1998, Lambert was surprised to see Shackleton in the directors' box at Burnley and remembers thinking, 'What on earth is Pete doing there?' In April, Shackleton invited Lambert and his son Nick to lunch in the James Hargreaves Stand at Turf Moor. Chairman Frank Teasdale and Ian Burns were also there.

After lunch, Teasdale left them to return to the directors' box and they watched the game from one of the corporate boxes, although Burns remained indoors. Lambert remembers the game, a 1-0 win against Bristol City with the goal scored by Andy Payton. If there were takeover discussions on this day, Lambert was not witness to them. What he also remembers is that Shackleton wanted to bring former player Paul Fletcher back to the club as CEO, but there was no contact with Fletcher and today Fletcher has no knowledge of this. The last time Lambert spoke to Shackleton was at the 2009 play-off final at Wembley when Burnley beat Sheffield United 1-0. To this day he remains totally sure that Shackleton was genuine and sincere in his actions.

Peter Shackleton's wife maintained that the failure of the deal devastated her husband. She was disparaging about Ian Burns and described her husband as 'gullible'. She says he would have made no financial gain himself from any takeover; he was not involved for profit but his sole aim was simply to help the club he supported at a time when it was needed.

His daughter says he was a genuine, talented and honest man, but taken in by the unscrupulousness of others. She talked about her father's love for the club and remembered the stories he used to tell her of the trips to Turf Moor travelling from Yorkshire. She maintained that he was immersed in the takeover project and massively excited, really believing it would happen. Today she still wonders how he could have been so taken in. He made no money from it and actually lost money. By the time the dust had settled it had cost them their house, their savings and his health. She is adamant that he lost his dignity and self-respect, occasionally attending a Burnley game but hoping not to be recognised. It left him with stress and depression and the family wonder if the cancer that came was the result of the suffering that he had been through.

What really happened? We shall probably never fully know. It is conjecture but he was perhaps just another trusting, gullible man, enticed by the prospect of helping the club he followed, and as a result was a clear victim of a fraud network, a network that included drug-running, stretching from the UK to the USA to Europe. Did he have any idea of what he had got himself into? An able man, but whose head was turned by the excitement and attractions of such an exhilarating deal, thinking he was about to become a key figure in the football world. Time and again in football, common sense flies out of the window when supporters become involved with their clubs and dreams. Nowhere is this seen more than at boardroom level when individuals who are top men and leaders in their fields of commerce can lose all sense of perspective and good business practice when they become enamoured by the supposed glamour of the game. It would appear that in 1998 certainly the chairman of Burnley Football Club was taken in by the Shackleton proposal, the scale of which was so dazzlingly huge.

* * *

In 1998 the club was in limbo thanks to all this, with manager Stan Ternent frustrated by Frank Teasdale. Only in December was it all sorted out, when Barry Kilby became chairman. At last the gaffer would see some money for new players, whilst I was about to be laid well and truly low by illness.

The ITV Digital fiasco came much later and was quite devastating. In between the Kilby takeover and the Digital finance collapse there were reasonably good years but the collapse of the ITV money left the club high and dry with the gaffer simply entering a survival period. Fast forward a few years to 2002 and by this time, I was back in the side and saw the effects at first hand.

An agreement had been made between the Football League and Granada and Carlton TV companies. It would give them exclusive rights to coverage of live games. This was a deal worth around £90m a year and Burnley's share would be around £3m, a tidy sum as they say. The contract was for four years and Burnley budgeted for the full four years. The money would come annually and it was assumed by all concerned that all was well and the deal watertight. But it wasn't and very soon it was clear to the TV companies that this was a deal they would have to abandon because they were losing so much money. Meanwhile, Burnley were one of many clubs happily spending the money on players and contracts and better wages. Alas, the football clubs found out that the contract was not worth the paper it was written on, nobody had really gone over it with a fine-tooth comb. Carlton and Granada, between them worth billions, simply abandoned it. Burnley were left high and dry.

Barry Kilby along with others looked at the legal situation, but in a nutshell the clubs were goosed. Carlton and Granada were sued by the clubs and the Football League even filed a claim against its own lawyers for not making the deal watertight. They sought £150m in damages but what they received was minimal. Overnight many players lost their jobs, clubs sought to cut costs and wage bills. At Burnley, Stan Ternent immediately told five players their contracts would not be renewed. It only reduced the wage bill by around ten per cent. Star man Glen Little had always been seen as a saleable asset but the bottom had dropped out of the market. Nobody was in a position to afford forking out large sums. Clubs just weren't buying.

Prior to the collapse of the deal Burnley had been securing their best players on longer contracts. I was one of them. The club was in the money compared to previous seasons. But now the club was badly hit because the ITV money was such a big percentage of the total income. An average weekly wage in the division was between £4,000 and £5,000. The club had a £5m-a-year wage bill and now needed to almost halve it. Clubs, certainly Burnley, fumed at the way in which their lawyers had never examined the small print.

A first-team group of something like 28 players now needed to be trimmed down to 21. Administration was on the cards for several clubs. Some clubs went into it to wipe out their debts, Leicester City, Bradford City, Ipswich and Barnsley being among them. The Football League cottoned on to what clubs were doing and so they imposed a points penalty system to deter them. Clubs tried to negotiate with players to reduce their wages with little success. Players were criticised when they refused. But then why should they be the ones to pay for the failure of others?

To rub salt in the wounds Carlton and Granada came back and offered just £5m to screen match highlights. Clubs accepted, being desperate for any kind of income. The whole thing had a massive effect on Burnley and destroyed any ambition to invest in players. As a direct result the aim was now survival and grimly hanging on to their place in the Championship. The Premier League dreams were dead.

All of this was tough on Stan. 'He was a brilliant coach,' said Andy Payton. 'And a proper players' manager. He was under-rated but not by the Burnley players. He knew how to run a football club. He was big on discipline. He may have appeared unfashionable but he transformed Burnley. He conjured promotion on a shoestring at Bury and performed miracles at Turf Moor.'

Graham Branch paid tribute to his man-management, although one pre-match routine bemused him. 'The night before a game the whole team went to the pub before being treated to a full English breakfast on matchday. We were scratching our heads but that was Stan for you. It was a big family. I struggled with confidence in my first season but had a chat with him. "You've got two choices," he said. "Prove them wrong or walk away." Stan wouldn't take any nonsense but he would walk to the end of the earth for you and he expected that in return. He wanted you to go to war for him and that's why we got promoted in the second season.'

Lenny Johnrose played for Ternent at both Bury and Burnley. 'Stan was incredibly tough and would hand out unbelievable abuse. Some players couldn't put up with him, he would destroy people and they would just have to go. However, I stood up to Stan and ignored the abuse. I was one of the best at taking people out. Stan would say, "Sort that fucking so-and-so out." And I would.'

There was no end of players who spoke well of Stan, despite him being likely to bawl them out just as loudly as anyone else he blasted. Andy Payton, Steve Davis, Mickey Mellon and Gordon Armstrong were unstinting in their praise, with the consensus of their views being: 'Every single day was intense … there were no days off … he was a leader of men who knew when to give the players responsibility and when it was time to lead … he was unpredictable at times and so kept you on your toes … he knew how to get teams out of this division … this is a big club with a fantastic manager.'

Glen Little thought the world of him. 'You have to be mentally strong and I've always been that. I've had my run-ins with Stan over the years at Burnley but that is part and parcel of football. He's swung for me a few times and you have your rows and square-ups, but as long as you don't take it to heart that is the important thing. I've been hit with a bottle, called everything under the sun and even had a right hook, but the day Stan stops shouting in your ear, that's the day you get worried. He might not be everyone's cup of tea and people might not like the way he does things but that's the way it is with him.'

It's true to say that the ITV Digital fiasco ended any hope that the gaffer might have had of getting the club back anywhere near the Premier League. It was a hammer blow. From that moment on it was very much a case of make do and mend. His man-management kept the club in the Championship.

Chapter 10

COLITIS FOR ME AND AN AILING CLUB

I COULD be flippant and joke that with me out of action seriously ill, the club was now struggling and losing games left, right and centre. Sadly, it was rather more than just me being unavailable. Stan Ternent had so many problems on his plate, but was still able to tell me to take all the time I needed and get well again.

Frank Teasdale had eventually reluctantly stepped down from the chairmanship, to enable Barry Kilby to take over but during all of that, Stan was barely speaking to the board, if at all. While I was battling Colitis, Stan was battling against a bottom-three place, it was that bad. If you look at an appearance statistics table, you'll see that he used 38 players in all competitions, a staggering number, although admittedly some made just one appearance, including me, before I was laid low. My one appearance in that illness-riddled 1998/99 season was away at Walsall and followed Stan taking action so drastic, it has gone down in Burnley folklore. Ray Simpson tells the story in his encyclopaedic book *The Clarets Chronicles*.

> It was a rant that will go down in Clarets folklore. Stan Ternent had already made his intentions clear on becoming

Burnley's new manager. But no one could have had any idea what was in store within months of him taking charge. Major changes needed to be made after the Clarets' last-gasp escape on the final day of the previous season. And if anyone knew that, it was Stan Ternent.

Just three games into his regime, Burnley fans everywhere were given a startling insight into his plans to reshape the entire playing staff. It was the third Saturday of the season and Burnley were looking to capitalise on their opening-day home success over Bristol Rovers. Andy Payton had scored twice on that day only for the Clarets to then suffer a blip in a 1-0 defeat at Chesterfield. Then, York City arrived.

They couldn't have asked for an easier three points than the ones they got at Turf Moor on 22 August. Burnley were outplayed in every department and the Minstermen could easily have gone back to Bootham Crescent with a far more emphatic scoreline. It proved to be the straw that broke the camel's back for four of Ternent's inherited side.

Afterwards he blasted, 'It's not personal, it's business. Steve Blatherwick, Lee Howey, Mark Winstanley and to a lesser degree Michael Williams, because he will never win the crowd over, will not play for Burnley Football Club again. They are not right for Burnley and they are not coming from where I am coming from. They are on the transfer list; they can go on a free transfer.'

'I need to bring some new bodies into the club,' Stan said. Clive Holt was left wondering how on earth the club could sell these players that Stan had so publicly disposed of. Board members were very concerned about the club's developing plight and maintained that Stan was not easy to deal with. Stan might have said just the same about them.

The prolonged takeover did affect the players, said Andy Payton. Ray Ingleby withdrew his interest and Peter Shackleton was gone from the scene. It was then new chairman Barry Kilby that brought Stan back to speaking terms. There was money available and an influx of players for whom actual money was paid: Steve Davis, Mickey Mellon, Graham Branch and Lenny Johnrose.

It was August when I went into Burnley General Hospital again. Something needed doing and with Stan having told me to take time off and get it sorted, in I went. There were two weeks in there, beginning a pattern of two weeks in, then out and then back in again. I was on more steroids and they began to work, so in September I was taken off them. Everything flared up again. It was back to square one. Now they wanted me on more drugs, different drugs with unpronounceable names and some of them with horrible side effects. Bear in mind, I'm just 21 and having to deal with all this on my own, my parents being far away in Worthing.

Maybe it's time for a few words about Colitis. Those with a squeamish disposition look away now. All of this is from the NHS website. I'm sure they won't mind.

Ulcerative Colitis is a long-term condition where the colon and rectum become inflamed. The colon is the large intestine (bowel) and the rectum is the end of the bowel where stools are stored. Ulcers form in the areas of inflammation.

The symptoms of Colitis are recurring diarrhoea which may contain blood, mucus or pus. (Not the 'pus' that sits on your knee while you stroke it and feed it mice.) There may be stomach pains. You may need to empty your bowels frequently. Colitis means you are desperate to get to the loo several times a day. (If I was driving home from the club to my house in Great Harwood, I'd have to stop at a Little Chef that was on the way and rush inside to do what I needed. Thank goodness it was there. It was a nightmare, all kicking off again.)

There may be extreme tiredness, loss of appetite and weight loss.

The severity of symptoms varies depending on how much of the rectum and colon are inflamed and how severe is the inflammation.

For some people daily life may be severely impacted. (You can say that again.)

A severe case may be defined as having to visit the loo and empty the bowels six or more times a day. Plus, there may be shortness of breath, irregular heartbeats, high temperature and blood in the stools. (When I first saw blood in my stools that was the worrying bit.)

Stress may be a potential factor. (If that is the case why did hundreds of Burnley fans not get Colitis during the 1980s and 1990s?)

What causes it? It is thought to be a breakdown of the auto-immune system. This is the way the body fights against infection. But if it goes wrong then healthy tissues are attacked. The theory is that the immune system mistakes harmless bacteria inside the colon for a threat and attacks the tissues of the colon, causing it to become inflamed. Nobody as yet knows why it does this. (Just one of life's little mysteries then.)

Maybe one in 400 people are affected in the UK and the condition can appear at any age though more commonly between 15 and 25 (me). It is more common in white people of European descent. Both men and women seem to be equally affected.

Treatment: (Ah well here's the thing. My early treatment, medication, did not work.) Mild to moderate flare-ups can be treated at home; more severe flare-ups need hospitalisation. Medication: you can have amino salicylates, corticosteroids or immune-suppressants. (You will be relieved to know you only need to know those off by heart if you are a doctor, nurse, or chemist.)

If medication does not work then surgery is needed (me). The small intestine will either be diverted out of an opening in your abdomen and you wear a bag; or can be used to create an internal pouch inside the body that is connected to the anus.

A word of caution: Do not confuse IBD with IBS. The former is Inflammatory Bowel Disease and the latter is Irritable Bowel Syndrome. IDS is Iain Duncan-Smith.

Back at the football club, the struggles went on with two awful consecutive home defeats, 5-0 to Gillingham and 6-0 to Manchester City. Home defeats, humiliating, belittling, embarrassing. Eleven goals in just two games with fans screaming for change and Stan's head. Chairman Kilby actually spoke to some of the senior players to ask them their views about Stan and what he should do. Gareth Taylor, who played for City that night and later signed for Burnley, remembered the game: 'Everything we did that night just came off.' And how it did. Burnley were simply mesmerised and the old film shows them unable to make a simple pass, time and again gifting the ball to City. A Manchester City fan sitting in one of the home stands will remember the game for a different reason. When he celebrated the sixth goal the pie hurled at him hit him full on his ear. Funnily enough, painful though it may be, watching that game again on YouTube is a reminder of how far the club have come since.

Stan stuck out his chest and announced that under no circumstances would he resign and that he was made of sterner stuff than Heath or Waddle. Paul Cook was brought in and one by one players were assembled who would eventually see the job through. But for the meantime there was a clear relegation battle facing them. All I could do was read the newspapers and listen to people who came to visit me either in hospital when I was in, or at home. I even managed to get to some of the games.

Come November and none of the medication was working. In came a group of doctors with the consultant, Mr Sandilands, as nice a guy as you could wish to meet. It was more or less ultimatum time;

carry on fumbling around trying this, and trying that, and nothing working, or have the bowel taken out.

The bowel taken out. It would take three operations. I looked at him. This was something big to think about. What were the implications? What would happen afterwards? How would it affect me? How long would recovery be? How do you replace a bowel and what with? A dozen questions are going around in my head but there's just me to make a decision. Think about it. You are just 21, you have a massive decision to make, yes or no, stick or twist.

He explained there would need to be three operations but this was the big one. Normally they would be well spaced out but he knew I was a footballer and needed to get back to playing as soon as possible, if indeed I ever did get back to playing. But the thought that I wouldn't never really entered my head. The proposed date for the operation was 7 December 1998, a date now imprinted in my head. It had been a year earlier when the first signs appeared and I had now been going on and on for a year with no sign of any cure or progress. Taking out the bowel was the only answer. Do it, I agreed.

Mr Sandilands was the saviour and got the operations right. Did I know the severity of it? One thing is for sure, I never thought it was going to end my career.

When I came around after the op, I was in intensive care for a short while. That sounds dramatic and the press made the most of it with headlines that suggested it was a life-and-death thing and that I was lucky to be alive. That was never the case. They had newspapers to sell and what could be better than a line that read 'it was touch and go for footballer Paul Weller'.

Back in my little room I surveyed what they had done. To say I felt queasy is an understatement. The artificial hole, the stoma, sat there on my stomach along with part of my bowel. It was gruesome. I passed out.

I was well and truly on the outside of everything in the normal world, looking in … and looking enviously … my world was made up of hospitals, doctors, surgeons and nurses. The word bowel became word of the moment. Intestine was another. Stools in this case were not what you sit on. Stoma is not a Norwegian football club in case you're wondering. A colonoscopy is a medical procedure performed by a surgeon in which the colon is examined. The patient lies on their stomach and the surgeon approaches from the rear to probe the colon via the rectum. The colon is a huge long wriggly lengthy thing that meanders about inside your body, long enough to stretch from Burnley to Brighton. It never ceases to amaze me that some surgeons specialise in prostate cancer where a finger is inserted in the rectum, or colon troubles where things are inserted even deeper. What is the attraction? It would be tempting to ask them, 'Does your mother know what you do for a living?'

During that two-week stint everyone rallied round; mum and dad came up, players, staff, management, were all regular visitors. When I came out on 21 December I went down to mum and dad's to rest and recuperate. Except now there was something different about me, I had a stoma and a colostomy bag fastened to it. From my little private room with nurses and auxiliaries to fuss and help me, now I was having to do all the necessaries myself. Normal life had finished. The things you take for granted about going to the loo were gone.

Or for a bath or a shower. How simple is that when you are fit and healthy and have nothing attached to your stomach to think about? I managed. Take the bag off and shower as fast as I could before anything began to leak out of the stoma. On one occasion back up in Burnley, just as I was stripped and ready to go into the shower, Andy Cooke came to the door. I opened it, stood there, starkers, holding the bag, with a tissue held ready for any leakage.

'Oh my God,' he said, and he nearly passed out. Those were the fun days.

Much later during a different stint in Burnley General, Glen Little came to visit me. He'd just had a hernia operation and was desperate to show me the scars. 'Hutch up,' he said and slid onto the bed beside me revealing his scars. I showed him mine.

'Ugh,' he croaked. Now it was him nearly passing out. He got off that bed as fast as he could.

Those first weeks with the stoma and the bag were so uncomfortable and being back down south, the faces I was so familiar with, the lads and the players from the club who had visited and kept me sane and cheerful, were all miles away up north. Sure, mum and dad were there but the nurses who had helped me change the bag and empty it, were not there anymore. I had it to do, not just once a day but several. You emptied the bag from the bottom down the loo. You fixed a fresh one every day. There were problems with leakage, the rashes that appeared, and simply keeping clean. No good moping, no good feeling sorry, no point sitting and thinking, why me? I had to do it and got on with it.

Driving was not easy. Bags back then were quite big so sitting hunched up to a steering wheel was very uncomfortable. There were only certain positions you could sit in to feel relaxed. Long journeys from Worthing to Burnley or the other way were purgatory with essential stops at various service stations to empty the bag.

The expression 'shit journey' takes on a whole new meaning.

The second operation was in February and we were into 1999 and the football team were struggling. This op was to cut me open again and make an internal anal pouch with the still existing small bowel. There is a fancy medical name for this but you don't need to know it. There was a new stoma and the colostomy bag remained. They would be there for a while yet.

Operation three was in April and was to connect the internal pouch they had made to the small bowel so that the outside colostomy bag was no longer needed. Instead of faeces going into the colostomy bag, it now went into the internal pouch and could pass through the anus. It was in fact a big moment and Mr Sandilands came in even on his day off to check me out. He was carrying a bike helmet with him. A bike rider. I thought the Hell's Angels had arrived. He knew of course that I was a footballer and a career was at stake. He knew how big this was for me. He was genuinely worried for me. It was Sandilands that told me I could still play even if I still needed a bag. It could be removed. The stoma plugged up and my abdomen strapped up. Four months earlier I'd seen the first stoma and bits of bowel lying on my stomach and felt ill at the sight of it. Now it was all sorted out inside me.

But, would the food I ate pass through alright? From eating, to passing stools through the anus once again. 'Things need to settle down,' said Sandilands after he'd sewn me up for the last time.

I'd opted to continue all the treatment in Burnley General instead of the private hospital in Gisburn that was on offer. Gisburn was more like a hotel, luxury facilities, carpets, TVs, more like a health spa. In Burnley General I knew everyone, it was easy for visitors. I was used to familiar faces and routines. Cocooned in my little room I whiled away the time with magazines and TV. In a normal ward you can set your watch by the regularity of all the daily routines. The opening of the curtains, the first cuppa tea, breakfast, lunch, pulse checks, heart rate checks, the afternoon cuppa, teatime, suppertime. All regular as clockwork. Such things in my little bubble passed me by. I was happy enough.

After the final op it was a waiting period. Nurses popped in. 'How's things, have you managed to go to the loo yet?' An hour later, 'Anything happening Paul?' Evening and no loo visits. Do I need to worry? Has it worked? Day one and no luck. Day two and they are popping in every hour again for a progress report. 'Sorry nurse, nothing yet.' Day two passes by and we are all wondering if I will ever pass anything. They are reassuring. 'Paul, don't worry, it takes time.' Don't forget I hadn't done a normal bowel movement for months. Now my insides were expected to start working again with what amounted to a new system installed. The night nurse on day two popped in. 'Any luck Paul?' 'No.' 'Maybe tomorrow.' We were all on pins. For everything to be successful I needed to be able to go to the loo normally as I had always done.

And the next day brought success. Day three I experienced a sort of pop and I swear I heard something. Something had passed through and it was on its way. The nurses were dancing and celebrating. Don't forget the proof of the pudding is in the eating, or in my case, the proof of the operation is the eating ending up where it should, down the loo, via small bowel, internal pouch and anus.

Now it was anal soreness that was the problem for a while because nothing had passed through it for months. I was having to walk around bow-legged, like John Wayne.

That season, 1998/99, could have ended so badly for the club. But it didn't. Eventually an 11-match unbeaten run ensured safety and the highlight near the end of the season was a 1-0 win over Fulham, the top dogs at the time, funded by Harrods' Al-Fayed. Supporter Tim Quelch was there to see Ronnie Jepson score the winner.

> Thank you, Ronnie. At seven minutes past five on May 1, you allowed my life to resume. My boss will be dead pleased. Of late my mind has tended to wander. How can you deal with budget crises when you are still waiting on Payton's fitness? But, on this day Burnley saved themselves and in so doing beat the best team in the division. It was a bit like ram-raiding Harrods' showroom. Fulham came in search of a record points tally. Unfortunately for them, Burnley were

> prepared to scrape and grapple their way higher. And it all ended happily thanks to Ronnie.
>
> Ronnie had come on for the second half. It was an inspired move with Branch prompting that inspiration. On comes Ronnie and makes straight for the thick of things. I've only seen him in fits and starts and yet I'm already in love. He may only have cost a dime but to me he's a million dollars. Today was his day. After 82 minutes, Cowan hurls in one of his long throws. Symons heads out but Cook heads back in. The header is deflected down and there is Ronnie. In one sweeping movement he flicks the ball round his body, swivelling with perfect timing, and volleying fast and low to Taylor's right.
>
> Turf Moor shuddered with relief and appreciation. Any goal would be good enough but this was a classy strike, one that a Cole or a Shearer would have been proud of. What a way to end your convalescence. Welcome back Ronnie.
>
> So, safe after all. None of us who endured the 6-0 City fiasco gave Stan and the boys a prayer. But they not only proved us wrong, they did it with something to spare. So, whom should we credit?

Barry Kilby was first name out of the hat, for investing his money, and for sticking by Stan Ternent. Second was Stan himself. He'd been criticised hugely, for the gang of four saga, his terseness, his outbursts in the press and for some of his selections and tactics. But in the end, he proved his critics wrong. He imposed his will, his stubbornness, his bloody-mindedness. He sorted the wheat from the chaff. He was a battler and it spread to the players. They were fighters. Finally, there was a team that looked good together and folks were thinking this might be a team that didn't need to just scrap for safety but might challenge for honours. They would be right.

Tim Quelch was a regular at our games despite travelling up from London. He was in big trouble for heading up to the Stoke City game. He came up on a very late whim and around midday asked his wife could he borrow her work BMW to get to the game but didn't actually say how far he'd be travelling. This was a 400 miles round trip. At 5pm she rang to ask where he was. Stoke? She exploded. To this day he says the doghouse treatment on his return was worth it, to see the 4-1 win and the Glen Little masterclass.

He saw the 3-1 home victory over Colchester at Easter. It was the game when the half-time entertainment was a troupe of dogs dressed up in female ballet outfits. There was a 1-1 draw at Lincoln, he recalls, where someone had an old air-raid warning siren they were using whenever they were on the attack. Lincoln had two huge front men so this was a game of high crosses. The aerial bombardment made the siren all the more appropriate. This is what it must have been like in those wartime games of the 40s.

Such fans are the bedrock of any club. There's a whole bunch of London Clarets who come up for every game. There are characters like 'Rocky' and Dave Burnley who hasn't missed a game for something like 40 years. There was always a good away following and in the Waddle season and then Stan's first season when we were hardly world-beaters, the way they continued to travel great distances was amazing. I got so many letters from them when I was in hospital. They kept me going.

There was never any shortage of visitors. Stan came on Sunday mornings. After a defeat I used to dread that. If I could I'd have hidden under the covers. He'd go through the performance and each player one by one.

There was one Sunday and they'd lost badly somewhere the day before, might have been 5-0. Yet still he came to see me. He would go through games and players and tell me this and that. I'd just sit there nodding. Glen Little's name came up frequently. But every Sunday Stan came and showed he cared.

If I was lying on top of the covers, he'd look at my legs with a look of horror … 'Come on you soft git. Your legs are wasting away. You need to sit on the end of the bed with some leg weights and exercise them,' he'd tell me. It was true, I'd lost so much muscle.

The nurses would tell him, 'Oh no, he's not.'

After his visits I'd text the lads. 'OK he's gone, you can come in now.'

All of these visits were one of the reasons I never got down and miserable. OK I felt like shit (if you'll pardon the expression) often enough but I'd just say 'well, there's plenty worse off than me'.

The fun times were when Andy Cooke and Glen Little would come and sneak me out. It would be great to say I was smuggled out in laundry baskets or down fire escapes, but it was never like that. You just casually walked out with one of them on either side, looking as if you were a visitor leaving the premises at 'closing time' along with the other visitors. Visits to the Chinese were especially welcome. Getting back in was the problem and getting by security.

'Oh, it's you Paul,' they'd say. 'Everyone's looking for you.' There'd be a bit of a telling-off from the nurses on the late shift, but they were always half-amused, as if to say, 'Footballers eh, what can you do with them?'

Andy Cooke remembers Sunday lunches with Stan Ternent. If we'd just beaten someone on the Saturday and Stan was in a good mood, he might say, 'Wellers, Cookey, Glen, my house tomorrow.' So, we'd go round on a Sunday and Cath would be cooking Sunday lunch and we'd be there with a nice glass of wine. He really looked after you.

Whenever possible I managed to be at the home games. That may have been a bit of a dim thing to do seeing as how stress can be linked with bowel problems. The 0-6 at home to Manchester

City comes to mind. The away end was full as they roared out their anthem 'Blue Moon'. You can see it on YouTube, an utter horror show. 'Feed the Goat,' they used to chant for City player Sean Goater. He duly obliged with a hat-trick. I remember the boos raining down from the supporters as they left early in their droves, and the abject depression afterwards. Before that there was the 0-5 at home to Gillingham and I seem to think that Stan remarked that things could only get better. If he had been psychic, it's something he would have avoided saying. If fans thought he would leave, he didn't.

'Those were the days,' say battle-hardened Burnley supporters today. The club has enjoyed consecutive seasons in the Premier League. The bank account is filled to overflowing, the training ground is state-of-the-art, no one can remember what thick mud looks like, the corporate boxes are oversubscribed, player cars in the car park look like a glistening motor show, the average wage is around £35,000 a week; it's all a long way from the days of Mullen, Heath, Waddle and Stan. Supporters say they were at this horror game or that nightmare game and parade their memories like a badge of honour. Darlington, Gillingham, Rochdale or York seem a million miles away. The seven years in the Fourth Division a distant memory.

'I'm just glad to be alive,' headlined the *Burnley Express* when at last all my health problems seemed to be over. It had been a year and a half since I first experienced the problem. In hospital, in bed, worrying about whether I'd ever play again, never came into my thinking. Thinking centred around one thing: beating the illness.

To be honest, the local press did get a bit over-dramatic. I'd stared death in the face, they said when I went under the knife for life-saving bowel operations (their words not mine). Did I really say, 'there was a chance I might not have been here at all, so any football is a bonus'?

But yes, they got some things right; I was told that the only cure for the ulcerated bowel was to take it out, form an artificial internal pouch and then reconnect everything up again. And yes, I was warned that something could go seriously wrong, so I was happy to get through it all to tell the tale. But you must be joking, I thought, when they told me that I could end up wearing a colostomy bag for life and then tried to cheer me up saying I could still continue playing. Today I have to smile when I see a supermarket sign saying 'bag for life'. I might have had one.

Can you imagine the dressing room banter if a player had a colostomy bag strapped to him?

'Hey Paul, going shopping?'

'What's in the bag Wellers?'

Can you imagine the perils of going into a flying tackle with Paul Ince, wearing a bag? Can you imagine the reaction if the bag burst during a full-frontal collision with Stan Collymore? What in God's name would Glen Little have ever said, the first time he saw it? A diving header and landing on the bag; it doesn't bear thinking about. Let me tell you now; if I'd had to wear a bag, I'd have given up the game. Obviously, the surgeon had never been a footballer.

The truth was, they told me that if I had to wear a bag, it could be removed temporarily, the exit in my abdomen plugged and then I could be strapped up. But no thanks, I thought. How could I possibly play like that at Championship level?

Chapter 11

BACK TO A PROMOTION SEASON

A PROGRAMME piece about my illness at the beginning of the new season, 1999/2000, summed things up neatly. What a season it would turn out to be, with promotion on the very last day and, prior to that, the arrival of legend, Ian Wright. Dave and I were chatting about him and his life since football: his TV career as a football pundit and his starring role in *I'm A Celebrity Get Me Out of Here,* where a selection of celebs exist in the jungle somewhere in Australia and have to perform gruesome tasks involving insects, snakes, slime, mud and eating the most revolting things you can imagine; and one by one they are eliminated. Ian, by all accounts, was not coming out of it too well, a bully and controlling, said the two old biddies on the treadmills next to Dave in the gym he goes to. 'I don't like him,' they chuntered. The *Daily Mirror* announced he was doing it to help him pay off a tax bill. Footballers and tax bills.

If true, he isn't the first and won't be the last. Tax bills or not, he was great with us at Burnley. And I never had big tax bills because I never earned big money.

The feature about me in a Burnley programme explained things:

Paul Weller's first-team comeback may have to wait a little longer than today's visit of Brentford. But when it happens it will be one of the most deserved in Claret history. Weller has faced one of the toughest fitness fights imaginable, without a medial ligament or ruptured Achilles tendon in sight.

The Burnley midfielder had to have his large bowel removed as one of three major operations, to not only salvage his playing career, but also to make his everyday life bearable. What was originally diagnosed as inflammation of the bowel turned out to be a serious ulcer problem. And when a course of steroids failed to produce a cure by last winter, Weller was left with no choice but to face a lengthy spell out of the game and three bouts of surgery.

'I tried to get fit and played two games but the pain was so bad I just couldn't go on,' he said. 'I just wanted to get it sorted out. I spoke to the physio and the manager who was brilliant and just said get it done whatever it takes. It got to November and I just couldn't go on and I'd had enough. I couldn't go on with the pain and I was going to the toilet about 20 times a day and losing so much blood.'

Weller was ready to undertake anything that would make him better but hadn't ever thought that he might not play again. However, it was apparent that the surgery was make or break for the 24-year-old's career. Happily, the treatment was a success and Weller, who managed just two games last season, was back in training by the start of pre-season and took his first tentative steps against Accrington Stanley in July.

'My stomach hasn't been a problem. I have always felt confident with that. I just felt nervous being on the pitch again for the first few games. I had to see whether I could still kick a ball,' added Weller, now itching for a return to

> league action after getting a handful of Pontins League games under his belt. 'I can't wait to get back on that pitch. I've got to keep playing as many games as possible to get my fitness back and force my way back in. It will be pretty hard while we are playing well but it's a case of waiting for my chance and snatching it when it comes.'
>
> Weller has been at Turf Moor for nine years, the last four of which have been a period of almost constant change. Ever since he has been laid low, Stan Ternent has totally overhauled his playing staff. But Weller is once again part of a squad which is at the opposite end of the table to the last one that he was regularly involved with.
>
> 'It felt weird seeing so many players coming and going. Not being at the club every day, although I did watch the home games, there were players walking past me I'd never seen before. There have been so many changes but the manager has turned things around and the lads are doing well. I mean we're top of the table.'

More or less two years after the first signs of this affliction had appeared on New Year's Eve during the Waddle season, it was now reasonable to say I was raring to go and the season was just starting for me. Restored, renewed, repaired, I was desperate to get back in the side. Trouble was, they were doing OK without me. To get back in I had a job on my hands. From the very beginning of the season they were never out of the top six, even though there were one or two blips along the way.

Getting back to fitness had been a relentless task; I was getting stronger and stronger and was desperate to get the feel of a game again. It came for the reserves at Accrington; the comeback trail had begun. First steps: it wasn't quite like learning to walk all over again, in some ways it was like riding a bike for the first time in a year; you don't really forget how to do it, but there might be the odd wobble for the first few minutes. It had been a long, long road, 'brave fightback', said reporter Pete Oliver. But the feeling I had was one of relief as well as enjoyment. I did just 50 minutes and that was enough for the first outing, and the young lads won 1-0. I sat in the small dressing room afterwards feeling great. A small step, but I was back on the grass. A bit of moral support came from the handful of players who came over, as well as a contingent of fans, and the reception I got was a huge boost. But there was still a long way to go to get back to full fitness and physio Ian Liversedge was determined to take it slow and steady. The gaffer was good, he knew that this was just a first step and he had no intention of hurling me straight back in again.

There were odd appearances here and there, against Wigan in a minor cup competition, then back in league football, the home game against Scunthorpe in October, then later against Bury and Oxford.

Oxford United was the end-of-the-Millennium game when Payts scored all three. The game before this had been memorable for all the wrong reasons, a 4-2 defeat away at Bury. It was touch and go whether or not the game would go ahead, the hail, sleet and rain had been so bad. One goalmouth was just about flooded. I read somewhere that Boxing Day is not the best day for Burnley, traditionally they tend to lose, and so it turned out in this game. I was involved when I was brought on as sub in the second half and I have a vague memory of someone scoring from a cross I sent over. Unfortunately, by then, we were four goals down and big Steve Davis had been sent off. The only consolation for me was that it was a few more minutes under my belt. Burnley fans were in three sides of the ground to make it almost a home game. It was no consolation for them.

The Millennium game was in front of 14,000 people and how much better things were just two days after the Bury misery. It was the day that Burnley legend, the great Jimmy McIlroy, was welcomed back to the club after a number of years' estrangement. Burnley Football Club hadn't always been the best at remembering or honouring its past players and managers. New man Barry Kilby was trying to do something about it. But the shaggy brown coat he wore came in for some ribaldry.

Here was Jimmy Mac on the pitch before the game started, along with most of the team that won the title in 1960. McIlroy and the others were there to officially open the stand that now had Jimmy's name, The Jimmy McIlroy Stand. Even some of the club's most hardened drinkers left the pubs early to be there. It was a moving moment when he said that for once he, an Irishman, was lost for words, and in fact it should be called not after him, but The Champions Stand, in honour of all of the team. And they weren't finished yet. At half-time Harry Potts' widow Margaret and Bob Lord's widow Hilda, were both presented to the crowd.

It was a key game following the Bury debacle but several players were shaking off the after-effects of flu. Or were they shaking off the after-effects of Christmas merriment, indulgence and plum duff? It would be a rare footballer that came in and admitted to Stan Ternent that he was out of sorts because he had over-eaten. It didn't prevent what was a decent win, even though Oxford scored and went 1-0 up within just three minutes. Andy Cooke was chopped down time and again as Burnley knocked the ball about but Glen Little had one of his unplayable games, some of his runs quite bewildering. At last Oxford chopped him down as well, this time in the penalty box. Andy Payton clipped it home. Games at this time of year are when supporters bring their cigars and flasks of brandy. You can almost smell the cigars from the touchline.

I was on the bench and when Paul Cook had to come off it was me that was sent on. More or less out of nowhere Oxford went ahead again, a free header from a corner. Bloody hell, lose this game and Stan will kill us on Monday, we think. Oxford probably had only three attacks and scored from two of them. One of those days, you think. Frustration on the terraces more often than not seeps down to the players and so it did in this game. By now, Glen Little was being kicked from pillar to post. Referees were supposed now to encourage attacking play with their decisions and protect the flair players. This one seemed not to know about that.

Stan changed things round a bit and moved Glen to his favoured right wing. And then a magic moment. He played me in, a gem of a cross from me to Andy Payton, he pounced, he struck, he scored, 2-2. The pass from me, I was over the moon as they say. And then it got better. We were desperate for the win, the crowd roaring us on, the atmosphere frantic and Glen on fire. He sent over a dozen tempting crosses and at last in the 89th minute, the predator, Andy Payton, stuck out a foot from a ruck of players and got his hat-trick goal. Once upon a time, a hundred years earlier this kind of goal would have been described as coming from a scrimmage. Today, a melee. Up went the injury-time board, Payton was named as man of the match, but really it was Glen's game. And for me, more minutes, more good play, a big contribution, but still a long way from being one of the first on the team sheet.

January 2000 and I was talking about how fortunate I'd been, in a heartfelt interview in the local press. A cup tie against Coventry was days away although I didn't play. Sometimes it most certainly hit me how lucky I'd been.

'Even if I'm substitute against Coventry and come on for the last ten minutes, I'll treasure every second. There was a time when I might not have been here at all so any football is a bonus. It was a frightening time because I was told the only cure for my ulcerated bowel was to take it out, form an artificial pouch then reconnect everything. I was warned something could go seriously wrong. I'm just happy to be here to tell the tale. Fortunately, here I am.'

They were frustrating times though. My fitness was back and I was raring to go. But there was no regular first-team place. I was 24 and with probably another ten years ahead of me, the peak years approaching, and felt hard done by. I was certain I was ready to get back in the side but Stan didn't include me.

We had more than one row and fell out several times. I'd tell him I was ready, and he'd say no you're not. Bear in mind I can be a fiery little so-and-so and I'm thinking he's talking rubbish. This went on and on. He knew I was disgruntled so the day came when he said 'right you can go' and put me on the transfer list. Actually, never one to mince his words, he told me if I didn't like it, I could fuck off.

People put two and two together and often get the wrong answer. Fans are quick to shoot a player down and so it was assumed it was me that had asked for a transfer. Ungrateful little so-and-so muttered the fans, getting hold of the wrong end of the stick. They'd seen the club had stood by me. I should have been loyal to them and shown gratitude, some folks thought, having decided I was being churlish.

Years later I heard a story that it was only Stan that saved me from being disposed of by the board where certain members wanted to cut their losses and sack me. But let's just suppose it was me that asked for a transfer. When that kind of thing happens, those who say a player should show respect and gratitude have no way of getting inside a footballer's head. A footballer wants to play; he wants to be in the first team. He does not want to be on the fringe. Maybe it's different today when they are so well paid and the bank accounts fill up, so that a footballer can think, well at least there's the money. Back in my day when the money was not so good it was less of a motivator.

But what do I do, I kept thinking? I liked it at Burnley. I liked the town. I felt at home. I'd been there for nine years. Leaving would be a wrench. Stick or twist.

It was in the away game to Oxford in April as the season was nearing its end that I felt I was really back. I was still on the list but Stan put me in the squad to travel for the game. What the hell is he doing, I thought. What's he dragging me all that way for, he's not going to play me. He's just playing mind games. He's gonna have me just carrying the skip. Then I saw later that I was down as sub, on the bench. I was as baffled as at any time since Waddle. From being ignored almost and put on the transfer list, which you could be forgiven for thinking was some sort of punishment, there I was down as sub. Even then I was still thinking, mind games, he's not going to play me, I'm just there as the odd-job man.

The prelude to all this was me assuming I'd be leaving in the summer so in February I'd had a knee operation and had ten weeks out to get fit again. I'm just a fringe player now, I thought, but nevertheless worked hard, and began to look really sharp in training and refreshed, whilst several of the others were beginning to look tired. Presumably, Stan had noticed.

By this time Ian Wright was at the club, and that's another story. I'd been playing plenty of reserve games but it's first-team games that you need to get up to full speed. You need quicker reactions, the bigger challenge, you need the buzz of a large crowd, the tempo is different. It's chalk and cheese. And then the buzz of a dressing room after a key win; and when you get the winning goal in such a game in the 90th minute, that's when you feel utter elation and triumph. With just minutes to go you could have been forgiven for thinking a horrible 1-0 defeat was on the cards but football, eh. It takes you by surprise, you never say never, you never stop battling, and just sometimes you get the rewards.

A wet and blustery day, squalls, from drizzle to downpours, but easing off by the time of the game. Supporters though, wet and cold. Those with a roof over their heads saying a silent prayer of thanks. Glen Little suspended. Me and Ian Wright on the bench.

And Burnley went 1-0 down to a poor Oxford side. Stan Ternent made changes at half-time, a couple of long-range shots, me and Wrighty still sat on the bench.

Wrighty turned to me and said, 'We'll get on here and change the game, he needs us now.' He told me that when we got on, when I got it, to run down the wing, cross it and he would head it in.

At last Stan brought us on, a last throw of the dice.

I'll always remember that chat, and that's what I did. I went down the right and crossed it over but I didn't get hold of it properly. Instead the ball went not to Wrighty but to Steve Davis near the edge of the box and Steve headed it in. 'Great ball,' he said but I was laughing to myself; it wasn't meant for Steve.

As scripts go, it was pretty good. Big Steve seemed to pick his spot, a headed goal from this distance is rare and has to be perfectly placed. Supporters roared, as much surprised as anything else, taken aback by the sheer unexpectedness of it. At least there was one point to take home and the evening was not a total disaster.

The injury-time board went up. Three minutes of extra time. Hold on for the draw maybe. But no. A ball was pushed forward and Ian Wright of all people chased after it even though it looked a lost cause. Here was a star, a galactico, once of England but grafting like a labourer. He wanted to win as much as any of us. No ego, no superstar huffing and puffing, no shrugging of the shoulders as if to say I'm not chasing that.

He caught it and banged it over. The final whistle was imminent and it was me on the end of it to score with seconds to go, getting in between two defenders and heading into the bottom corner. Crap game said the fans but they didn't care and neither did we. Scoring a winner in injury time is just the most amazing feeling. Stan Ternent had changed our mentality. Under Heath or Waddle we'd not have won this game. We were a nice club that played nice football but we were never going to win anything with either of them. Stan T made us a hard side to beat. He instilled a definite cussed mentality into us. The first thing he said to us, was that each player had to win their individual battle and if each player won their own battle, we would win games. We never used to fight enough, we were too nice, a pretty team but Stan made us into a proper team that really wanted to win. He had a winning mind; he was focussed and he made us focussed. So, we never gave up lost causes and that was why Ian Wright chased that ball that was going out, and caught it and crossed it. He wanted to do it for Stan Ternent and said so more than once.

I got a fair amount of ribbing on the way back; it was my first goal for two years. Heading had never been my strong point and this was a headed goal. The stats say there were over 2,000 Burnley fans there; that's some following. It was also the third time in four games we'd scored in the last minute. Dream day is an understatement. The press churned out the clichés; hero of the hour, never say die, and Roy of the Rovers. There was a big emphasis on how I'd been out for so long, the three operations, got back, then a knee injury on top of all that, on to the transfer list and then off it.

The other Paul Weller and The Jam used to sing about 'the five o'clock hero.' The five o'clock hero on Saturday at Oxford United was me. You can't beat it, the feeling, the thrill, the satisfaction. They say everyone can be famous for 15 minutes. That's the beauty of being a footballer. You can have more than just one chance to be a hero. And famous, even though it might only be in East Lancashire.

The feeling was one of tiredness but also accomplishment on the coach on the way home. The spirit we had was unbelievable. And by now we wanted promotion. We were always in the top six, we were close, we could smell it and feel it. Just five games left and win them all and there was automatic promotion.

But, was I still on the transfer list? Er no. I found out not from Stan, but from the press. 'You've been taken off the transfer list, Paul.'

But football can kick you in the teeth so easily as we lost the next game at home 3-0 to promotion rivals Gillingham in front of an astonishing 17,000 people. Joy one minute and disappointment the next. The fans exited the stadium with downcast faces, looking like they'd lost a fiver and found a 50p. It knocked us for six.

Their manager Peter Taylor made a comment after the game to Stan, that Stan stored away in his mental Filofax. Taylor must have thought, right, that's it, that's sorted our promotion then. You wouldn't have blamed him for thinking that or for any Burnley fan thinking we had blown our chance of automatic promotion.

'Don't worry Stan, you'll get it right eventually,' said Taylor. Genuine or smug, condescending or sincere; that was not the kind of thing to say to Stan. He was livid and would get his own back at the end of the season.

And so to Scunthorpe, last game of the season, top six assured. Automatic promotion only if Gillingham lost and Burnley won.

A crowd of 7,000 supporters watched on the big screen back at Turf Moor, people without tickets wandered round Scunthorpe's ground hoping to sneak in; days before people had queued in the rain back in Burnley to get tickets. But the day of the game was bright and sunny. Scunthorpe were already relegated but even if Burnley won, there was still no guarantee of automatic promotion. Gillingham, them again, could still scupper the chance if they won at Wrexham, managed by Burnley hero Brian Flynn. After the Gillingham defeat Burnley had won the next three games to keep hopes alive. Burnley have a long history of end-of-season games that are 'deciders'. Here was another.

Cometh the hour, cometh the man. Glen had experienced a mixed season, genius one day and journeyman on another. In this game he was brought on with the score at 1-1. Supporter hopes had vanished like a burst balloon when Scunthorpe went ahead. Mickey Mellon equalised. Supporters' heads and hopes were lifted.

News came that Wrexham were beating Gillingham. Supporters were chewing fingernails to the bone and then enter Glen Little. With around 20 minutes left to play, a clearance by the Scunthorpe defender came to Little 20 yards out. Without a pause he volleyed it back and into the net for a superb off the cuff, instinctive goal. He just wellied it. It was stunning, the match-winner … and the promotion winner. His goal sparked a pitch invasion. As that was cleared Ian Wright came on from the subs' bench. A goal would have been the icing on the cake for him. He tore through the defence and only an unkind bounce of the ball robbed him of a real scoring chance.

I was watching from the stands. Two minutes remaining of normal time were torment. Fans congregated at the front of the stands ready to race on. The referee indicated THREE minutes of injury time. The crowd groaned. Whistles for the ref to blow for time were ear-piercing. Watching a game can be torture. We players don't always get that. Now I knew what it was like to be on the waiting end. Wrighty wasted a bit of time by the corner flag. A huge punt down to the Scunthorpe end wasted a bit more. And then, at last, the whistle. The players raced as fast as they could to get to the tunnel, those that didn't quite make it were mobbed.

My view of what went on when the final whistle eventually went was blurred only by the people standing up in front of me going wild. Around 2,000 Clarets poured onto the pitch in a state of utter euphoria. The green grass was obliterated by a sea of claret and blue. They jumped, they hugged, they ran, they did cartwheels and somersaults, they danced and screamed and shouted and stayed until Stan and the team came out into the stand to receive the roars they deserved.

Only two years earlier they had come away from the final game against Plymouth joyful but relieved to avoid relegation.

The news came through that Gillingham had indeed lost. Now Burnley had been promoted. A second roar of joy came from the hordes of fans.

Ian Wright was as joyful as anyone. His first goal for the club had come in the last four minutes at Gillingham; he celebrated like it was his first ever. He suffered appalling racial abuse at Colchester. He could do a lovely fake northern accent that had us in stitches. But his cars. He had a superb Bentley at a time when no footballer at Burnley had anything remotely flash. How it wasn't nicked is a mystery. Perhaps folks knew who it belonged to. He did stop coming up in it eventually and had a Mini as well. What a way to finish his last season in football. What a memory to add to his long list. What a swansong.

There's no question Stan was flexible with him in terms of training and attendances at Gawthorpe. He more or less did what he liked in training and any rigorous diet went to pieces. He certainly took a liberty with the truffles when he visited Stan one day at his home. Ian tells this story in his newest biography.

> Once I went to his house and he had this box of truffles put out. I bit into six or seven of them. I'm not sure I really liked them and replaced them in their lovely individual containers and then put them back in the box. Later, he called a family meeting about the truffles with his wife and sons, Chris and Danny, who were all fantastic people. He went mad.
>
> 'Who's done this to my fucking truffles?'
>
> They told him. 'It was Ian did it, when he came here the other night.'
>
> At training I told the lads what I had done just before he came in for training, screaming, 'Wright, you fucking bastard.'
>
> I had so much fun at Burnley.

We knew Wrighty was taking a few liberties but never lost our respect for him. We were winning and he was helping us. It was great just having him around the place. It became clear he couldn't last the pace of a full 90 minutes so Stan used him as an impact sub. It worked. But the racial abuse he suffered at Colchester was unforgiveable.

Glen Little in an interview with Chris Boden, remembered him well: 'There was a bit of banter and he was a noisy bloke but to be fair Ian wasn't there too often. He had his TV shows and the like but he came up whenever he could. He didn't half give us a lift and I think we all thought, right, you've been playing with Bergkamp, but we're not bad players ourselves. I remember not long after he came the press were slating us saying he was more used to the likes of Bergkamp but I thought that was a bit of a slight on the players we had because he did have chances and missed quite a few before he finally came good. The established players deserve more credit; he never really played that well and the first few games were a nightmare. He was struggling with an injury so the gaffer made the brave decision to put him on the bench and he did much better in the cameo role, scoring his first goal at Gillingham and then getting some other crucial goals. The masterstroke was putting him on the bench. We were in the play-offs anyhow and I think it's unfair on the lads to say he got us up, but every bit helped and his goals were vitally important.'

Stan wanted him to do one more season, he says in his book, but he said no. How could he top finishing his career helping an old mate and winning promotion? He was 36 and he'd had 15 years as a professional and at some grounds he got an ovation because they knew he was retiring.

What we didn't know was anything about all his angsts and anxieties, problems he'd had during his chaotic and oppressive childhood, a cruel stepfather, impatience and anger issues. There were rejection issues, both from his family and from football clubs before he was at last signed by Crystal Palace at the ripe old age of 21. There were stages of his life that he hated and early fame that he found hard to handle and resist the temptations of the hangers-on. It took a long time to reconcile with his mother.

At Burnley we knew none of this, and to this day would have no idea but for an article in the *Guardian* about him. With us he was just 'Wrighty', a fun-loving guy who joined in with everything. We looked up to him and he never let us down. Never once did we think what is he doing here? When Gazza came, we thought it frequently.

After the promotion game at Scunthorpe, at what other club could a bunch of inebriated supporters journeying home on the train to London whip out a mobile phone and speak first to vice-chairman Ray Ingleby and then chairman Barry Kilby? Only at Burnley. Sozzled by bottles of champagne and gallons of ale, hardly able to think straight or speak clearly, the London Clarets were in fine voice and full flow. The train conductor (they used to have them years ago) was even helping them open the bottles of champagne.

There was a civic reception, at which, when interviewed, Ian Cox said that when he came to Burnley (his wife was from Preston) he couldn't believe that all the players actually got on with each other.

Stan, meanwhile, got his own back on Peter Taylor and faxed him. 'Dear Peter, keep going son, you'll get it right eventually, Stan.'

The end-of-season jolly was to Portugal. Burnley wasn't the richest club in the world so someone joked that we were going with Hazard Airways. Funnily enough there was a fault somewhere on the plane; it then had to come back and land after it had taken off. Huge disappointment all round of course but Wrighty solved the problem of boredom. Steve Davis remembers he took himself from the waiting area once we had all got off the plane, and then came back carrying a huge ghetto blaster that he'd been and bought. On it went and the entertainment commenced while we waited. It went all the way to Portugal as well. That was Wrighty.

Not many people know that there was a late attempt to scupper the deal to bring him to Burnley. It was Alan Pardew that tried to persuade him to join Reading but Wright did not want to go back on his word to Stan Ternent, someone of whom he said he was petrified at Crystal Palace when Ternent was a coach there. Pardew made a late call. Wright then went on to score against Reading and Pardew.

Years later he revealed that maybe he'd made a wrong career choice. 'Stan wanted me to stay and if I'm honest I wish I'd stayed in football. If I'd stayed with Stan, he would probably have got me involved in the coaching side. But I had agents who were leading me towards television. That was the problem I had. The more I think about it I'm very disappointed that I made that decision. I don't know what could have happened. But it was a great decision to join Burnley and I'm very proud of my time there. Burnley speak about me with a lot of fondness. It was a time when we had a little bit of success and, to be fair, Burnley haven't looked back from that. And that's credit to the people involved.'

He still speaks so fondly of the club, the players, the camaraderie, the banter and the dressing room atmosphere. The way he fitted in, the acceptance, and the good laughs. 'To get promotion was the icing on the cake.'

Promotion: it was a triumph for the gaffer, a vindication of his efforts, the tough decisions he had made, and the sheer hard slog he had put into the club.

Chapter 12

PLAYER OF THE YEAR AND TWO SPECIAL GAMES

ON THE day that we met again, it was Frank Casper's birthday; he was 75 and still sharp as a pin. Once again, we were in Tubbs talking. He had a simple maxim for young players. 'Look smart, play smart.' He was always smart himself and few if any people had a bad word to say about him. His career came to an end prematurely thanks to a tackle in a game against Leeds United at Elland Road when Norman Hunter took him out well after the ball was gone. Facebook is notoriously inaccurate at the best of times, a place where people can put all kinds of accusations, so maybe you take with a pinch of salt the guy who wrote that Hunter had told him he remembered the tackle, and said that the Burnley centre-halves had been winding him up and the red mists came down. The 70s we look back at as a glorious age for football. But it was also a time of tackles and aggression that would not be tolerated today. There was a simple rule back then when there was real brutality: if the referee doesn't see it, it isn't a foul. There were some wonderful players and you stopped them any way you could.

It was also Chris Waddle's birthday on the day of the Burnley versus Newcastle game, the previous weekend. Burnley won 1-0 by the way, in foul rain and sleet and a biting wind. There was a programme feature about him. Twitter was filled with clips of his time as a player, and boy could he play with magical skills in his prime. We may have been baffled during his time as manager at Burnley but as a player he was peerless. We should not forget that. Watching some of those clips was an education.

* * *

Football is all ifs and buts. If Burnley had won one more game in 2000/01, we'd have been in the play-offs. If I hadn't been so ill and had all that time out of the game … if I'd been signed by West Ham … if I'd been offered a contract before Stan Ternent left the club … you could dwell on this kind of thing forever.

But 2000/01 was the season I was back, properly, with 43 appearances for the side. All that work, all that training, all that effort, all that determination through three operations. And back then, how many times had I inserted that damned squeezy thing up my rectum? Every day for months and months. But how it paid off. The 'rebel' tag was gone. I must have been doing something that was right. By the end of the season I'd won a shedload of supporters' player of the year awards.

It was in the October that Stan said, 'We need to get you signed up. What do you want in a new contract?'

'More than so and so,' I answered. 'I'm better than him,' and named one of the players. Not that I had anything against that player, it was just that I knew how much he was on. Eventually I got what I wanted, and even better, it went up each year. Looking back, I should have had an agent. Lots of the lads did back then but not me. After I was player of the year an agent would have knocked on the door and said 'Look, he's player of the year, he deserves more.' In truth, I'd never thought of having an agent; I was happy where I was and was always confident enough to talk about wages. But more importantly, later on, maybe an agent would have looked out for me far better than I did myself as my final season there wound down.

There were no after-effects following the illness other than needing to get to the loo pretty quick but that was controllable by timing my eating. I'd go to the loo before a game and several times was sat on the loo with the door open so I could hear Stan's final team-talks. Sometimes I'd need to go at half-time.

It's funny how things work out and even repeat themselves. In two seasons Burnley were seventh and missed the play-offs. In both those seasons the final game was won but the penultimate game was lost, one against Sheffield United and one against Grimsby. You can look at those two games you lost and think 'if only'. There can be a dozen defeats in a season so why pinpoint just one of them as being the cause of disappointment when you just miss out on success? They are all equally disappointing. But, it's so often the games at the end of the season that define things. You might have lost ten games in a season but you can still point to one in particular and think 'that was the game that cost us'.

In this particular season, 2000/01, Fulham were the money-bags team and won the title. But our East Lancashire rivals Blackburn Rovers were now in the Championship; they had been relegated the previous season from the Premier League and the sole topic of conversation for Burnley fans now was the two games against them in the Championship. Unfortunately, there was a problem. They had millionaire Jack Walker and loads of money and Burnley were scraping to make ends meet. But Burnley fans were now ecstatic to see Blackburn come down as Burnley went up, despite the inequality. Blackburn fans had looked down their noses at Burnley for long enough; Burnley fans consoled themselves by accusing Rovers of simply buying their way to the Premier League and a league title. As far as they were concerned, it didn't count. Promotion or a title had to be earned, not bought. Today, Burnley's progress to the Premier

League has been careful, prudent, unexpected even, when it first happened in 2009. 'Built not bought' was the Burnley slogan.

This is why today, Burnley fans are so delighted to see Blackburn Rovers in the Championship with barely a penny to their name, while they, Burnley, enjoy another season in the Premier League, at least while we are writing this. It is why they are so pleased to have the current bragging rights and have won the last three games against them. Never have goals been so loudly cheered as those scored by Danny Ings, Jason Shackell and Scott Arfield at Ewood Park. November 2020, and Burnley are most certainly the dominant team in East Lancashire. In 2000/01 it was very different. For 18 years Burnley fans had waited to be in the same division as Blackburn Rovers and now they were. Five years earlier Rovers had been the Premier League champions. Now they had suffered the ignominy of failure.

You can make a list of the great derby games that make fans sit up and take notice; Manchester City versus Manchester United, Liverpool versus Everton, Rangers versus Celtic, but Burnley versus Blackburn Rovers is up there with them all for its intensity, passion and vitriol. It's the one that when it takes place today fans are escorted and bussed from ground to ground. No one is allowed to make their own way there. Abuse and bigotry are rampant.

The 'cotton mill derby' we played in 2000 was the first for 17 years. Two of the oldest clubs in the league, only eight miles apart, would be slugging it out again in a game that dated back to throbbing industry, workmen's clogs, cloth caps, tobacco smoke and steam railways. The first ever derby was won by Blackburn 7-1. In the bad days of Burnley's life in the old Fourth Division, Blackburn fans hired a plane to fly over Turf Moor with a banner emblazoned with STAYING DOWN FOREVER, LOVE ROVERS. One particular game at Ewood Park was marred by Burnley fans rioting when rivalry went far beyond anything normal. The two games we played in 2000/01 did not end well for Burnley. But oh, how things have been turned around since then.

Before the first of the games, in December 2000, there was a joint press conference asking for calm. 'Stay away if you intend to cause trouble,' said Stan Ternent. There were genuine fears that real violence could break out both in the town and the stadium. If Rovers fans might have felt disdain after all their years of superiority, then Burnley fans felt real resentment at these cash-rich, bankrolled opponents. Rovers fans, previously, even had the nerve to say their derby games were now against Liverpool and Manchester United and sneered that Burnley were just an irrelevance. Today, the football boot is well and truly on the other foot.

The Rovers manager was Graeme Souness, who had seen intense derbies throughout his career. He was warned that this would be on a different level altogether. The build-up most certainly spread to the players. Of course, we were keyed up for a game nobody wanted to lose.

The derby was at Turf Moor. We'd been doing reasonably well in the new division, only a 0-5 against Nottingham Forest had marred things. But now it was Blackburn. Packed house, sell-out, tickets impossible to get. Feverish, frantic atmosphere inside the ground, light the blue touchpaper, stand well back. Andrew Firmin was at the game, seated right behind the away dugout and Souness, and his report for the London Clarets' magazine showed he clearly relished the verbal jousting he had with him. Even the warm-up was febrile. But:

> What an anti-climax this match was. All the build-up, the genuine anticipation and excitement and the hype on top of it, the shocking nervousness that ruined Saturday night's sleep, the worrying about tickets, transport and drinking arrangements, the endless discussion and careful planning,

was all for nothing. After 17 years of hurt, in a moment we'd all yearned for and often suspected might never occur, Burnley didn't play. We didn't get going. The opposition, who were far from spectacular, deserved to win. What could be harder to take than that?

I'd like to stop this report at the moment the teams ran out and fireworks erupted over the Cricket Field Stand partly because that was a magical moment, but also because it was all downhill from there. They were there, in their dreadful blue and white shirts, playing us at home for points. This was it. And then the game started.

There was an early promising move but that represented the game's high-water mark. The opposition settled down faster and got on top of the game. We looked hurried, too nervous. The ball was a hot potato and some players couldn't get rid of it fast enough. We weren't holding on to possession and we weren't passing. Some players, senior players, who you look to, to show the way, evaded their responsibilities. Chief culprits were in midfield where the game was lost.

How we missed Little, more than in any other game he has missed. A bit of derring-do, something out of the ordinary, was what it would have taken for us to win this game. I'd have loved to see him taking someone on down the touchline. My heart had sunk to see he wasn't even on the bench when the team sheets were doled out and we desperately lacked width in this game. Weller was stymied by being played in a defensive position.

This left us with a hard-working but ball-starved front two. Payton did his best with the scraps that came his way but we rarely tried to use Moore's pace and touch. If you spend a million quid on a striker you have to work out ways to get the ball to him. Thankfully whilst having the edge, our opponents looked less than great. They had more of the ball but didn't particularly threaten with it. They were poor in front of goal and their crossing was dreadful.

The opposition bench in front of us was now getting desperate for a helping hand from the officials. Perhaps they've had this in the past and expected it now. I should explain we were on the front row right behind them. Their manager cut a ludicrous figure, strutting along the touchline, timing his runs from the limits of his technical area to coincide with the linesman's absence, rarely still for long, protesting at the injustice of everything expecting the referee to give all. One of the more satisfying things in life is when you've always disliked someone and you turn out to be right. I've always loathed him and when he joined his current club, I said it was a perfect match. They go together nicely. He epitomises them.

It was on one of the opposition manager's frequent scurries that I lost my aplomb. Those nearby may have been surprised to witness a be-tied fellow leap from his seat to bellow 'get back in yer fucking area'. This was to be the start of a good period of discussion with the opposition bench which came to a head when the man bounded from the area to insist on a handball penalty when the ball had struck Steve Davis' chest. He stormed over to the nearby Sky man and demanded to see a replay on the monitor. A clear penalty, proclaimed he. At this point we were told to watch the game. We pointed out that what was stopping us was this jumping fool bounding about in front of us, and merely observed it would be better if they observed the rules. It was all quite enjoyable and served to help what was a poor half, pass quickly.

The tone of this report would be very different if it wasn't for what happened half a minute from half-time. From nowhere, the other side scored. Cook failed to deal with an innocuous throw-in, and as the defence froze and the goalkeeper watched from his line, an opposing player was allowed to head home. It happened in slow motion. It was a soft goal and a shocking goal to concede in the context of a big match. Seconds later, the whistle blew and the game had changed horribly.

It was clear early in the second half that no great improvement was happening. They started brighter while Burnley just didn't get going. The opposition manager started the half in the stand, before bounding down to the pitch-side within a minute of the half starting. We were thankful for their dodgy finishing at this stage. And then Kevin Ball decided to inject some passion into the game. His tackle on Dunn was two-footed and so late it could have come by Virgin Train. The ref brandished an immediate red card and it seemed fair enough. It wasn't enough for the opposition manager. He charged from his area and onto the pitch to intervene. Ball walked.

After that, it got quite heated on the pitch and the referee paid the price for his earlier laissez-faire approach. As it started to boil, he found it difficult to keep a lid on the unpleasantness. He could have sent Davis off. This time Ternent charged on. If Davis had gone the game would have turned into one long brawl. Oddly enough, we played some of our better stuff when Ball was off. I'm not sure about the old ten-man cliché so I assume it was because we realised that attack was all we could do now.

When Maylett picked the ball up for a throw for some reason this incensed the other lot and some tough guy knocked it from the kid's hands. To no one's surprise it quickly turned into a heated session of close-up finger

> pointing between Ternent and the other manager, which the fourth official broke up, pushing Stan gently back to his own bench. The fourth official had a bad game. Minutes earlier he and the opposition manager had been bawling nose to nose.
>
> They put the lid on a dismal game with the second goal on 90 minutes. I ask you. More stood-off defending and motionless goalkeeping produced the grim finale. Nik parried rather than held and the rebound was tucked away. That was it. I couldn't get out fast enough and it was out into the police state of Harry Potts Way.

Bad things went on in the town that night that represented more awfulness piled upon the day. There were things not to be proud of. A day to forget. Burnley didn't do themselves justice and the opposition were not really that good, by no means unbeatable. Maybe we let the occasion get to us and in so doing bang went the unbeaten home record.

The Kevin Ball tackle on David Dunn has gone down in Burnley history. Red card but it was not a deliberate attempt to cripple Dunny. It was the way Ball played all the time, in training as well, no holds barred. His advice always stayed with me. 'Train like you play,' he always said. 'Don't just think you can turn it on, on a matchday.' Good advice and absolutely true.

After the game Bally said it was 'just a clash of shins' and it was never a red card. Glen Little begged to differ. 'He was lucky he wasn't arrested,' he said in disbelief.

The result was disappointing but, on the day, they had the luck and the better players. There was no great backlash from supporters against the team; they appreciated just how far we had come. And they were always able to say that Blackburn had a millionaire backer and Burnley didn't.

The illness behind me, it was just wonderful to be back in the thick of things. Illness under control and stomach pains gone. Stan Ternent must have been psychic when he said to me in the summer that this would be my season; that the Championship would be good for me. I went on to win several of the supporters' player of the year awards, and made a real mark in the first home game of the season against Wimbledon, a game that began with a firework display.

Weller Shows He's Back to His Best, headlined one match report. 'Paul Weller scored one of the goals of his life. To Weller it was the end of a nightmare and the chance to hang on to a shirt for which he has fought so hard. The little wing-back missed almost two seasons with a serious stomach illness and three operations. Many felt he might never get back to his best again, but now he was back with a vengeance determined to make up for lost time.

'"He's a tough little cookie," said manager Stan Ternent. "It was a case of could he get back to full strength and fitness; now it looks as if he has never been away. It's like signing a new player."'

Andy Cooke was probably cursing me for not crossing to him. Instead I took on the defender and shot. And scored. And yelled and celebrated. What's better than scoring a goal? Selling a shirt or a tracksuit, Roger Eli used to joke in the club car park when he opened up his car boot for us to see what he had on offer. For me today, maybe selling another car from the W18 showrooms in Colne.

Dons Have No Stomach for A Fight, was another headline. Clever that. 'Miracle man returned to the Burnley team to give Wimbledon a bellyful of problems. Wimbledon must feel that they have been kicked in the guts.' Three one-liners, full marks to that reporter.

Another one wrote that I'd sprinted from the halfway line into the Wimbledon penalty box, shaped to pass but cracked a great shot for a super winner. They're in the scrapbook my mum kept putting together. This game was a big occasion, the first start I'd made at Turf Moor in two years. Two years of pain, exhaustion, sickness, hospital, the operations, recovery, getting fit and grimacing for weeks when I felt fit but Stan Ternent said I wasn't. You say all the right things, the clichés, and practise modesty. Pete Oliver wrote the best report:

> No wonder the national newspaper boys loved it. The Paul Weller story is already well known in these parts and the Burnley faithful have long recognised his courage in overcoming a potentially career-threatening illness. But with First Division football now attracting the nation's media to Turf Moor, Weller's wonderful winning goal ensured it received a major airing over the weekend. And who could begrudge Weller his moment of glory. For over a year, the 25-year-old didn't kick a ball in anger after undergoing three major bouts of surgery to remove most of his large bowel. Before last Saturday he had played just two league games in two seasons and on one occasion last term was so frustrated he ended up on the transfer list. The nationals don't know everything.

Now I had to show I was worth the boss's faith in me. But inside all you think is, 'Don't you dare bloody drop me now.'

Next up was signing a new four-year deal. Things were good. Back in the side. Health under control. Another goal, this one in the last minute against Portsmouth to save a point. The adrenalin rush when you score is unique. Winning is brilliant, but scoring, especially a key goal, is up there with everything. Scoring the last goal in, let's say, a 5-0 win (not many of those at Burnley by the way) is almost a waste of a goal, it's almost a casual celebration, unlike that last-minute winner way back away at Oxford that meant so much. What's it like to be an out-and-out striker when you score on a regular basis, an Andy Payton, who today can pretty much remember every goal he has scored? Most strikers say they can do that.

What a collection of goalscorers Burnley have had over the years: Ray Pointer, Jimmy Robson, Billy Hamilton, Frank Casper, Roger Eli, Andy Payton. And today Ashley Barnes and Chris Wood. Just two big lumps, Chris Wood's words not mine. Football is a team effort but it's strikers that get the glory. A striker's misses are soon forgotten if he scores in the next game. A keeper drops a clanger, De Gea at Watford, more recently against Spurs, and it's remembered for weeks. Funny that.

A knee injury kept me out for a spell, as if I hadn't suffered enough. Back I came and results were pretty good until Boxing Day at struggling Barnsley. A 1-0 defeat sent manager Stan berserk. There was a massive Burnley following on a bitter, freezing day. The gaffer was utterly furious. Barnsley, the land that time forgot, a bit of a graveyard for Burnley over the years.

Believe it or not I was the club's longest-serving player and despite a run of poor results we were tenth. Not bad for a newly promoted side, the club in the best state since I'd been there, new chairman and a bit of money coming in, from the brink of relegation with Waddle to doing OK in the Championship and looking to get in the top six, and Turf Moor a great stadium. Playing against better players, as we were in the Championship, makes you a better player. Our standards were going up all the time.

Grimsby next and why shouldn't we win there?

Because it was bloody Grimsby, that's why. What is it about some places that depresses you before you even get there? This isn't supposed to be a book with nothing but a procession of match reports in it, but you come away from some games that have been lost and you just groan, even years later. Supporters who travelled to the game were welcomed by a sign on the edge of town. 'Welcome to Great Grimsby.'

The stadium sits just a couple of feet above sea level and is thus the lowest ground in the country. Global warming and the rising of sea levels could drown it. Just across the railway lines alongside the ground is the North Sea and the views from the top of the stand out to sea are said to be spectacular. The view from ground level during the 1-0 defeat we suffered is less than brilliant, mostly mud and Grimsby legs disappearing down the other end. The main stand used to be called the Findus Stand (maybe it still is) in honour of the local frozen fish company that paid for half of it. Which of us with young families have not enjoyed the delights of Findus Frozen Fish Fingers? There's a book of football grounds that says: 'You don't just go to Blundell Park for the football, you go for Grimsby, the town, the people, the smell of fish and the sea.' It would be nice to go there one day for a win.

The ground is actually in Cleethorpes, a place that resembled a typical little seaside resort. Sounds nice, but our fans were well miffed at the poor conditions they had to endure, cramped seats, horrible toilets, poor food and extortionate prices. A state-of-the-art stadium this was not. Not only that but on the way home, fans who hoped to buy decent fish and chips from Britain's premier fishing port were sadly disappointed. There was not a piece of cod to be found.

We lost this one thanks to a Chinaman aided by a Dutchman, who scored against a Greek. Dany Robson was the reporter. Her dad is Jimmy Robson, the great Burnley striker of the title team of 1959/60. The Chinaman was called Zhang Enhua, a centre-half, and in 2001 there weren't many Chinese players around in English football. It was just our bad luck. He scored the winning and only goal. Dany summed it up in the opening paragraph: 'It left a sour rather than a sweet taste and this Chinese takeaway stuck in our throats.'

'We are getting caught with our pants down,' said the gaffer. He always did have a way with words. 'The goal we gave away was Towneley Park stuff.'

And then we won the next game against high-flying Fulham; a night game under the floodlights somehow seems to raise the pulse rate and the adrenalin. No fans (or maybe even players) expected this, but win we did, and even the next game as well. Consistency was never our strong point. If it had been, then Burnley would have reached the play-offs rather than a frustrating seventh.

The return game against Blackburn was in April and was the first time that Burnley's fans were to be bussed to the ground. Skipper Steve Davis was optimistic, suggesting that Blackburn were due a defeat. Many years earlier, way back in the 60s, fans travelled side by side and even stood side by side. There was a mutual respect despite the rivalry. All that had changed in the 70s with a growing divide and bitterness. By the time rivalries were renewed it was deemed unsafe not to strictly segregate fans and even the way they travelled. Ancient double-decker buses lined up at Turf Moor, Lord only knows where they dug some of these boneshakers up, and those with a ticket had to travel on them. Cattle trucks, some fans called them. A Bubble match, the police designated it. There are intense derby games all over the UK but Burnley v Blackburn is one of the few where bus transport is compulsory.

Having already lost the first of the games, this next one assumed new importance. Blackburn wanted to rub Burnley noses into the mud and Burnley wanted to redeem themselves. Tony Scholes, who today runs the influential website *Up the Clarets,* wrote a brief and pained report on the game. It was entitled 'It Hurts; it Hurts like Hell'.

> What an horrendous day it has been. A day when anyone with any feeling at all for Burnley Football Club can hardly

lift their heads, a day when the worst possible thing that can happen, did happen. The day started poorly with Clarets fans made to look like third-class citizens by being sent to Ewood Park on buses that you simply would not use on a local route. Just over a week ago the club's PR manager said that the club wanted to provide the same service that their (Blackburn) fans received for the game at Turf Moor. They came on coaches for free, we paid £4 each for this shabby transport. I didn't see our PR manager travelling on them. Was the club at all concerned that we were laughed at when we arrived on these things? Somebody has been ripped off here. If the club have paid £4 per head, it is they who have been 'done'. And surely, they wouldn't want to make a profit out of it, would they?

As for the game, did we really compete? There never appeared to be a 50/50 ball. We just lost out every time. I can accept teams being better than us but today we didn't even look up for it and that is unacceptable. Steve Davis and Paul Weller showed great commitment throughout the 90 minutes today and they can take pride in that.

And finally, to the Clarets fans today. I have great memories of trips to Derby, both grounds, Coventry, Spurs and the like when the supporters did us proud. Today though, for most of the time the support was minimal with the chanting either aimed at Jack Walker or racist. The performance was awful for sure, but couldn't we have just got on with trying to support the team?

Supporter Phil Whalley was also at the game and had provided a match report for the London Clarets' magazine *Something to Write Home About*. He had once lived in Blackburn during the 80s and was of the opinion that MP Jack Straw had never had the slightest interest in Blackburn Rovers. Once they had won the Premier League title, however, he was a Blackburn supporter. Writing nearly 20 years ago, Phil made a prediction. 'Take comfort dear reader. One day we shall have back the Blackburn Rovers we used to hate far less.' Psychic or what? Today the positions are reversed with Blackburn now the impoverished neighbours, and Premier League Burnley with their jar on the mantelpiece brim full. Twenty years on, Phil emailed me his thoughts on that black day at Ewood.

> I volunteered for that match report with something of a devil-may-care attitude, thinking I could conjure up some kind of consolatory, philosophical perspective on the whole thing, but I found it quite beyond me, such was the complete misery of the day. Come the Sunday morning, we turned up at Turf Moor to be met with the most laughably decrepit set of buses you could imagine. Ours could barely get up the hill on the dual carriageway out of Huncoat.
>
> My overriding memory of the game is Burnley being completely open down our left flank almost from the off and us screaming at Ternent to do something about it. Afterwards came the bizarre explanation that Graham Branch had twisted his knee which meant he couldn't twist or turn hence the classic 'he could only run in straight lines' excuse.
>
> And then if things couldn't get any worse the Burnley fans started singing about Blackburn being a town full of Pakis. *[Today of course this would result in whole swathes of fans being ejected and prosecuted. In the last game at Ewood prior to this one, Burnley fans had actually rioted and reconstructed one of the roofs.]*
>
> I think my main aim in the match report [20-ish years ago], was to put into perspective the achievement of the club to be back in the company of monied sides like Blackburn,

> who were years ahead of Burnley at that point and really shouldn't have gone down in 1999 given the squad they had.

In his actual match report Phil had written about the shamefully one-sided second half with Blackburn five goals to the good and threatening to score with every attack. The Blackburn fans sang lustily. 'We've beaten the bastards 5-0,' but this in fact was with an air of disbelief and joy. Phil took comfort from this since it signified that it almost expressed a sense of relief because Burnley, heaven forbid, wonder of wonders, were perceived to be an actual threat. Superior they might have been but 5-0 was never a result they expected.

There were, of course, a few sporadic Burnley threats; there was a Burnley goal disallowed for a close offside, the Blackburn fifth was clearly offside, but in truth the Clarets struggled. Phil wrote that Burnley didn't compete, looked yards slower and this was simply a bad day at the office. Blackburn, meanwhile, had acres of space, ran up a real head of steam and this was essentially Nationwide toilers against Premier League quality. It wasn't often that Ternent's defenders came in for criticism but on this day, it was sadly chronic. There's half a memory of David Dunn, complaining that we were all trying to hurt him. He was never popular with Burnley supporters on account of him choosing Blackburn over Burnley as a youth player.

As far as the players were concerned it was a game to take on the chin but again, they seemed to have all the luck going. We played the best Burnley team we could and there were no excuses from us. You just have to stick together, not let it get you down, and react in the next game (which we did and won 3-0).

The gaffer tried to take the hurt out of it afterwards, saying the result needed to be put into perspective, that Blackburn were the best team in the division, that we were beaten fairly and squarely.

Now, in 2020, there is no doubt which is the top side in East Lancashire. The 5-0 defeat was years ago and long forgotten; the positions today are reversed. They were light years ahead of Burnley back then but today it is the Burnley supporters that are crowing and always have the final word by simply saying, 'You bought that title and had a rich sugar daddy, but look at you now.'

Interesting too, that Phil in his email, referred to the Ternent sides always having to play at 110 per cent to get consistent results. He saw the side of 2001/02 as particularly swashbuckling, top by five points at one stage, but unable to maintain the momentum. Today it is much the same with the Sean Dyche sides. They win when every player, or most of the players in any game, perform at maximum capacity.

Only one of the last nine games of that season was lost. Those nine games included six wins. It was a fantastic run and if only there had been a win at Sheffield United in the penultimate game, Burnley would have been in the play-offs. Bramall Lane is one of those grounds that is a bit of a graveyard for Burnley. Why is it that at some grounds a team just never does well? This one was no different except for one thing, the row that erupted between the two clubs and the two managers over alleged spying … Bramallgate I suppose. All the players remembered it. For quite a while the two managers hadn't exchanged Christmas cards. Events at Sheffield took their dislike to a new level. An apprentice was sent to eavesdrop at the door to Stan's half-time team talk. On hearing that this was happening, Stan kicked the door open and it was Kevin Blackwell, the assistant manager, he collared down the corridor, not the apprentice. Blows were exchanged. After the game Stan T was seething.

'At half-time Neil Warnock sent someone down the corridor listening behind our dressing-room door to my team talk. That's cheating. That is the lowest of the low. If that is the sort of lengths that managers have to go to win football matches, I'd rather be out cutting my grass. I need to say that and it is wrong. I'll be writing a letter to the FA and to the Football League and reporting him for that because it is not in the true spirit of the game. And if I was chairman of a football club, he wouldn't be working for me.'

Who'd be a manager?

If we were disappointed as a team, then on a personal level it had been a super season for me, hoovering up a table-full of player awards at the end of the season. From lying in a hospital bed studying my navel, the new stoma to be exact, thinking what the hell is that, to getting up and down more times than a fiddler's elbow to walk up to the presentation stage to receive awards one after the other. Thirteen or fourteen of them, can't remember exactly. With a red felt tip, my mum headlined the page in the scrapbook … 'What A Season 2001'. 'These awards make you feel wanted by the supporters,' I said to the local press. All this silverware, plaques, glassware, wine, the icing on the cake after the draining time I'd had.

The press churned out another potted history of the ailments, the operations, the recovery and rehabilitation with a few words from me.

'When I was ill, I was worried whether I would be able to play again. But the gaffer was so good and said "take as much time as you want". It took a long time to build my strength afterwards, the whole of last season. But the gaffer said "this could be your season".'

My season: yep, it had been great. As a team we'd hoped to finish midway in the table after promotion but we ended up missing the top six by one win.

'You look forward to these nights and because I haven't been involved in the last couple of years, to be involved this year and to get these awards has been great. It's very much appreciated.'

Nor were the good times over just yet. Another good season was just around the corner and with a surprising new addition to the squad.

Chapter 13

HOW TO WIN AND YET STILL LOSE, WITH A BLOKE CALLED GAZZA

JUNE 2001 brought race riots in Burnley and they were the prelude to what would be a great but near-miss season. They were labelled race riots at the time but subsequent reports would identify other factors that were significant. It started with a stabbing in Daneshouse, an area of Burnley, and then a taxi driver was assaulted with a hammer. Before long, it had all escalated out of control. Homes were petrol-bombed and families attacked. The Duke of York pub was burned down. A weekend of violence on the streets saw gangs of up to 200 strong, of whites and Asians fighting with police. It was on TV news, particularly the attacks on the police.

The troubles were blamed on racists exploiting what were at first minor incidents around the town. The immediate analysis was that this was racial tension being the root cause. But, subsequent reports focussed on the town's problems of drugs, crime, education, housing and the generally poor social environment. Disenchantment and dissatisfaction were prevalent in wide areas of Burnley. It was inaccurate to say the causes were solely racial.

What was certainly true was that Burnley was seen as a segregated town with distinctly white areas and clear Asian districts. Feelings were high that public money was being spent in some areas to the detriment of others.

Whatever happened, and whatever were the catalysts, official reports pointed to some fights being between Asian gangs amongst themselves, and a turf war between rival white and Asian drug dealers. The level of violence and the nature of the aggression also suggested that the participants were essentially from the criminal community. Exaggerations and wildly inaccurate stories compounded the spread of the violence.

And the relevance of all this to the football club? Burnley FC has tried to encourage the Asian community to feel part of the club and to attend games – with little success, it has to be said. Plus, when Stan Ternent tried to sign Peter Crouch from QPR, it was alleged that one reason why the deal fell through was that his wife was concerned about the 'race' riots. Stan's book *Stan the Man* refers to it.

At the point when I had stopped playing and was working for the community section of the club, we did work in schools, coaching, and several of those schools served Asian communities. We did what we could to spread the message and those kids loved their football but somewhere further down the line that interest was somehow diluted and we could rarely get them to come to a game. Looking at the make-up of Burnley crowds today, and how few Asian faces there are, it seems the problem might still be there.

Stan had been chasing Crouchy, who was then rated at £1m down at QPR. He was brilliant in the air – he recently described himself as just a head on a stick – and considering the shape of him was better than he looked with the ball at his feet. Stan managed to get him to head north and they met at Stan's house. His kitchen was where many a deal was made or the foundations laid. Unfortunately, with Burnley looking more like Beirut, coming there was not the attractive proposition Stan tried to make out. The inevitable phone call from Crouch's agent came a few days later. He would be going to Portsmouth, possibly preferring a derelict stadium to a derelict town. It's another of football's 'ifs'. If Peter Crouch had come to Burnley that season …

In 2019, years later, he did indeed come to Burnley for a loan spell, from January to May, from Stoke City. Was he 37 or 38 by then? By all accounts he thoroughly enjoyed things, was great around the training ground, but made only a handful of cameo appearances without scoring. By and large fans asked what was all that about, just what was the point?

My bowels, a progress report. Fine, no problems, save for the need to get to the loo on time. Everyone was perfectly used to me sitting with the door open while Stan gave a team talk. This was a small dressing room, by the way, barely room to swing a cat. Up to 15 sweaty footballers in there, the odours were horrific enough sometimes, without me sitting with a loo door open. Liniment, body odour, underarms, socks, sweaty feet, you name it.

Things were so good, top at Christmas, fans over the moon, how far could we go? But then came the Maine Road mauling. The gaffer had been named Manager of the Month for November 2001, and no more than he deserved, and at Christmas, Burnley were five points clear at the top of the division after ten games unbeaten, including six wins in a row. This was terrific stuff. Even the Grimsby match had attracted over 18,000 to Turf Moor; but always with an eye for a bargain, the £5 entrance fee was very tempting to Burnley folks. Going on in the background was the vote of professional players to go on strike unless TV revenue was distributed more fairly. The dispute was settled. We would not be going on strike.

Arthur Gnohere was the newest cult hero; fans called him The King. When he scored twice at Preston in a 3-2 win his performance was outstanding. He seemed to arrive at the club out of nowhere and would later fade away in just the same way. A one-season wonder you might say. Those of a poetic nature, such as supporter Steve Corrigan, described him as 'a mighty colossus bestriding the Lancashire turf'. And, 'an almost impassable barrier upon which the waves of Preston's many attacks floundered and made little impression'. Arthur was brilliant at what reporters might describe as 'a powerful surge'. Alas this was a game when a perfectly decent goal in the final minutes was disallowed. And this in a season when one goal would frustrate a top-six place. 'Dingles, Dingles, top of the league,' sang the ecstatic fans.

The wildest rumour of all was that David Ginola was joining Burnley. Women supporters of all shapes and sizes swooned. Robbie Blake seemed a more likely target, but Robbie alas, short of stature and almost portly looking, was never a serious rival to the charms of Monsieur Ginola, had the latter ever arrived.

Burnley top! What on earth was going on? And for me, from a hospital bed not that long ago, stomach crossed with cuts and scars, and now top of the league. Unfashionable, hard-up, unglamorous: something was happening that wasn't supposed to. Manchester City and Watford were supposed to be the top dogs with their celebrity managers, Kevin Keegan and Gianluca Vialli. Who the hell were Burnley when they were at home? Who the hell was Stan Ternent? There was even a feeling that we should be apologising for having the effrontery to be top. And then came Manchester City at Maine Road, and we were still four points clear at the top. And that was where the good news ended.

Burnley lost 5-1.

Barry Heagin of the London Clarets provides the report. This was a defining game so it's worth including the best of it.

I suppose it was inevitable that the run was going to come to an end at some stage. But yet again, we failed on the big stage. I genuinely believed we could do something here, as did most neutral observers. The manner of the defeat was surprising after a reasonable start to the match. The pressing game that is the mainstay of our most impressive results against good teams, deserted us. Ian Moore hassled, as always, from the front but that was often the only challenge to the Wanchope/Goater combine harvester combination. Could the Claret Premiership dream be the biggest piece of fiction since the inclusion of fidelity vows in a French marriage ceremony?

Anyway, a nice sunny day at Moss Side's finest stadium. A midday kick-off but a generous helping of ale to ward off the vision of the City Orcs a mere three feet of netting away. The stands here are of course, hideous, designed by the same firm that did Stonehenge. A couple of thousand Clarets were giving some serious oral abuse to the arrogant City prats, before the start of 'our Cup Final'.

The first 20 minutes provided some fairly slick, attacking football, almost all of which was from the Clarets. One small problem though. We were one down after two minutes.

The half then began to run away from the Clarets and there was no great surprise when the City third came after 37 minutes. Wanchope hammered home a fourth. Half-time to pies with the texture of cat's vomit. Game over.

So then, huge disappointment again after a Man City match. A certain amount of gallows humour in the local hostelry decreed that a slight variation of the normal method of choosing the London Clarets' Man of the Match award was required, primarily to cheer ourselves up. Usual scoring system to apply, two points for the winner and one for the second.

(And if one day these awards become available to the public, we do hope that the recipients will accept them in the spirit of supporter humour intended. Nothing personal, they are all very nice blokes I'm sure.)

First worst: Glen Little, more holes in his game today than a statement from a Transport Secretary.

Second worst: Gareth Taylor, did the work of two men today, Laurel and Hardy.

Third worst: Alan Moore, a good player but with more Achilles heels today than the average biped.

Fourth worst: Kevin Ball, raced hard for the ball, but time's iron grip had a firm hold of his shirt.

Fifth worst: Tony Grant, there are amoeba on Saturn that display better ball control.

Sixth worst: Dean West, everything over his head today, so should look for future employment as a limbo dancer.

Finally, one couldn't possibly finish the piece without a comment on good old Kevin Keegan who was taking some serious stick from the City fans in the pub before the game. As the psychiatrist once said of Basil in one of the later episodes of *Fawlty Towers*, there is more than enough material there for a dissertation.

The New Year, and despite losing at City, fans were happy, indeed one of them described this as a new Golden Age. Fans were agreed it had been a fantastic year for the club, one of the best for years, almost reminiscent of the 70s and Jimmy Adamson's team. But if Adamson had players he had inherited from Harry Potts, Stan's team was created solely by him. Tyrant though Stan might have been with us, bullying, cajoling, threatening and fining us, the team that was top at Christmas was his team, his creation. Nobody was getting carried away though, least of all Stan. If fans were dreaming of trips to Old Trafford and Highbury, the players weren't. Fans were already wondering if we got promotion again would we come straight back down; and there were still 20 games to go. But, the players knew, football can kick you in the teeth so easily. Things can change so quickly. A couple of defeats when you least expect them are always just around the corner.

In a roundabout sort of way Stan blamed me for the defeat at City. With a throwaway comment he suggested it was a game I should have played in. With that remark was the almost accusation it was my fault we'd lost. I'd got a fifth yellow card and with that came suspension. He probably wasn't serious, but then maybe he was.

There were strange rumours. March and the rumours were a bit more solid. A bloke called Gazza was on his way to the club. Gazzamania was fast approaching. The theory behind it was sound enough. Loads of publicity, the waning season gets a boost, bums on seats and extra ticket sales; and the maestro with his genius sees us through into the play-offs with Gazza having his last hurrah back in the Prem with little Burnley. The theory was great: the end-product not so good although we weren't to know that.

TV was full of it; the papers were full of it. The man was a legend. The club shop stocked up on Gascoigne shirts. A prankster extraordinaire; never stand with your back to him or you ran the risk of him pulling your shorts down. Or watch out for the laxatives in your tea. Fans were being interviewed. Excitement was growing. Was it really happening? Could Stan pull it off? And if he did might he have the same impact and effect as Ian Wright? He wouldn't, but no one was to know that just yet.

Everton manager Walter Smith couldn't make up his mind whether to let him leave or not but when Smith was sacked the way was clear. Fans were sceptical; was it just a publicity stunt? Was it just to boost morale? Whatever: Gazza arrived in a blaze of publicity making Burnley big news and leaving us players in fear and trepidation of being drowned in fart powder or having our shoes nailed to the floor.

Tony Grant was delighted at the news: 'Gazza was my idol growing up. I had played against him and was now playing with him. I only have good things to say about him. Humble, funny and an unbelievable footballer. He was still a genius and it was the rest of us who weren't up to his standards.'

Gazza declared he was pleased to join because Stan T was as mad as he was and they were both Geordies. He declared he had already had a few laughs with him and it would be a race to see who had a heart attack first. On his first appearance in Stan's local, the Kettledrum, within 30 minutes the place was a chaotic mass of heaving fans and worshippers as news spread that he was in there.

Stan T knew what he was letting himself in for; a player who was unreliable, unpredictable, drinking heavily, in need of real guidance and counselling. On a personal level I was absolutely made up. As a Spurs fan he'd been one of my heroes and he was on his way to Turf Moor. I loved him to bits; he was a superstar.

The fines system at the club was a bit of light relief and one story involved Gazza. Fines were handed out for various sins during the week: bad clothes, bad parking, bad haircuts, bad language and bad behaviour. Each Friday the players were gathered together and the charges were made. If someone disagreed, he could summon friends or witnesses to support his case. These were few and far between. The courts and trials could become quite heated. The fines were no more than £10 but honour, or humiliation, were at stake. To one or two players losing a tenner was worse than losing a limb. Dean West was particularly reluctant to part with his money.

Gazza was fined for handing out the gaffer's cakes one day. We gave him hell. We cut up his socks and all his gear, but he said nothing. We should have suspected something. He would want revenge but when would it come?

He got his own back. One morning he was handing out cups of tea he'd made for us. We were quite touched. But then suspicion descended. If he's made us all cups of tea, he's up to something. We were right. The giant teapot had been filled with great spoonfuls of laxative.

Stan, who knew about the socks and his gear, asked him at that week's fines meeting, 'Paul, is there anything you want to say?'

'No gaffer,' said Gazza and pulled out a half-empty bottle of laxative from his pocket.

'No gaffer, I got my own back. Yah knaw that tea ah made yers all this mornin'?' He waved the bottle. We looked at the big pot on the table. Gordon Armstrong looked ill and spat out a huge mouthful of tea he was drinking.

'Aargh I've had three cups of the stuff,' he groaned.

Another of his tricks was slicing up bars of soap into thin slivers and slipping them into people's sandwiches.

It was brilliant, if not nerve-wracking, having him around. But on the pitch, he was a liability. We saw it in the first day of training, that he'd lost that magic touch and timing. It was possession training where reflexes have to be razor sharp. He struggled. Just occasionally in training there was that flash of something special or something out of the ordinary that he could still do, a reminder of the genius that he once was.

It was a menace having him sat next to you in the dressing room if the gaffer was having a go at someone. On one occasion he was having a go at Bally, a game at Grimsby if memory serves, and we knew Bally could give as good as he got. But Gazza is there sitting alongside me nudging me and trying to get me to laugh. So, I'm doing my best not to. If Stan had seen me laughing, I would have been next for the hairdryer. It was the game, I think, when we were losing at half-time and Stan was furious. He told Bally he was coming off. Bally said, 'No I'm not.' 'Yes, you are,' said Stan.

'No, I'm not,' said Bally. This went on for a couple of minutes until eventually Bally was replaced.

Football pranks are a way of life, or at least they were back then. Do they still cut up each other's ties in the Premier League, cut the toe ends off socks, glue pockets together, hide shoes, swap clothes round on the pegs? Footballers, eh?

The best one I ever did was on Vince Overson. He'd egged my car, my pride and joy, eggs smeared all over the shiny exterior. I bided my time and I defy anyone to better what I did. I made a sign for the back of his car printed nicely on card.

'I'm gay so give me a honk,' it said.

It was a time when he was up from Stoke and had to drive back down the M6. Car after car honked at him as they passed by with some drivers even waving at him. He waved back of course and some honked again. He assumed they were honking because they recognised him as a famous footballer, well mildly famous I suppose, and smiled at them as they waved. It was his wife who told him about the sign on the back when he got home, because he still hadn't spotted it. I'm proud of that one to this day.

Sam Ellis was another target. And this was the classic fish prank. How many footballers have done this over the years? Dozens I'll bet. Simply nicking his wheel trims wasn't enough, we felt, so David May and myself went to the fishmongers and bought a large fish. We had it cut up into slices, got into Sam's car and hid the small pieces all over the place; under the seats, in the boot, in the dashboard cupboards, in the door pockets, in the engine. How many, maybe a dozen? The smell of fish, bad enough in your kitchen but in a confined car, horrible. It hit him straight away when he got in and he knew what somebody had done. He found a couple and thought that was it. But still the smell was there. He found more pieces, but still the smell was there. It drove him mad and it was days before he found the last one.

'Which bastards have done this?' he demanded to know. Meanwhile, we were in hysterics. Egg you can wash off a car; it takes a lot of effort, but you can. Fish smell you cannot get rid of for days. To this day he has no idea it was me and David May. Perfect.

Seven games to go. The top six our target. Gazza here to help and motivate. He didn't even know the names of some of the players in the side and made his debut against Bradford City in a 1-1 draw in front of a near full-house. It was his first proper game in about five weeks and the pace was too much for him. Sadly, he didn't pull up any trees. He may well have retained his crown as football's biggest loony, but his best days as a player were far behind him. It wouldn't be long before we realised that terrific though he might have been on the training pitch, on a matchday he was a shadow. There was a game away at Sheffield United when Stan ought to have taken him off within 20 minutes or so. He took him off at half-time, we suspect to spare his embarrassment.

Now, however, the Burnley bubble was in serious trouble. The ITV money for broadcasting games was about to vanish. ITV Digital was about to go into administration. The implications for such as Burnley were huge. Football assumed that the owners of the football channel, Carlton and Granada, would bail things out after poor viewing figures and money losses into the millions. But they did not, and wiped their hands of it. Threats to sue them came to nothing. The contract had more holes than a sieve, in fact it had never even been signed properly. Someone had boobed, big time. The TV companies were able to walk away. Barry Kilby likened Granada and Carlton to a couple of Del Boys, shiftily denying responsibility. A contract is a contract he added, but alas this was a contract not worth the paper it was written on.

He went on to explain that the club did its budgets looking two or three years ahead and the TV money was about 30 per cent of the income. £3m out of a projected income of £10m. The next season had already been budgeted for on the assumption that the next TV lump sum of just under £2m would be arriving, but there was now no chance of that money appearing. Robbie Blake was on his way for £1m and this was due to come from the now non-existent TV money. An improved deal given to Glen Little would lead to the eventual need to offload him. 'Let's just hope we get into the Premier League,' Kilby said almost plaintively. His wish was several years away. A poor compensatory deal was eventually reached between the Football League and the TV companies. It left Burnley high and dry and the knock-on effects would be felt in the next season.

It is one of the great truisms of football that goals change games. You can add to that, they can also change seasons. But it is not only the goals that are scored that change a season, but also the perfectly good goals that are scored and disallowed. There had been one already away at Preston in a 3-2 win, when a fourth good goal was chalked off for some reason that only the referee understood. We thought little of it at the time, having no idea of its eventual significance. But the goal scored by Gareth Taylor against Wolves at Turf Moor that was ruled out, had a massive impact. Massive inasmuch as we lost the game 3-2. Talk of it filled the dressing room afterwards.

'I've watched the video,' said Stan, 'and Gareth's was a perfectly good goal. I don't know who disallowed it but by his performance today, it must have been the referee. Referees are like God. They aren't always right but they are never wrong. A professional sport is being run by amateur people. I don't want to talk too much about the referee because I haven't got enough money to pay the fine.'

Managers, in their old age, and Stan is now in his 70s, must I'm sure, sit in their armchairs thinking about this and that, and goals and games and players, and moments that were big moments. Stan's dream was always to get Burnley into the Premier League. It was a dream denied to him and if he does think about things, then the disallowed Taylor goal he may remember more vividly than others.

It was Easter Sunday with Wolves in an automatic promotion spot. The game was a sell-out and we had been in the top six all season. We had just lost at Sheffield United with Gazza having a stinker of a game.

A crowd of 22,000 supporters was crammed in at Turf Moor. London Claret, Andrew Firmin, was there. Firmo has a bit of a cynical, caustic streak in him and has never been one to mince his words. He also belongs to a group of supporters who, when Burnley go three goals down, leave and head for the nearest pub. This game was no exception.

> We always lose to Wolves. Civilisations live and die, empires rise and fall, continents drift, but some things remain. When Burnley play Wolves, only one team wins and it ain't the one in Claret. That's the way it is and there doesn't seem to be much we can do to change it. And so, it came to pass, the run went on. For the second game running we shipped three goals and Gascoigne was once more a liability …
>
> It all started so well, when we took an early lead. Only referee Barry Knight didn't seem to think so. Taylor rose and headed towards goal. Goalkeeper Oakes fell. It was in. Then we realised that Knight had decided not to give it. If there was a foul, he was the only one to see it. None of the Wolves players appealed. Knight can't have been anywhere near it, after fussing about the placing of the wall, he'd walked backwards towards the middle, away from the action as soon as the free kick was taken. But somehow, he'd seen a foul. I suppose if you are a goalkeeper and you know you are beaten, it's always worth going down when the attacker is near you. It was an injustice and how we paid for it.

> Now we were struggling, injustice there may have been but we weren't doing ourselves any favours. Wolves were on top now. Gascoigne remains a problem. He produced one stirring run when he took on and beat a couple of men before getting in a shot from the edge of the box. For a moment it was as if he had remembered how to turn on the magic even though it was hard to imagine the shot going in. Then he settled into the routine of dwelling on the ball and being caught napping. It's terribly sad to see a legend reduced to this.
>
> Wolves' third goal came when they broke from midfield, their finishing was ruthless.
>
> Stan showed that he does not shirk the hard decisions by taking Gascoigne off at half-time. We heard the roar of Burnley's first goal as we walked towards the town centre. We missed a stirring comeback. David Johnson went on to score a second near the end which caused a few tense and gung-ho final minutes.
>
> There's no shame in losing by one goal to a side which may be playing in the Premier League next season but for once the other results didn't go our way. While we remained fourth, everyone edged a little close. The gap that we once enjoyed has long gone.

Four games remaining and still a top-six place was clearly possible. If memory serves, had we won three of them that would have been enough. We won two. The God-awful defeat at Grimsby is in another chapter. At Portsmouth there was just a point.

'Keep an eye on Gazza,' said Stan to me in the hotel at Portsmouth. We knew by then he would drink at most opportunities if not all. He had a little bag he carried round with him with a clasp at the top, rather like one of those old-fashioned doctor's bags. We once tried to look in it but it was locked and when we picked it up it rattled and clinked. You knew straightaway what was in it.

'Make sure he's down for the coach at 1.30,' said Stan. He knew my room was next to Gazza's.

Come 1.25 and I knock on his door. When the door opened, I could see in the room and that the mini-bar door was open and every bottle had gone. Steve Davis recalled that you never actually saw him having a drink but you'd know if he'd had one.

You can say it over and over again; where you finish at the end of a season is down to an accumulation of all results over a full season. It's not just one. But over and over again you can say that certain results stick in the memory. Some goals are more important. Some defeats are worse than others. They don't go away. How did we possibly lose at Grimsby of all places before we beat Coventry?

Fans will tell you that sometimes there is a depressing inevitability about watching Burnley. Here we are at the moment, as we write, in the Premier League and they're still saying it, having just lost 2-0 to Manchester United. Maybe all fans say it about their teams (unless they are one of the top-six super-clubs), that their team manages to bottle it when the pressure increases. Players don't set out to play badly, they don't deliberately choose to have an off day. But some days are just stinkers and the Grimsby game was one. It was an angry dressing room afterwards and at half-time. It was the half-time when Gazza had tried to get me to laugh at the row between Stan and Bally. Not the best time to be amused.

Come the Coventry game, the last of the season, hanging on by our fingernails to a play-off place. Since Christmas we had won just six games. There was the problem. It just wasn't good enough. Top at Christmas by several points and now scrabbling in the last-chance saloon, and even then, dependent on the results of other games. Barry Heagin was at the game and wrote down his thoughts. Most people he met in the pub before the game were cynical about the prospects of success. It needed Stockport County to win at Norwich for starters. It was not to be.

> A tense start to the game. Free kicks gave the Coventry goalkeeper Hedman easy catching practice. News came through that the Stockport keeper had been sent off very early in the game. Our heads drooped. Weller cleared a Coventry shot off the line. Faraway Norwich went one up. Gareth Taylor came on, brilliant with his head. He scored with his first touch. It couldn't have been more exciting if Elvis Presley had come on as sub. Coventry responded with a move as slick as Minestrone soup. Norwich took a two-goal lead and Burnley were sunk from that moment on. Coventry nearly equalised, our Greek goalkeeper stranded, having clearly lost his marbles. A standing ovation for the boys at the end but they looked about as happy as a penguin in a microwave. Weller had an excellent game. David Johnson was great, to the extent that if we'd had him at the Battle of Hastings against the Normans, the Frenchies would have gone home.
>
> Weller had an excellent game … Sickening to think however that having led the table for so long, the play-off pot of gold had disappeared into the abyss. Unsurprising in some ways considering the relatively poor form since Maine Road. It could be worse I suppose, as we are officially the 27th best team in England and of course you should never take life too seriously as nobody gets out alive. It didn't quite stop the tears on the long trek home, back to the Smoke.

And from the Dave Thomas book *It's Burnley Not Barcelona* a truly heartfelt piece, written the day after the game. I reckon it's how we all felt.

I feel like I have a hangover. But that isn't because of any wild celebrations or a few bottles of wine. We did win 1-0 but it wasn't enough as all other teams in contention won, and Norwich scored more than us.

Norwich scored one more goal than us.

I can't stop saying it in disbelief. For the first time in months, on the very last day of the season, we slipped out of the top six by just one goal. That's how crucial yesterday was when Norwich scored two and we scored just one. Words like heart-breaking and anguish just don't seem enough. There's 16 weeks to the next game in August and it's going to be a long 16 weeks as we wonder if this will be the closest we ever get to further success.

For the second season we are seventh but this time with 75 points. There's an irony. In any other season, 75 points would have been enough for a play-off place. It was hard to swallow that Burnley played as well as they did for weeks and hammered and pressured the Coventry goal.

Then Gazza came on for the last ten minutes in the hope that chances of free kicks would occur. And yes, they did. Twice he had magnificent and accurate free kicks from outside the box heading like arrows for the bottom corner. On any other day one would surely have gone in, but this was a day when fate decreed that goalkeeper Hedman would make wonder-saves and keep them out. On any other day against any other keeper Burnley would have scored three or more. Today the man was unbelievable. Gazza and the rest of us hung our heads in despair.

Meanwhile, at Norwich, the gods had decided that this was to be their day, not ours. After just 40 seconds Stockport had their goalkeeper sent off. In what other game, all season, has any team had their goalkeeper sent off after just 40

> seconds? When we heard this on pocket radios, we just knew this was not to be our day. But even then, up until the 75th minute it was Burnley in that golden play-off place. The scores were 1-0 at both grounds.
>
> And then Norwich scored again.

The Coventry goalkeeper said after the game that they were relieved that Gareth Taylor hadn't played the whole game, they were so concerned with his heading ability. Fans called him Golden Bonce, top man, heart as big as a house, and in a survey of the season he was top scorer with his head, along with Peter Crouch. In the first half we'd banged crosses over but there was no Gareth. In the second half on he comes and scores with his first header.

If this had been Melchester Rovers then somehow, we would have nicked a 90th-minute winner with one of those Gazza specials. He could not have struck them better. Or there would have been another bullet header from the man with the golden head. But there was to be no bit of magic, no special moment, no incredible extra goal of the sort that makes this game of football so special.

After such a game you ask yourself what more could you have done? You look at certain games or certain moments. Goals you missed, draws that should have been wins.

But the bottom line is, we missed out. This was the reality. So near, so far, so close, but so far away. It was Heartbreak Hotel.

In the book that Gazza released in 2004, he wrote of his time at Burnley in none too complimentary a way and went on to complain about the time he spent with us. He said the club was unprofessional behind the scenes and the football was kick and rush. He claimed he was owed money from the sale of replica shirts bearing his name, and this was a part of the deal he signed. Next, he went on to claim he was even promised a share of the gate money. Chairman Barry Kilby stressed that Gazza had received every penny he was due.

'I didn't really enjoy my football at Burnley, their sort of football wasn't my style. Perhaps I'd lost a bit of the necessary pace but whatever the case, I wasn't comfortable with it. The lads were fine,' he said.

Poor old Gazza. A magnificent career but a sad story at the end.

Chapter 14

IT'S BURNLEY NOT BARCELONA

FOR ME the 2002/03 season was a season of injuries, but the bowels were holding up. I'd been playing now for ten years and the niggles, tears and strains were starting. There was a knee operation in the summer that set me back in terms of training. In pre-season, playing catch-up I ended up with my foot in plaster. Once back from that, there was a tear and pains in the groin. I was annoyed and sulked, silly really, it happens to all of us, nothing you can do. Stuck in the treatment room and not training it's hard to keep your spirits up and it just seemed to be one thing after another. You get back into the side but you're not 100 per cent fit. You've lost a bit of sharpness, you're that bit slower, the fans don't know and get on your back. You play as long as you can but then you need to be subbed because you are running on adrenalin and then eventually there is nothing left in the tank. You give the ball away a couple of times and the crowd moans. Dispiriting. There is no such thing as instant fitness. It builds up in pre-season and if you miss that, the effects linger on. Once the season starts you are playing catch-up and it can take weeks to get fitness back in full.

It led to confrontations with Stan when he wanted me to play, or be on the bench, when I just wasn't match fit. But credit Stan, you could have a row with him and that was it. Done with. Flare-ups and confrontations, never made him vindictive. If he was that way, half the players in the club would never have got another game. I can't think of a player he bore a grudge against. Other managers – maybe.

It was the most weird and whacky season, a complete contrast to the one before that had ended so close to success. It was a season that began with the club over £4m in the red, and was simply the strangest for years. It sometimes thrilled fans, sometimes left them in despair shaking their heads. It frequently had them wondering which Burnley team would turn up, the one that rolled over, lay down and lost so easily, or the one that turned up and won handsomely. It was a season when supporters wondered what would happen next and it sometimes left them open-mouthed with anguish, or speechless with admiration, or smiling with appreciation, even though it was a season where we let in just one short of 90 goals.

The exotic Isle of Man was the scene of a number of pre-season workouts. Ah, the joys of the Isle of Man. When last I looked it had roughly the same population as Burnley but was far prettier. It seems it is also a good place to live and pay low taxes. About the only other thing I knew about the place was that the Manx cat is a breed of cat with either a stump for a tail or no tail at all. Believe it or not there are wild wallabies there, following an escape from a wildlife park. We didn't see any.

It was certainly a step up from pre-season trips to Devon and Exeter. Nice hotel, golf course, taxi into the town centre; mind you we had to pay for that ourselves if we wanted to go out. Strict curfews of course. The Exeter curfews had caused mayhem. After that, and players being told to leave, no one broke them again. These were the days when few clubs went on expensive pre-season trips abroad and Dubai was just a few buildings in the desert, so when Kevin Ball flew in for the first time, he looked around the rather nice hotel and remarked, 'How good is this?' We'd lose games out there because it was seen as the time to build up fitness rather than just to win games. The running I remember. Stan wasn't bothered about who won, who was first back to the start or how fast we went. In fact, he'd tell us to slow down and concentrate.

'Just get your form and your rhythm.'

The season proper began with very early games in sweltering heat and four defeats, just one goal in the first five games, and Stan Ternent in despair. The fourth of those defeats away at Reading produced a performance so abject from us that Stan was withering in his criticism and threatened resignation. He ripped into us in the dressing room but we were as upset as him with the poor results. There is no worse loser than me and you don't have a great Saturday night when things are going so badly. Stan's rant was brutal.

'I am going to have a chat with the chairman and see where we go from here. Tonight, I was embarrassed to be their gaffer because that performance is a reflection on me. Everyone knows the players are not performing, a blind man on a galloping horse can see that. A lot of people have spent a lot of money to come down here and watch that, and I am embarrassed.'

At that particular point the despondency on the terraces was depressing yet these were the same players that had finished seventh the season before. An occasional supporter still wore a shirt with Gascoigne on the back. Sad.

'Where next for sorry Clarets?' was one headline. With cash in short supply, was this the season the chairman coined the phrase, 'the jar on the mantelpiece is empty'? The club was even phoning supporters basically asking for money. There were stories throughout the season that the club was close to administration.

Those on decent money were worried, some of them on £8,000 a week, maybe even £10,000. Not me though; £5,000 was the best I ever got. I was a bargain; they could afford me. We knew a little about the money problems and supporters demanded to know the facts. Players were being given one-month contracts. Yet players that cost £1m each were sat on the bench: Ian Moore and Robbie Blake.

The purse strings were so tight there wasn't even a goalkeeper on the bench for one of the early home games. It was Barry Kilby and other directors propping up the club with loans that kept things ticking over but there was never money to buy players. The clubs, meanwhile, were threatening to sue their own lawyers for the shambles of ITV Digital, suing them for negligence. One of the friendly pre-season games was in support of the financially stricken Bury Football Club. They went out of existence as we wrote this book. I had a spell there after I finished playing, on the coaching and community side. It was badly run at the top, and a financial mess even then, with money disappearing to no one knew quite where.

This particular friendly at Bury was marked by the frequency of substitutions, so many that the few spectators there wondered if incontinence was the problem. At this point the club had a Greek centre-forward, Dimi Papadopoulos trying to establish himself, but one problem was his lack of English.

Stan, asked if his English was improving, was never short of a quip and answered, 'Whose? Glen Little's?' It was apt enough, none of us could ever understand the cockney motormouth either.

With such poor results through August, we were bombarded with abuse and foul-mouthed tirades from the terraces. Sometimes you could even hear the laughter of derision. Cruel. Who'd be a footballer? Where's the beautiful game when you are bombarded with obscenities? Where's the dream in that? It's funny that spectators will hurl abuse and criticism for players having a poor game, but how would they feel if people stood and watched and abused them for doing a bad plumbing job if they were a plumber, or for building a wobbly wall if they were a builder?

As for me, I was what you might call a Marmite player, target for the boo boys one minute, hero the next game. It was during that memorable game against Walsall in Heath's time, when the lights went out at half-time that, and I hadn't been playing that long, Jamie Hoyland said to me I would be OK, there was a footballer inside me. He said that because I knew I was having a poor game, he knew I was having a poor game, but he recognised that I never gave up, never hid, never shirked. It wasn't in my nature.

One coach told us one day, and I've never forgotten, to just ignore the crowd. 'Forget about that lot. One is your binman, one is your postman, one is your window cleaner, one works in a factory, one stacks tins on shelves; they know fuck-all about football.'

And yet despite the sorry start to the season, despite defeats of the magnitude of 6-2, 7-4, 6-5, 5-2 and 7-2, all but one at Turf Moor, (just have a think about the size of those defeats) there were good runs, times when we flirted near the top six and two wonderful wins over First Division opponents in the cup to get to the quarter-finals. Mind you, the display against Watford in that quarter-final was abysmal.

No wonder Stan tore his hair out that season. There's even a book to go with it, the aptly titled, *It's Burnley Not Barcelona,* four words that Stan conjured up in response to supporter criticism, and there was plenty of it that season. You have a home game and lose it 6-2. You have a home game and lose it 7-4. Players and fans went home equally embarrassed. These were not nights to be going out on the town clubbing if you were a player. Following another spate of supporter grumbles he said they had champagne tastes but only beer money. Nice one.

It was the season Robbie Blake came good. But very early on Stan T was savage in his opinion of him … hopeless … said he looked like he was wearing diver's boots. But at last, in the sixth game, away at Derby, and the first win of the season, Blake blossomed and showed all the skills, tricks and twists for which he was renowned and that he had demonstrated before he came to Burnley. With him in the side and at his best, you knew you would see proper football. Not many years later, the great Jimmy McIlroy said he was the only Burnley player he would pay to go and see. For his first few months at the club, supporters wondered just where £1m had gone. He would go on to become an icon and a hero of Wembley 2009.

Slowly things improved, we clawed our way off the bottom of the table but then came the game away at Bradford that had the Gaffer and supporters incensed. Don't blame me, I was injured and could only sit and watch. Dave Thomas was there and described the game in *It's Burnley Not Barcelona,* which for reasons of brevity can now be referred to as *IBNB*.

> The sun is shining. The sky is blue. The ground is colourful and bright. Two sets of bedecked supporters are in good voice and here is a fine spectacle in prospect. Drew 2-2 which on the surface looks a good away result at Bradford City as we watch a game from the privileged comfort of a warm, food-laden, drink-filled corporate box. Non-playing spectators Paul Weller, Andy Payton, Graham Branch and Gordon Armstrong sit in front of us, close enough to speak to.
>
> Bradford score first. First half did we have a shot? But two Bradford players are sent off. The home crowd is incensed. We score two and lead 2-1 against the nine men. At half-time Mrs T and me go and see the four Burnley players and think of something to say. One of them is

Left, the best I played with. Right, Steve Cotterill – from him I learned on the eve of my wedding that I was no longer needed. Cotterill picture by David Atkinson.

Adrian Heath, I learned such a lot from him but back in those days it was hard to find a shirt that wasn't two sizes too big. Both pictures courtesy of Burnley Football Club

The magical Glen Little, a six-foot winger, who could weave his way round players as if they weren't there and scorer of wonderful goals. In the dressing room you could never keep him quiet. He is a born story teller with some wonderful stories on the Under the Cosh podcasts on YouTube. His performance against Tottenham in a Carling Cup game at Turf Moor when we won 2-1 was memorable. When he, myself and Dean West were on form together down the right-hand side, we put on some great displays. Glen was and still is a fans' favourite. Picture courtesy of Burnley Football Club.

With Glen Little and matchday mascot, his son Keiron.

Captain for the day away at Brighton, with my nephews left to right, Charlie, William and Thomas. I used to send Thomas my shirts. Both pictures courtesy of Burnley Football Club.

Chris Waddle arrived at Burnley in a blaze of glory and great things were expected. Alas things didn't turn out that way. Picture courtesy of Burnley Football Club.

With Imogen, Flynn and Lenny Johnrose at a fund-raising function. I am filled with admiration for this man and the way he has coped with Motor Neurone.

The best world XI. This was a regular programme feature. When it came to my turn, I decided I would only choose players that I had seen play. That knocked out great people like Pele and Bobby Moore. Courtesy of Burnley Football Club.

Both Wrighty and Gazza arrived in a fanfare of anticipation. Only one of them left leaving good memories. It was Wright that left grateful fans. Both pictures courtesy of Burnley Express.

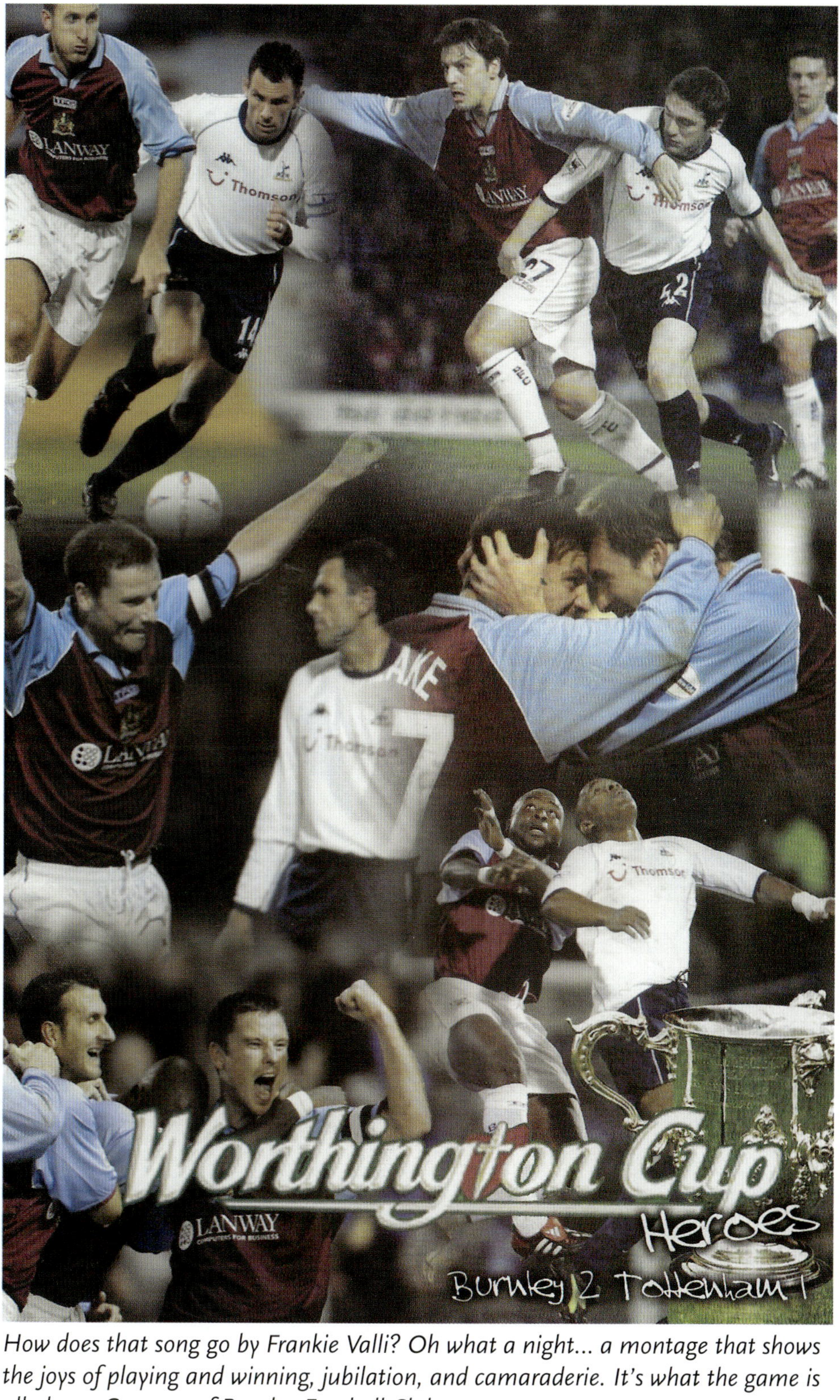

How does that song go by Frankie Valli? Oh what a night... a montage that shows the joys of playing and winning, jubilation, and camaraderie. It's what the game is all about. Courtesy of Burnley Football Club.

In the thick of things and never shirked a tackle or a challenge. Pictures courtesy of Burnley Football Club.

scoffing chips he has scavenged from another corporate box near us. They are not galacticos and decidedly ordinary but they are footballers which makes them different to us. The four musketeers maybe, Aramis Branch, Porthos Weller, D'Artagnan Armstrong and the Payton Padiham Predator. We say something along the lines of:

'Aren't you playing today?'

Well of course they're not playing. They're in suits and sitting in the stand. It's about the dumbest question you could ask. I take Mrs T's picture with them and tell them I once used to teach our swashbuckling full-back Dean West.

'Tight fisted bugger from Yorkshire,' says one of them. Footballers eh.

One of them tells me that, yes, Burnley were indeed two days away from administration. The Padiham Predator tells me they need to sell a player to raise some cash, but nobody is buying. Clubs are in the same boat these days. Broke. Premier clubs couldn't give a hoot. They all look hungry and I wonder should I ask them back into our box to finish off the food. But it's not my box and anyway, it belongs to a Bradford supporter.

Half-time ends and we settle to watch the game again. The bare facts of the game hide the real story; that a brave referee that you could never call a homer sent two home players off, and indeed could easily have sent the Burnley Greek centre-forward off for his antics. The fact that he was still on the pitch incensed the locals. You feared for the safety of any Greek restaurants in the city that evening. Stan Ternent took him off for his own safety. Burnley were already well remembered from the year before when our corporate host assures me that we kicked Bradford all over the place and the local paper said Burnley were physical, ugly and brutal. You may deduce that Burnley are not well liked in Bradford.

The game began in the traditional Burnley hoofer style and got nowhere thanks to the usual sloppy goal given away to give themselves a challenge. The second half changes saw the artists come on in the shape of Alan Moore, and Robbie Blake. We then played football and it seemed certain that Burnley would score more against a nine-man side. Eleven against nine and the game was more evenly balanced. Anything less than the win seemed ridiculous.

But: disgrace, embarrassment and torrents of Bradford derision set in with roughly about 15 minutes to go. Every Burnley supporter left that ground baffled by what we did at the end. We spurned the chance of a gift three points by ignoring the chance to keep the ball in the Bradford half and going for a third goal. With the Bradford players on their knees Burnley elected to play showboat stuff in their own half with the inevitable slip-up when they gave the ball away. Off Bradford went with glee and scored with maybe five seconds remaining on the clock. My mouth dropped wide open, big enough to swallow Vince Overson.

Thus, was the draw snatched from the jaws of victory. Burnley fans demanded that the players be docked their wages. It was pretty much a contest between two hopeless sides and Bradford websites said everything abusive you could expect about cheating Burnley. Burnley fans slunk away although Mrs T and I stayed awhile to finish off the top-notch chicken, salad and moussaka.

The Bradford manager was loud and vociferous in his condemnation of the diving Dimi Papadopoulos. We couldn't disagree but kept quiet. It was a huge skill of his, falling over at speed. Dimi had this natural ability to go flying and end up on the floor looking wronged. Some players just have the knack. They still do today although in today's game it is not called diving, it is called simulation. Somehow using a fancy word makes it more professional. Dimi will be in his forties now and I wonder if he does his supermarket shopping or takes a stroll along the beach, and does a quick dive every now and then for old time's sake. Old habits die hard. He would be priceless in today's game when diving for a penalty is an art form. But don't tell Sean Dyche: it is the bee in his bonnet.

It is impossible to present a picture of that curious season without describing more of these unique games. Another was in late October, close to Halloween, and was referred to as Fright Night. Grimsby 6 Burnley 5. What is it about Grimsby? The Grimsby marketing department had gone into overtime. Before the teams came out, the tannoy played the theme music from *The Addams Family*. The night was advertised as a Halloween Spooktacular. Kids were given free sweets.

It was a new way to lose; by scoring five quite good-quality goals but then just letting the opposition score when they felt like it. There was more absenteeism in the Burnley defence than an old British Leyland factory. It would be an insult to kids to say that this was schoolboy defending. For supporters this was the game in just 90 minutes that summed up the let-downs, heartaches, perils, trials and tribulations they endured following us. The previous year it had been a lad called Michael Boulding who had skinned us and as good as ended the play-off aspirations. The year before that, it had been a Chinaman. This time it was a lad called Steve Kabba who they had on loan from somewhere.

Even when we'd beaten Walsall 2-1 in an earlier game there were signs that someday, some team would give us a thumping. But Grimsby? They were second-bottom of the division, had scored just four goals at home so far, had just one win at Blundell Park and were the perennial strugglers. Who in their right mind could think they would score six that night? We were well and truly lost at sea.

It was French/African defender Arthur Gnohere who copped the blame that night as Kabba ran amok, and when Grimsby scored the third the gaffer hauled Arthur off. His early promise as a great defender and cult hero had gone. Without being much more than 6ft tall, he still looked like a man-mountain with a barrel-chest, shoulders wide enough to knock a door frame down, upper legs the size of tree trunks and a shaven head so burnished it shone. He looked like a god. Sadly, he didn't play like one. Alas, for the time he was on the pitch at Grimsby he was Gnohere to be seen. Stan shuffled the pack, moved players round; the Dutch called it Total Football, at Grimsby it was a total disaster. Astonishingly we could have scored seven or eight ourselves but stopped at five ... Arthur had a little English but three words he soon learned were 'liven up Arthur' which Stan frequently bellowed at him from the touchline. One of his better moments was planting a kiss firmly on Stan's forehead during one of his good games. He scored the equaliser in a 1-1 draw and charged over. It took a while for Stan to recover.

After the Grimsby match Stan was reeling with rage and went absolutely mad. 'I'm gobsmacked. It's the first time in my career anything like this has happened. I'm lost for words.' We all sat in the dressing room afterwards stupefied.

'I took him off because he cost us three goals,' bemoaned Stan of Arthur. 'The only place he is injured is between the ears.'

Arthur made Stan particularly mad every time they had a row and Arthur reverted to speaking French. Picture the scene, it would make a good comedy like Basil Fawlty and the hapless Manuel. Stan would berate Arthur for some gaffe he had made or try to explain patiently. It would get heated. You could see Stan getting more and more frustrated and Arthur getting more and more confused, to the point where he would blow a gasket and start jabbering in French. Arthur eventually began to turn up in a huge BMW, in fact he had two. They must have cost a fortune so we assumed he bought them on HP because we certainly weren't paid that kind of money.

The only good news that day was that a deal was reached between the Football League clubs and ITV with a bit of cash. Eddie Lea was at the Grimsby game. He'd driven 150 miles to be there.

> A mild, damp and windswept late October Tuesday evening. The journey was a crawl via the M42 and M1 until Sheffield. Then it was a clear run along the M180. Racing along the flat north Lincolnshire plain, one's nostrils were alerted to various different aromas; the foundries and smelters of Scunthorpe, the petrochemicals of Immingham, and finally the fish of Grimsby. Indeed, even a blind man on a galloping horse would have known what part of the country he was in.
>
> Yes, by George, one must have fish and chips in Grimsby. Not only was there a vast chippy within vinegar-sprinkling distance of the ground, there was even a parking space in the side street next to it. There was a cod so big my teenaged daughter and I struggled to finish it and chips so hot they burned your mouth. 'That'll be £3.50 luvver,' said the woman behind the counter in a strange accent. At the turnstiles the kids were given free sweets. No one at kick-off could have dreamed of what we were about to witness.
>
> Phew 2-2 and only half an hour gone. Five minutes later and we were 4-2 down. Stan decided to shuffle the pack and took off the King, Arthur, who by now looked a busted flush. He then put the Joker at centre-half, di Branchio. Subsequent events on the pitch only confirmed that his move made precious little difference.

> Meanwhile, Robbie Blake continued his transmogrification from 'what a waste of money' to 'Burnley's best-ever buy.' Controlling and blasting the ball in for our third just before the interval, he underlined all that is good about his play. He has close control, is useful with both feet and wrong-foots defenders with quick thinking. He plays good one-twos if there is ever anybody around alert enough nearby. He is beginning to look well worth £1m
>
> Half-time and I opined that the next goal would be the crucial one. Make it 4-4 and we could well win it. Into the second half and the lads duly obliged: 4-4. But dear reader this is Burnley we are talking about. A harsh penalty is given and penalties change games more often than any other refereeing decision. 5-4. Worse was to follow. 6-4. Into the last ten minutes and Papadopoulos went down under a challenge. (Have we not already mentioned Papa's skill at going down or diving?) Penalty, Blake scored. 6-5.
>
> If you concede six you deserve nothing. I've been following the Clarets for 40 years and saw three things I'd never seen before. Eleven goals in 90 minutes, seven goals in one half and Burnley scoring five away from home. It's more often than not a trial supporting this club. A 300-mile round trip, getting home at 1am, and not a point to show for it. God help us.

But the fish and chips were outstanding, mused Eddie as he motored home down the motorways.

'At the moment we're just pansies,' said Stan in another memorable match summary after we had lost 3-1 at Preston. Losing to Preston is a close second to losing to Blackburn. Apparently, the whole team was on the transfer list, I'm not sure we even knew; but nobody was buying as money was so tight at every club. Crowd trouble at the Burnley end was the icing on the cake. We'd no idea he'd called us pansies; we avoided reading reports.

It was probably not the best time to be playing Spurs in the League Cup, having just shipped nine goals in two games. They had a team filled with household names and were managed by Glenn Hoddle who placed great faith in a medium called Eileen. Stan the boss had more faith in Holy Water from Lourdes, that he once sprinkled in the corners of the pitch to try and improve things in his early days there as manager. Games between Spurs and Burnley back in the olden days had assumed mythical status when legends played for both sides in the 60s. Revenge for losing the Cup Final of 62 to Spurs would be sweet but who on earth gave us a chance of winning? They were, as well, my 'other' team from boyhood days and now I could play against them. Couldn't wait. None of us could.

For most players, success is staying in their division another season, with maybe a good cup run. It was certainly the case at Burnley as we hovered around mid-table, with just an occasional flip to just below the top six. Then a couple of defeats would restore the rightful middle-of-the-ground place. A game against a top club under the floodlights, and on TV as well, was therefore a little bright interlude in an otherwise mundane season. Mind you, we were already discovering that this particular season was not going to be mundane, with the results we'd had. TV brings a bit of fame, with extra coverage, interviews and all the build-up. My mum and dad might watch. The press takes a bit more interest in a game like this. Our 15 minutes of fame, as it were, or 90 to be precise. The names of Jimmy McIlroy and Bob Lord were dredged up from the past when Spurs and Burnley really were genuine rivals at the top end of the football table.

On the TV, or magic lantern as the gaffer referred to it, Chris Waddle was one of the studio experts. On TV he could talk for England. A group of London Clarets, unable to make the game, watched in a Covent Garden pub, jeering his every word. Football fans don't forget. They saw Gus Poyet score for Spurs, who, as a manager at Brighton in later years would come in for even more derision from Burnley fans. They drank enough beer to float a battleship and noted that Glen Little was simply extraordinary. Sadly, there were only 13,500 at Turf Moor. A report of the game and even a bit of Wordsworth, is in *It's Burnley Not Barcelona*.

> My God, we won, on a magnificent, magnificent
> glorious night.
> Shout for a mighty victory is won!
> On Burnley ground the invaders are laid low.
> The breath of heaven has drifted them like snow
> and left them lying in the silent night
> never to rise again … the work is done.
> Come forth ye old men, now in peaceful show.
> *Greet your Clarets. Drums beat and trumpets blow …*
> (With apologies to William Wordsworth, *Anticipation*,
> October 1803)

How did William Wordsworth know nearly two hundred years ago that such a night would occur and a feeble first half-hour Burnley would be transformed when sub Glen Little came on in an early reshuffle and totally transformed the game. If this wasn't his best ever game in a Burnley shirt, or in his lifetime, then I haven't seen it.

Never let it be said that Uncle Stan is afraid of making tactical change when a game plan isn't working. One of his trademarks has been the early substitution in light of the failed game plan. It was inspired and Little's introduction transformed the game. Little and Weller, Little and Blake; these two players play so much better with him.

It was a night of magic, emotion and deserved victory, transformed by Glen Little, leaving Glenn Hoddle initially almost speechless and wondering just where it went wrong after they had been one-up and coasting. For the record, Blake scored with a rasping shot from 18 yards and Steve Davis with a thumping header from a corner. Blake, what a player, two good feet, close control and an ability to turn and twist as good as any Chubby Checker. Spurs despite the changes they made were simply by-passed by Little, Blake and Weller.

What can be said about the second half? We were terrific. We played superbly and we deserved to win. There's an old saying that you need to score when you're on top. And we did.

'Fans roared at the final whistle, roared into the night air and turned to the Spurs end. They had largely disappeared melting into the night. Their coach journeys home would have been long and miserable. Beaten by a side that had just lost 6-5 at Grimsby. Fans waved goodbye to the Spurs coaches. Childish, but amusing.

'Caught like rabbits in headlights as the Burnley juggernaut gave them a battering,' it said in the *Sun*.

All that, plus 1970s legend Ralph Coates at half-time, now looking a little like one of the Roly Polys but at least minus the trademark hairstyle wherein a few long strands of hair were carefully arranged over the scalp from left to right (a la Bobby Charlton and which on a windy day trailed behind him by several feet).

From the glamour of a game against Tottenham Hotspur and on telly, to the drabness of Rotherham. Such is the life of a footballer. The Chuckle Brothers came from Rotherham. Sadly now, there is only one of them. Quite where they got the name Chuckle Brothers from is a mystery; it couldn't have been Rotherham where there never seemed much to smile about when we played there. Fans, to get to the away end, needed to walk down what is known as a ginnel in these parts, a narrow alley with the ground on one side and old derelict industrial buildings down the other that could have come off the pages of a Charles Dickens novel. At the bottom end used to be scrapyards filled with old railway stock and rusting locos. Radio commentators would say football at places like this is what the game is all about. Yep, the fans sat in seats with so little legroom they were sure to get deep vein thrombosis by the time they got home.

If the Tottenham match was all that is good about the game, Rotherham was the opposite: dire, dreadful and unpretty with the ball in the air most of the time, hoofed and punted mercilessly by both teams. And that was just the warm-up. After that it got worse. We kicked, lumped, hoofed, punted, scrapped, scraped, lurched, muscled, pushed, shoved and muddled our way to a 0-0 draw. Rotherham were big, tall, square-jawed, physical, robust, muscular and hard. And that was just the women. But they hadn't met our colossus King Arthur, le Roi, Monsieur Gnohere. We could even have snatched an ugly win but I fluffed a golden chance when the ball came to me waist high, by the far post. Perhaps I was just mesmerised by the awfulness of the game. And anyway, a goal would have spoiled the total bleakness of the afternoon. Living the dream eh? Sometimes there is just not one jot of glamour to be found in a game especially in the freezing cold dressing rooms at Rotherham. This was one of them.

Ups, downs, a win here, a defeat there, enough wins to keep in sight of the top six if you think a six-point gap is within sight. A home defeat to Manchester United in the League Cup in front of 22,000. These are the good nights. They took their chances. We didn't. You live for the games like this when they come around.

Chapter 15

DEFINITELY NOT BARCELONA

IT'S ONE of the worst things a player ever has to do; attend a fan's funeral with his or her family, on a sombre day of mourning and remembrance. It was a dreadfully sad occasion when the funeral of Nathan Shaw took place, after he was murdered in Burnley on the December day that we played Nottingham Forest at Turf Moor.

Not many days before this we had played so well against Manchester United and earned praise from the media. Now the name of Burnley Football Club was besmirched and shamed. Burnley prided itself back then on being a family club. Now it was disgraced as the news spread and it became clear that a teenage Forest fan had been attacked in the Yates Wine Lodge and then outside, before the game, and died later in hospital. It followed on from trouble at Leicester and Preston as it became clear that a gang of thugs had attached itself to the football club.

All the good things that had happened – the United game, the win over Nottingham Forest, the club clawing its way back to some semblance of financial normality – all of it became meaningless the minute that boy died. The club was tarnished and the town disgraced. Some Christmas that was going to be for the boy's family. Clubbed with a bottle by a thug who was later charged with manslaughter, Shaw collapsed and died later.

During the afternoon of the attack, unknowing fans sat in the stands and enjoyed the game. We, the players, had no idea. The next morning, we still had smiles on our faces, but as facts emerged in the following days, we were shocked. No one should go to a football match and lose their life. It wasn't the first incident of its kind and others over the years have followed, as supporters have followed their teams.

Prior to this, people had been slow to acknowledge that Burnley had a growing hooligan problem. Nothing had been done about the growing number of yobs who had attached themselves to the club. The culprit for this particular crime was found swiftly and that was the only consolation.

An impeccable minute's silence was held at the next home game against Rotherham. It was a demonstration that the normal fans and we, the players, disassociated ourselves from violence and hooliganism and in so doing showed our condemnation. It was a sincere gesture to the boy's family.

After that chastening minute, Burnley lost to the giants from Rotherham, 6-2. Of this home game we will say little other than Stan's book had just been published and in it he revealed the story about sprinkling holy water on the pitch to improve things. After the game there was a suggestion that he should dunk the team in a barrel of the stuff. Freak result, you might say, but it hadn't been the first had it that season? And it wouldn't be the last.

The government announced that people could work beyond the age of 65 and still receive a pension. We joked that this was good news for Paul Cook and Andy Payton. We relished training at Gawthorpe, which was quite simply a mudbath; most days when we came off you had no idea who you were talking to as all of us were black from head to foot. Stan and the club were still regretting the dire effects of the ITV Digital contract fiasco as we went to Gillingham, a fixture that ranks up there, or down there, with Grimsby, Rotherham and Barnsley. Another four goals flew past us. The very first Gillingham ground years ago was situated right next to one of the country's biggest manure heaps; there is probably a good joke in there somewhere, but after losing 4-2, no one could think of one.

Nathan's funeral was in January and was attended by Burnley's CEO Andrew Watson, myself and player Gareth Taylor who still remembers the hugely emotional day and the few words he had with the family. Forest manager Paul Hart was there with Forest players; the coffin was draped with a Forest flag and the boy's cap. The family sent a heartfelt message to the club afterwards.

> Hello and a big thank you to all who have left messages in Burnley. At this sad time for our family and friends, we find it so difficult to comprehend the mindless act of violence that took place on December 8, 2002. All Nathan wanted to achieve that day was the enjoyment of a game of football with his friends. After all, it is only a game. We have received messages from far and wide and all are standing united as we try to come to terms with the tragic loss of a grandson, son, brother, boyfriend, friend and football supporter. Please don't let Nathan's death be in vain. Always think of Nathan from Nottingham at all future sporting events. Once again, a big thank you to you all.'
>
> *The Shaw Family*

Just as you thought it might be safe to assume another Boxing Day defeat was on the cards, what do we go and do but beat Wolves. Football, you can't fathom it out. We do our fans no favours though, with a superb first half and then a second half where we vanished and a final ten minutes of nerve-wracking, nail-biting tension with the score at 2-1. Sometimes a team doesn't know what to do when it is two goals up and we floundered around hanging on for grim death at the end. It was the first win over Wolves for 40 years. Chairman Barry Kilby reminded everyone that five years earlier Burnley drew a drab game 0-0 against Chesterfield but here we were comfortably mid-table in the Championship – albeit skint.

The Withdean Stadium was next. What a strange place that was, an old athletics stadium where Brighton played their games because the place that they used to own had been flogged. Set in a residential area, anything like music was banned at the Withdean. The twee people of the area were far from pleased that football fans now descended and disturbed the peace. People spoke in nothing more than a whisper but the oddest thing was a bloke who used to lurk in the trees and set off a rocket every time Brighton scored. This was fine and quite amusing until the day came that one rocket landed on the pitch and nearly decapitated one of the players. The result was 2-2 by the way after we'd thrown away a two-goal lead in the last five minutes. Three days later the West Pier at Brighton collapsed.

Nothing much changes at Burnley. Today the club bemoans how hard it is to bring new players in just as the club did back in Stan's day. The only difference is, back then they really did have no money. Today in the Premier League the club has money in the bank. It really was hand-to-mouth stuff in the last couple of years I was there, and would get even worse. It was a vicious circle; if results were poor, attendances fell, if attendances fell there was even less money, less money meant no fresh players. Lack of new players impacted on results. Mind you, you could also argue it was our own fault. If we hadn't screwed up certain results when we'd been in winning positions, we'd have been just one point behind the play-offs again. 'If' – there's that word again.

And all the while in the background were supporters who always wanted more. They were a demanding lot. Many of them still harked back to the good old days of grandeur when they were a great team. Twice in fact, winning the title in 1960 and then producing that team of the 70s. The club had a great history so there were expectations and ambitions despite all the years in the old Fourth Division. There was a fine ground and great traditions. It was all a heavy burden. Burnley had scaled the heights and seen Europe and the Isle of Man, we joked. It meant that we were expected to beat teams like Grimsby and Rotherham and Barnsley and Gillingham. Too often it didn't work out that way and Burnley fans were a hard lot to please.

It was good then, to wallop Grimsby in the FA Cup, 4-0 at Burnley after a 2-2 draw at Grimsby. Funnily enough that draw was yet another game when we were 2-0 up and then ended up with the 2-2 draw. 'Burnley have only themselves to blame for not winning 8-0,' said a Grimsby report. Stan Ternent had just a few more grey hairs.

The treatment room was becoming a familiar sight. If memory serves it was where I heard the draw for the next round of the cup in the days when it was on a Monday lunchtime on the radio, although you could still see it on TV. Brentford away was our next game and we disposed of them comfortably, probably to the surprise of supporters who always feared the worst with our performances.

The physio was Ian Liversedge, a nice guy that I liked a lot, but he always seemed to be a bit in awe of the gaffer so it seemed to me that when he should have been backing me and saying I was not fully fit, he didn't. There was the time he told me that Stan wanted to see me. Hell, what for, I wondered. What had I done; had I been out drinking? Ian came with me. It was the day of a game against City, if I remember, an evening game and I was at the ground.

'Are you fit to play?' Stan asked, to my astonishment. I said 'No' and assumed that Ian would back me up. This was just a couple of hours before the game.

'Well, you're on the bench tonight.' I looked at him incredulously.

'But gaffer I'm just not fit,' I spluttered and looked to Ian to back me up. He had vanished out of sight, not on my left, not on my right. He was in fact standing behind me. He's bloody hiding from Stan, I thought. He's not gonna say anything. And he didn't. I hadn't even taken my boots in, so convinced was I that I would not be playing.

'But I haven't even got my boots,' I told Stan.

'Well go and get them,' says Stan. My jaw was hitting the floor by now as I called Zoe to go and get them from Gawthorpe whilst the team were all doing the warm-up.

So, the game started, with me on the bench with a hamstring that was still not right, and I knew it wasn't right. Stan had assured me I wouldn't actually play, and I was praying that he did not bring me on. He did. I couldn't believe it.

'Are you mad?' I asked him. There was no way I could run properly or flat out, so all I could do was run around like a fairy in case it went again. Fans think you're just not trying or not interested. They don't know you shouldn't even be on the bench, let alone on the field. *If only they knew.* What a good book title that would be.

There are, in fact, some nice stories in football and one of them, from the bizarre 2002/03 season, concerned full-back Dean West, the lad from Leeds whose first words as a toddler were 'HOW MUCH.'

Gawthorpe was frozen solid so we were training in the gym at Turf Moor. In the same building was a rather decent café. Gone now, it never made any money, but it did a good bacon bap. Co-author Dave Thomas was in there having a bacon bap (what else) while we were in the gym training, and tells the story:

> Inside the café was a bunch of athletic, good looking, (well some of them) blokes in black training gear. They looked

like SAS rejects. Normally the café is filled with OAPs and hangers-on who love to be near footballers, and schoolkids or an occasional player who has sneaked out of the treatment room for a brew. Anyway, here's this black-garbed crew, who close up, have knobbly knees and hairy legs just like the rest of us.

Anyway, to my surprise I saw a familiar face. Well, half familiar maybe, it was buried deep inside a bobble hat. The face beamed. It called out:

'Mr Thomas?'

'Dean West,' I called back, amazed.

And yes, it was the lad I used to teach 20 years ago and the last time I saw him he was only this high. Over he came with a grin like a Cheshire cat, friendly, good natured, modest and sociable. He's the only lad in 20 years of wet Saturday mornings or a freezing afternoon after school that made it into professional football. The lad who more or less single-handedly won us second place in the school league in his final year, against schools three and four times the size of the little village school where I was head. After one particular mudbath game against a team of giants, from somewhere in the murky depths of Wakefield, (and believe me there is real murk in Wakefield), when he ran the show and kicked everything that moved, I jokingly told him I'd get him a trial at Burnley one day. It impressed neither him or his dad, both Leeds United supporters. Our little school was on the edge of Leeds but played games against schools from Wakefield.

That was back in the 80s and Burnley in the 80s were far from impressive. These were not the vintage years. No wonder he grimaced at the suggestion. He and the team were on the way across to the main stand to watch a video that

Stan had prepared, he said. God it was cold at Grimsby he added, he hadn't played, just sat and froze. He couldn't figure out why this was a team that could go ten games unbeaten and then go to pieces.

My bacon bap arrived. They do two sorts, undercooked and nearly black. I always go for the black. I ate it and drank my coffee and pondered on how being a headmaster is like being a football manager in many ways. The only difference as far as I can make out is that I could never sack people on the spot or tell them they were shite.

The big debate at Burnley around this time was over whether the Gawthorpe youth system was worth continuing. I was the only youth team product in the current first team and it had been ten years since I last set foot in a youth team. Before me there was Trevor Steven and he dated back to 1983. Chris McCann and Kyle Lafferty were two others brought through in Stan's time but were eventually sold. Richard Chaplow was another product but had to be sold. I'd signed as a pro in 1993. Others had made appearances or sat on the bench, but most just faded away. Paul Smith might have made it but illness cost him dear. The gaffer was adamant the youth set-up and reserves should be disbanded and the money saved, used elsewhere. His opinion was that the club should look at young lads that the big clubs might discard: far more cost effective. Dwight McNeil, currently lauded as home-grown, was in fact a Manchester United reject.

There is still an argument today that the money spent on the hugely upgraded Gawthorpe facilities will never be cost effective. The best young players go to the academies at the big clubs of which there are so many in Lancashire. Dwight McNeil is the only product to have come through Burnley's youth team to gain a regular place, since Jay Rodriguez way back in 2008/09. And even then, McNeil was only given his chance because of so many injuries to the other wide players. Without that, it is more than likely he would have followed the path of so many other young lads from Gawthorpe and been sent out on loan. And once on loan few of them have made it at any senior level. Rodriguez is the only one to have been out on loan and then returned to the first team.

Stan was firm in his views. 'Better to have one squad of 20 players and then trawl the academies at other clubs and get their young players at 18 or 19. The youth team is very complicated and a long-winded item of discussion and is a subject close to my heart. The problem is that Burnley can't attract the best young players. We are just not producing kids and Burnley was always known for producing its own players. I was one of them. But now, the best kids want to go to the Premiership.'

Even with Burnley in the Premiership, the best kids are hoovered up by United, City, Liverpool and Everton. Millions have been invested at Gawthorpe to improve facilities and raise the academy status. And still, I can't see any prospect of Burnley's first team, one day, being comprised of a hard core of home-grown players.

We used to have this little lounge under the stand we used after a game. 'Lounge' gives the wrong impression. It was more of a large broom cupboard with a sort of a pinky striped wallpaper, peeling away in one or two places, with a few framed pictures and faded newspaper clippings. In one corner there was a tiny bar with just whisky, brandy or lager. A huge hot water urn balanced on a small table from which we could brew a tea or a coffee. There was always a warm and welcoming atmosphere for the wives and visitors. Wives at Burnley back then were nothing like the ones you get now, bejewelled, walking fashion icons.

We had this new guy called Drissa Diallo that Stan had unearthed in Belgium. His club had gone broke and he was available on a free. Stan snapped him up. A tall, spindly, black guy, he looked more like a Harlem Globetrotter basketball player. And then you saw him play at centre-back. Somehow, he found his way to Burnley by train, no mean feat for anyone really, but Drissa was a total stranger finding his own way and spoke French. I suppose it was a miracle he found Burnley and not Barnsley. One day a visitor came to the little lounge and engaged him in a conversation in French. It sounded quite impressive, although every now and then Drissa would look a bit puzzled.

Drissa came over afterwards and told us his worries. 'Zat man who speak to me. He tells me he loves me. What should I do?'

Funny how footballers bump into each other after football. Jamie Hoyland was scouting in Belgium recently and was sat next to a guy who was also obviously on a scouting mission. They got to chatting and told each other they were ex-footballers. The second guy was Drissa, who Jamie had never met before. 'I used to play in England,' explained Drissa. 'For Burnley.' 'Well so did I,' answered Jamie.

We disposed of Grimsby comfortably at Turf Moor in the FA Cup. They were awful and left us wondering just how they had always managed to beat us at Blundell Park. On a Grimsby blog there was a fine explanation.

> The Town players moved in strange and unusual ways, like they had never met before. Burnley were a whirling dervish of tricks and flicks, surges, crosses, Clarets to the left of them, Clarets to the right of them. More crosses, more blocks as Burnley danced around the Town penalty area. The game had the tension of a geography lesson on a wet Tuesday in June and the fascination of the inner ring road in Scunthorpe.
>
> Town were unable to keep up the high tempo sleepwalking of the first half settling into a groggy, stumbling, barely conscious lethargy. Burnley plainly got a rollicking from Stan the Man, foregoing the tip tap showbiz football. They

> were intent on scoring the perfect goal, wanting to walk the ball into the net only after each player had touched it once. They swirled in dizzying patterns that confused the old and infirm, which was half the Grimsby team of course. Burnley, Burnley, Burnley, all up the other end. If only they could shoot straight, they'd have had seven.

Meanwhile, Ian Moore was in and out the team and sometimes got a bit miffed. He'd go and see Stan for a talk and told us, 'They haven't been quiet meetings, but I seem to go in and come out none the wiser.' How many footballers have said that at clubs everywhere after they have had a chat with the manager?

Gazza had flown off to China to try and pick up a lucrative deal. We were still constantly reminded of his ill-fated stay with us. Pictures in the press usually showed him in a claret shirt. All of us loved his man/child personality, his foolishness and impudence. We took him to our hearts and willed him to rediscover his old magic. But it was long gone. He was much loved at every ground we went to and the welcomes he received were generous and affectionate. It was as if they knew they would not see him again. He seemed to belong to all fans. Who could forget his tears at Italia 90? If only one of those free kicks had gone in against Coventry. He ended up at a team somewhere in or near the Gobi Desert. Sad.

Another of the poor results was Burnley 2 Reading 5. Fans left early with the gaffer saying he wished he could have joined them but he was obliged to stay to the end. There were worse to come. The thing about this game was the incredible time-wasting of their goalkeeper Marcus Hahnemann, driving us and supporters absolutely crazy with a referee who did nothing about it. His placing of the ball was in slow motion. He retrieved the ball from wherever it landed behind the goal in slow motion. He set up his kicks in slow motion. Then he took the kick in slow motion. It was utterly infuriating; how there wasn't a riot behind his goal was a mystery as the crowd screamed at him. They took their revenge by hurling all manner of objects at him. Coins, bananas, sandwiches, pies, a bottle and a bag of something that nobody could identify. He took the coin and the pie to the referee. The referee kept the pound and threw the pie away. They were good pies as well. With a pie, a banana and a sandwich, Hahnemann was only two tomatoes short of a picnic.

Time-wasting never bothered me. If we wasted time it was fine. Today it's called game management to make it respectable.

By coincidence at this time the club had teamed up with the Samaritans. Glen Little had a leading publicity role. An unnamed source said that Burnley were the perfect club to work with, on account of all the poor results and that after the Reading game everybody was suicidal. Arthur Gnohere was particularly out of sorts around this time, so the boss sent him home to Paris with his family for a short spell to get his head back on.

Stan explained. '*Il pete plus haut que son cul.*' Or put it another way, '*Il a la tete dans le cul.*' Both mean just about the same. 'He has his head up his arse.' 'He needs a rest mentally,' explained Stan in a kindlier tone. 'See his parents, dodge around for a few days.'

Fulham in the cup, managed by Jean Tigana, another Frenchman and bankrolled by Mohamed Al-Fayed, the Harrods owner. Some managers smoke 40 a day. Tigana chewed matchsticks. The first leg was a 1-1 draw with the press drooling over our performance. Around 3,000 Burnley fans went down there. And how well we played in the replay at Turf Moor.

Taylor, a poacher's goal, Ian Moore a chip over the goalkeeper and Drissa Diallo with a thumping header. Little teasing and twisting, back to fitness and on for the last ten minutes. Ian Moore, Taylor, Grant or Diallo, if these four were superhuman then the rest were not far behind. Diallo, as a defender, a great free signing. Not a man wasn't on top form, denying Fulham space and time to breathe. I replaced an exhausted Cook, who had run himself into the ground. Beresford hardly had a shot to save.

Let's be honest this wasn't samba football, or the neat intricate dazzling stuff that ripped Tottenham apart. This was what we might call power football, gritty, resolute, determined, all hustle and bustle, a bit of flair when you needed it, and then some showboating at the end. None of us could have predicted such total superiority and one of the two best results of the season. How did we play like this, and then fail so miserably against Watford in the cup just a couple of weeks later? Football can drive you mad, especially when a side is so inconsistent.

Tigana moaned that Fulham were tired. He moaned that Burnley had targeted their star man Boa Morte. He moaned about the refereeing. The pundits agreed that Burnley were superb, even Mark Lawrenson. Two weeks later he'd be saying that Burnley were one of the worst sides he'd seen. We didn't know if owner Al-Fayed was there. There were stories he wanted to convert Craven Cottage into luxury flats. After this game he probably couldn't wait to start.

Into March and thoughts of the cup tie to come at Watford were entering our heads. Dean West scored a stunning goal at Stoke, stunning because this was a ground so windy the ball kept blowing back at us. We were battered by wind and hail but who cares when you win 1-0. The gaffer was still in his phase of not playing Blake and Little. Glen Little's nickname was Blakey because he bore an uncanny resemblance (said some) to one of the characters in an old TV show called *On the Buses.* So, if ever they were in the side together and Stan was shouting and balling instructions, 'Blakey get stuck in … Blakey shift yourself … Blakey you're fucking hopeless …' it was a fair bet neither of them knew who he was shouting at.

The Millwall game was another one where Stan had a memorable rant about the referee. 'If that's the best he can do he should be on Hackney Marshes.'

And then our 15 minutes of fame arrived. Watford and a chance of glory and the FA Cup semi-finals on the horizon. Cup fever was mounting. Supporters were urged to wear flat caps and make it a special occasion. The clubs, both skint, agreed to share the £400,000 prize money whoever won. The stadium, built on the site of old gravel pits, was famous for the holes that used to appear from time to time, the result of subsidence. But the last one had been in the 1980s. The streets outside the ground were a mass of colour and noise and the sun shone from a blue sky making the colours quite brilliant, even the cemetery on the other side of the road.

'One of the worst spectacles of football at this stage the competition has witnessed,' said one report. 'A desperate quarter-final bereft of drama and entertainment or anything resembling quality or class,' said another. They weren't wrong.

The draw for the next round was a reminder to us of what we had missed. Southampton, who were beatable. Seeing the name Watford in the news over and again rubbed salt in the wound. For us, no more attention, no more limelight, no more minutes of fame. If only ... those two words again. It was back to the bread and butter stuff again and someone joked that if we won every one of the next ten games we would be in the play-offs. I had missed the Watford game, but who knows, if me, Blakey and Robbie had started that game, to this day I say we would have won. Glen and Robbie, two of the best match-winners I ever played with ...

The press dragged something into the open that had supposedly been kept quiet: that way back in August every player had been put on the transfer list in response to players refusing to take a wage reduction, via the bonus system, to help with the financial crisis at the club. The bonus scheme was decent, and as a group we'd said 'no, we're hanging on to it', to Stan and the chairman. It's the bonus system at many clubs that tops up the wages to something acceptable. Some players, the careful ones, put the bonuses on one side for when the day comes that they leave the game.

Stan responded: 'Having thought long and hard about it, I may have made a mistake. I asked the players about revised bonuses but they decided to stay on what they were earning. I said if that's the case, then everyone is for sale. I wouldn't do it again.' It caused quite some consternation amongst supporters who knew nothing about this. Looking back, I'm not sure or can't remember, if we knew either.

Chapter 16

BEWARE THE IDES OF MARCH

THE ITV Digital fiasco was still wreaking its impact on finances and it's easy, looking back, to say that our season was as good as finished after we lost that cup game at Watford. Of course, you don't know it at the time and with 13 games left you could imagine a few more wins and you could carry on with conviction and purpose, especially with Stan Ternent to drive you on. Slacking was not an option.

Who knows, put in a really good run (footballers are always optimistic) and the top six was by no means impossible. But in truth it was a dire end to that season. Add in to the mix that several players were concerned about their futures, certainly the players who would be out of contract; add in to the mix that it wouldn't be long before Glen Little would be loaned to Reading, and the recipe was there for the disheartening final few weeks.

Probably the last game anyone would have chosen to be next was away to Sheffield United. It had the loudest tannoy system in football and teams came out to the thundering din of the *Star Wars* theme. The theme from *Steptoe and Son* might have suited us better. Yet again there was an astonishing number of away supporters. With nothing else to do they derided Neil Warnock incessantly.

We lost and trudged off, thoroughly outplayed, as Sheffield had whistled four goals past us.

When Walsall won in the next game, we knew both in our heads and hearts the season was over. Several players knew it was the end of the line for them. Walsall represented the last chance for us to keep the season alive but it was a 3-2 defeat.

In the space of just seven days in March, it was all over, finished. At the beginning of the month we had looked forward to extending the cup run, maybe inching our way to the play-offs, glory or gloom. Gloom won in the end. Stan was fuming. We were woeful.

'They are having a laugh,' he said of us. 'There is no spark, no brightness, there is no enthusiasm. I am absolutely sick to death of it. They are nicking money while people are paying their hard-earned cash to go and see them. They are not having a go, and they are bone idle.'

One fan, Eddie Lea, was livid and wrote: 'A bad couple of weeks. One point from three league games and a non-performance against Watford in the cup. I'm worried now that we've been found out after three decent seasons in this league. Plan A seems to be team spirit, work hard, close down the opposition, hoof it to Taylor. There's not much evidence of a plan B. The squad continues to age. Where are the eager, young, fresh faces banging on the first team door? There are none. It doesn't bode well for the future. Next season could be very difficult.'

Written in 2003, 17 years ago, you could now write those exact same words to describe the current Burnley side in the Premier League, although you'd change the name Taylor to Barnes or Wood.

Back in 2003, for every person that was critical about Stan, there were others that sprang to his defence, reminding us of what he had achieved, the rescue job he did, and the limited resources he worked with. Today the debate is much the same about Sean Dyche as he explains yet again how hard the transfer market is, how the club seeks to find value for money and how bargains are hard to find. The club does have money today, but is fearful of wasting it.

Fans were certainly critical of us back then and angry at the way the season had fallen apart in this awful month. This little snippet is from *IBNB*.

> Here's a scene from the Turf last night as we sit in our seats. Behind us to the right is a large fat bloke stuffing a pie into his mouth while standing up hurling abuse at the players. His face is a mask of fury and bile. His eyes are narrowed and venomous. He is twice as big as me so I stay mum. What's interesting is that this tirade is during the warm-up. The game hasn't even started, it's still ten minutes to kick-off. For this he has paid £19 and whatever it is for a pie these days. Most of the pie has finished up on the collar of the person in front of him. God forbid that we lose; he might bring the whole pie back up.

Meanwhile, the gaffer fumed when a newspaper said he was quitting. 'Nonsense' was the gist of his answer, while it was still mathematically possible to reach the play-offs.

But after a 1-1 draw with Grimsby (ah that name again), that was it, that really was season over, everything following just an anti-climax and going through the motions. On this particular day, the sun shone beautifully and those that were there almost got a bit of a suntan. Whilst we actually played, people read their programmes or discussed the day's news. One or two people did actually fall asleep. Pigeons settled on various parts of the pitch, there was so little going on. Grimsby were so bad it was a mystery how they weren't marooned at the bottom 90 points behind everyone else. And we weren't much better. The game had all the passion, interest and excitement of listening to Iain Duncan Smith. It was the classic end of season game when there is nothing to play for when neither fans nor players are interested. Burnley 3 Fulham 0 seemed light years away.

And still the gloom went on. Now it was a home defeat to Bradford City as March wound down. But before it did, Glen Little was loaned to Reading and supporters were incensed. It was a money-saving exercise thanks to ITV Digital but they were angry enough since the team had gone into freefall after the Watford game; now, this was the last straw. Despite his inconsistency he was a hero, legend, cult figure, talisman and an entertainer. He was also my mate.

As fans raged about this and that and everything under the sun, journalist Tony Livesey in *IBNB* tried to talk some sense into them:

> As they say in all the best Baghdad knocking shops, stone me. Here we are heading for our fourth season in Division One and you lot are stringing yourselves up. I'd hate to think how you'd react if we were relegated. It's Glen Little who's gone, not your wife. I'm not sure if some of you realised how critical this season was for Burnley FC. Clipped with debt, however much we like to think our individual season ticket purchases help, the club was only ever going to limp through. Survival was the only real option. Of course, Stan wanted more, who wouldn't? But taking stock now: two decent cup runs, safety, recouping well over a million that ITV picked from our pockets, you have to admit the season is a success. Yes. Success. Don't kid yourselves either. Next year will be more of the same. If we can possibly survive that, then contracts can be re-negotiated and the club may just have a future.
>
> As it is, take a look around. Derby, Coventry, Ipswich, Sheffield Wednesday, Bradford, all wobbling. I've watched

> Burnley for 33 years. It's a long haul folks. I've read on here about people wanting to protest or go to Ewood instead, or not buying a season ticket for next season. It beggars belief. I for one will be in the Turf Moor trenches for the next 33 years. God willing. Does that make me a mug? Nope. It makes me what I am, a Burnley fan. Not a boo-boy, not a fair-weather supporter, not someone who expects to win every game. Just a fan who recognises that if some of your howls of outrage reach the ground on matchday, you may well frighten away the people who currently keep our club afloat. Don't forget I am the man who organised the 3.33 protest. I recognise failure when I see it. I don't see it at Burnley. But I do see it in the attitudes of some impatient, impractical supporters.

We'd had a ten-day break because of a postponed game at Portsmouth. Paul Cook already knew he had played his last game for Burnley. Out of contract and now with an ankle in plaster, he faced that time that comes to all footballers, the unknown, uncertainty, the old question, just what do I do next? Like Tony Livesey, in the press he defended Stan and his record.

Cookie wasn't the only one worried about the future. Clubs were still reeling from the ITV disaster and desperately pulling in their horns. One chairman warned his players 'to brush up on their dustman's skills'. It was thought that 800 players would be looking for work. Every Sunderland player, for example, was on the transfer list.

We didn't do much to help Stan, or soothe supporters, in the next game. It was Burnley 4 Watford 7. SEVEN. Not since the days of Queen Victoria had Burnley ever let seven goals in at Turf Moor. Goalkeeper Marlon Beresford was shamefully barracked. Cries of 'Super Glen' rang round the ground. It was the first game Watford had won since they had beaten us in the quarter-final. Gareth Taylor scored a hat-trick and still lost. The crowd at the end didn't know whether to laugh, cry, boo, or just shake their heads in disbelief.

The big question was, if Gillingham got four, Reading got five, Rotherham got six, and Watford got seven, how many would Preston get in the next game? Poor Burnley fan Paul Johnson drove from Essex a couple of hundred miles to see his team play, saw them lose 7-4, drove 200 miles all the way back, and had a puncture 11 miles from home.

Astonishingly we won 2-0. Fans turned up wondering what to expect. But the gloom was lifted. A ray of hope appeared. The squad was decimated and had three kids on the bench but pulled off the win. In the Kettledrum pub, Stan's local, the landlord was telling folks that Stan had come in with a headache after the Watford game, he'd had so many season tickets thrown at him.

We flew to Norwich on a plane funded by the supporters who accompanied us. They joked with us that for the same price they could have had a weekend in New York or a week in Corfu. We flew from a small airport at Warton near Blackpool. Stan had his usual fag outside reception. All of us, players and supporters, mingled in the tiny departure lounge. This was the weekend when we might have been playing in the FA Cup semi-finals but you get over it and move on. A short flight and a bit of breakfast, two sausages springs to mind, and thinking we were going to land in a field full of turkeys. But no, it was the field next to the airport. Flying was a bit of a novelty for us. 'We can pretend we're in Europe,' somebody shouted.

The feelings after the game have been expressed in the opening pages of this book. Suffice it to say here, we lost, and that sometimes there is the unwritten law that the home side wins simply because they are the home side. This was just such a day. Sometimes you come back from a game and there's not much said, not many laughs; the season is clearly winding down and you can't wait for the summer to come and a chance to refresh and then start all over again. It's also a time to worry whether you will be offered a new contract if it is running out. Something like half of us limped back on to the plane, we'd been whacked and kicked around good and hard on a day of stifling heat when the sweat poured off us.

We lost away at Portsmouth next as well. As we approached the stadium you were hit by the graffiti. I never knew there were so many ways to spray and decorate the word fuck. Inside, the ground was a bit of a time warp and our fans were at the uncovered end, on fortunately, a dry night. Yet again we looked at the vast numbers of them who filled the away end. You could only marvel at the lengths they travelled and the money they spent, even to distant games where there was nothing to play for. We earned their support on this occasion despite losing 1-0 to the side that would be promoted. For Portsmouth it was a night of triumph and celebration whilst we were just the sacrificial lambs. It was an overnight coach journey home, long, monotonous, endless motorways, when all you want is to get home. Who says football is glamorous when there are downsides such as trying without success to doze on a long coach journey, after yet another defeat, at the end of a season ending so poorly? Living the dream this was not.

This was a time when the leagues were not really awash with French Africans with their exotic names. Yes, there were overseas players but nothing like the numbers there are today. Gillingham came, though, with Nyron Nosworthy, Mamady Sidibe, Akwasi Edusei, and Jones Awuah. We had Dean West. Astonishingly with almost a scratch side, we won 2-0 with Gareth Taylor scoring a goal like no other he had ever scored. Gareth was so good with his head he could put spin on his headers. Goals with his feet were rare. This one was the rarest of all for him, a volley. And a volley that was accurate. It was unheard of. His last one had gone over the stand at Norwich. This one took him so much by surprise it took him several minutes to recover. He actually ran to the touchline to show Sam Ellis his successful foot and boot. And Graham Branch, he had once been the target of crowd disapproval but now at centre-back he was majestic. When he was named most improved player of the year we were gobsmacked. He was 31. In this game he was renamed Kaiser Branchenbauer, a far cry from the names he was called a couple of years earlier.

Gazza, by the way, was now in an Arizona rehab centre, as we proceeded to lose the final three games of the season. It might not have mattered too much except to depress supporters even more and to make us even more eager to head for the summer break. But one of those defeats was a shocker. Before that, though, the club announced the retirements of Paul Cook and Andy Payton. They would go their different ways and Andy would experience all the downsides of leaving the game over the next few years, before his impressive recovery. Paul is now ex-manager of Wigan Athletic. In some controversial manoeuvring with Far Eastern owners, Wigan went into administration when by all accounts they had no need to.

The penultimate game: Burnley 2 Sheffield Wednesday 7. SEVEN. 'Sufferance is the badge of all our tribe,' wrote Will Shakespeare. The Claret tribe certainly suffered that afternoon as they had done on several previous Saturday afternoons. I was missing (thank goodness) from this game along with several other regulars. The goals-against column was 89 by the end of the season, needless to say the worst in the division, but there was little thought that a side already relegated would slam another seven past us. Football fans can be cruel. They joked we had the defence of a pub team. Others replied that a pub team was better organised.

Stan was blunt as ever and said he couldn't wait for the summer to change things. He said he'd known for some time those he wanted to get rid of and those he wanted to keep. Those at the end of their contracts shivered a little more at this ominous news. Gordon Armstrong was another one. I still had a year left on mine and was playing reasonably well. There was no reason to suppose that I wouldn't be offered another one in a few months' time. Before the game Paul Cook and Andy Payton came out and waved their goodbyes to the crowd. It was emotional. Payts had saved our season with his goals during the Waddle reign.

Cook always looks back on his time at Burnley with gratitude. 'Burnley saved my career. I wasn't going anywhere at the time and all of a sudden, I was 32. Everyone got on so well, there were no cliques, we enjoyed each other's company and there was laughter around the training ground. You couldn't wait to go into training with the banter and the good runs of form. We all got on so well and we all loved our football. And Stan knew how to get the best out of everyone. He was great and his man management was second to none. If you worked for him and gave the best for him, then he would give you the best of him.'

'The end of the season can't come quick enough,' the gaffer announced. He wasn't the only one thinking that.

The game itself was described as a banquet of goals, a feast of football, a harvest of clangers, unfortunately all at the wrong end of Turf Moor. The goalmouths were a sea of sand reminiscent of Blackpool Beach so that when one shot hit a divot and literally sprang up in the air it took Nik the Greek by surprise. Nik was another one on his way at the end of the season. Remember, Sheffield Wednesday were a side already relegated and they went on and on scoring, with their packed fans in the away end singing and roaring like they'd won the cup. I have half a memory they were singing 'Always Look on the Bright Side of Life'. Burnley fans were noticeably quiet. There was a certain novelty value to Burnley 4 Watford 7, but this one was just a sad way to end the season at home. Supporters, websites, message boards, people in the pubs, people in town, were just numbed.

It just so happened the awards night held by the supporters was just a few nights later. We'd just lost 7-2 at home and we had to attend an awards night, the last place you wanted to be. You felt embarrassed and needed a thick skin to attend with a smile but fans still wanted pictures and autographs. Gareth Taylor swept the board this time. At the last one it was me that had collected trophy after trophy at the end of a season where we'd done well, so it meant something.

I can't say it often enough, that players don't deliberately have a bad day. We all have them whether you're a teacher, plumber or a footballer. But it must be the only occupation where you have 15,000 people watching and criticising. Think about that for a minute. That is Pressure with a capital P. And yet we have to shrug it off and go out and perform. It's a heavy burden especially when you are going through a rough patch and confidence is low. When confidence is high you do the ambitious pass, take a shot when you get the chance and rip into tackles. When it's low you make the safe pass, you pass instead of shooting. And something else at Burnley; this is a club with a big history and some wonderful teams. Supporters remember them and make comparisons. The history of the club can be a burden. We have the same hang-ups and problems as anybody else. A bad night's sleep, a toddler that is up all night, toothache even, mortgages obviously and bills to pay. We worry just like anyone else in our daily lives. And yet the word 'footballer' gives us an image that we are somehow different, that we are fair game. But, do I stand behind the bloke mending my guttering yelling abuse at him?

You do worry. You worry that an injury can end your career and then what do you do? Overnight, your livelihood is gone. It happened to Frank Casper's son Chris. A dreadful injury at Reading. Career over.

The final game bordered on the meaningless. We lost 2-1 at Wimbledon. Wimbledon had no home of their own back then so we played at Crystal Palace in front of under 2,000 fans. Vast empty spaces, almost silent terraces, the perfect epitaph for a strange, strange season that we couldn't wait to end, but which had included the two memorable games against Spurs and Fulham. It was the final game for Steve Davis, now plagued by injuries: the skipper, the rock, a superb centre-half, cool under pressure, elegant and unruffled, scorer of so many outstanding headed goals, always seemed to have control and time and space; a great career coming to an end although he would soldier on at other smaller clubs for a while, and then return to Burnley as a coach with the next manager.

That summer, 13 players left Burnley, seven of them having been the backbone of the team over the last few seasons. Some of them were good friends and remain so to this day. But others you say goodbye and know that's the last you'll see of them. Stan's list included both goalkeepers; who would he bring in, we wondered.

There are always players who continue to live in the Burnley area, myself included. Others still here are Vince Overson, Chris Brass, Andy Payton, Steve Davis and Jamie Hoyland. Add to those all the players from the 70s and 80s who are still here. It's that kind of place.

It's changed during the 20 years or so I have been here. When I first arrived, you could certainly say it was a grim and almost derelict place, neglected by the government, but now much of it has been rejuvenated and huge areas of the town renovated. OK, there are still social problems of need and petty crime and it carries a stereotype view to this day of cloth caps and cobbled terraced streets. You could say the town itself isn't a pretty picture-postcard place but the surrounding area, hills and uplands and moors are beautiful. There are plenty of fine, attractive places, tiny villages, hamlets and narrow valleys filled with woodlands and streams. The

Trough of Bowland, Pendle witch country, the Dales and Settle are not far away; Clitheroe and Skipton are close by. But sadly, when a TV company comes to film, they still look for mill chimneys, empty properties, and the shabbier streets. It's a few years ago but when Ian Wright arrived, they found two blokes with cloth caps and whippets to interview. Priceless.

'Would the real Burnley please stand up?' That was the title of one piece written about us and who could argue with it at the end of the strangest season. 'Seesaw Season' was another. I certainly came in for a bit of criticism. Inconsistent, not the standards of the season when he was player of the year. But then this had been a season of so many forced changes to the side and a few players not at their best in several games. And we go back to that same thing: players worried about what the new season would bring, a new contract or not. Of course, it has its effect. Fans were hugely critical of Nik the Greek after the Sheffield Wednesday drubbing, even accusing him of faking an injury so he could leave the pitch.

Whilst all this was going on, the town was in the news because of the success of the BNP in the local council elections. It was headline news. The British National Party was a far-right, almost fascist group. Mention the name of the club, and the BNP successes were inevitably mentioned in the same article or news item. In its simplest terms, ordinary people were fed up with the minority groups getting the regeneration and Lottery money. The backlash was voting for the BNP.

'Eight seats for the BNP,' screamed the headline in the local paper. The BBC must have known what was coming as it announced the results from the Turf Moor Leisure Centre of all places. 'And now over to Turf Moor,' announced TV commentators more than once in the evening. It was sad to see Burnley now labelled as a racist town but racism was not the sole reason for the voting. It was very much a protest vote against a poorly functioning town council. But it was sad to see the club tarnished and the town seen as the BNP capital of the country. Now, 17 years on, the BNP has vanished from the town.

The season ended. No illness recurrence, no relapses. Half the established team had gone. Robbie Blake was wondering if he'd be sold to Wigan. Gareth Taylor wondered if he'd be sold to Nottingham Forest. We'd no idea if Glen Little would come back or if Graham Branch would stay. We had finished the season on such a low, we now had no goalkeeper, no money and disgruntled fans.

But apart from that …

Chapter 17

WINNING AND ALL GOOD THINGS

IT WAS my father's funeral on a cold January day of wind and rain. All good things for him had ended a while ago with the onset of dementia. For me it was a time to remember how he had only come into my life when I was 11, even though he was my real father. But he was a good man. He was supportive and there to drive me up to Burnley when I needed him; and until the dementia curse ended any normal life, he was proud of me. He'd been a county level footballer himself, another Spurs fan, and he and mum would come up to London to see me play when they could. The family that gathered together included a brother I hadn't seen for ten years; this was our day of family thanksgiving that his awful illness was over. You remember the good things, not the shell of a man who lay in his bed totally unaware of what was going on around him, or who was in the room.

All good things come to an end as the saying goes; and for me and Stan Ternent, this 2003/04 season was the one when all good things certainly did come to an end. There was no success, no cup runs, no money, and certainly nothing to write home about. It was a season of incessant struggle and a tale of just scraping along. But Stan would say it was his greatest achievement.

Much has always been said of the Orient Season when Burnley nearly went out of the league in 1987 and the season before that when Burnley were close to insolvency. In 2009 administration was avoided only when the team were promoted to the Premier League. But the final Stan Ternent season deserves special mention for the way in which the place in the Championship was saved. It seems to me it receives few mentions in the great scheme of things. Supporter Andrew Firmin wrote:

> This was, I suppose, a season which was always going to be about the end. All season long, the question was whether, come May, we'd be stopping up or going down. I always felt it might be tight. Coming into the season, I was prepared to define survival as success; failure would be relegation. And, as it turned out, it was about the end. We did stay up – just. And the season was defined by the way it ended. It ended with the end of an era. I do say in football it's always the end of an era somewhere, but here was one of the more significant ones. After six years, Stan was no longer our man.

Supporters can look at wins from any season and say that was a key win, or this one was massive. They talk about Wade Elliott's goal at Wembley or Martin Patterson at Reading and then think of the wins on those days and argue that these were two of the biggest wins ever. But without the wins in season 2003/04, and there weren't many, there wouldn't have been wins at Reading or Wembley. And there were two in particular at the dreg-end of the season, that saved the club and the place in the Championship.

At the end of August, Burnley were in the bottom three but then somehow scraped clear. From the mid-point of the season Burnley flirted with the bottom three, never actually in there but were hovering on occasions just one place above. Those seventh spot places we finished with a couple of seasons earlier seemed like the distant past.

Two wins in the final four games were crucial with Graham Branch the unlikely hero. Before those there was an amazing win at Bradford with a last-minute goal, and when keeper Brian Jensen had the game of a lifetime. Prior to that, fans chewed fingernails and feared the worst. I'd played my part in the season in 33 of the games but the end was approaching for both me and the gaffer, although neither of us had any idea.

With a week of the season remaining, the chairman informed Stan that his contract would not be renewed. In the meantime, mine was running out with me hoping, if not assuming, there would be an extension. I was approaching that moment that comes to all footballers when they ask, what's going to happen to me? What do I do next? But I was only 28. Plenty of life left in me even if the injuries did interfere every now and then. I've said it many times, fans have no idea of the number of games that you play when not fully fit and, in this season, it was more often than not. But you are picked so you play. Fans demand that you give 100 per cent; on some days you just can't. The critics are then out in force.

A 6-1 defeat away at Ipswich was maybe the lowest point; they had scored five before half-time. It's a long way to get back to Burnley with no fast, direct route until you hit the motorways halfway home. A silent coach, the half-light, feeble attempts at conversation until you can nod off. It's no bundle of laughs being a footballer on a night like that. And the last thing you want is to meet a supporter the next day. Wandering round Tesco is not the best idea.

Today you look back at this game and realise it was an example of how clubs were getting away with going into administration without any penalty. Ipswich back then cleared their debts at a stroke, local businesses lost out badly, and they were not the only ones. Leicester

City did just the same. Ipswich even poached Burnley player Drissa Diallo, being able to offer him better wages. It was wrong. Today clubs cannot get away with this without suffering points deductions that can easily result in relegation. Administration is now a last desperate resort.

With no goalkeeper on the books Stan had signed a giant of a bloke called Brian Jensen from West Brom. They called him the Beast down there and it was easy to see why. The jury was out on him for months, brilliant one minute, less than brilliant the next. But his game at Bradford was one of the best ever with their manager Bryan Robson saying he had been world class. Over the next ten years he had a great career at Burnley, and was part of the Owen Coyle promotion team to the Premier League. No one will ever forget his penalty saves in a League Cup game at Chelsea at a time when Chelsea were near invincible; yet were knocked out of the League Cup on their own ground by Burnley who were still a Championship side.

A huge miss was big Gareth Taylor and his golden bonce when he was sold to Nottingham Forest for £500,000, but he had to go. The chairman or the gaffer, I forget which, said it was either that or the club faced possible administration. The comings and goings were so frequent that we had a new revolving door fitted. Following the exodus at the end of the previous season, King Arthur was shipped out to QPR, more of a liability than ever now that his first impressive season was behind him. Glen Little was loaned to Bolton Wanderers to the dismay of fans, but then came back again. In came David May and Luke Chadwick, both ex-Manchester United. A sprinkling of loans who barely featured made up the numbers, but of the total squad, probably only 14 could be described as regulars.

The make do and mend nature of this season was illustrated beautifully by the signing of Dele Adebola towards the end in an attempt to fix the absence of a big target man. Dele was a man-mountain, tall and muscular. He had to duck to get under any doorway, but he wasn't the answer. If I remember rightly, he wasn't fit when he arrived but Stan used him like he used me, on the bench when he shouldn't have been, because he wasn't fit. But with Dele it backfired spectacularly in one of the end games at home against Watford. Stan was banned from the touchline and was sitting up in the stands but sent the message that Dele should go on. Dele refused and we had one of Stan's minions running into the stand to ask Stan what to do. Total confusion was an understatement with one of the assistants running back and forth, up and down the stairs, like a madman. With Dele being something like 6ft 6in and built like the proverbial outdoor toilet facility, he was not a man to argue with. Watford won, by the way.

Somebody remarked that 'no stone was unturned to improve the squad cheaply'. But still we limped along and scraped results here and there. You could say the same applies today with Burnley trying to compete in the Premier League without spending silly money.

Pre-season was in the Isle of Man again. Does that count as an overseas trip? Stan singled me out for the hairdryer after a 4-1 defeat to Wrexham. He was furious and pointed the finger at me. 'There were some players tonight who didn't put out which disappoints me. But they won't play, it's as simple as that. They didn't put out and they're having a laugh so I'll get other players in. Paul Weller wasn't putting out for me so I took him off. He was nowhere near, miles off the pace and if he doesn't shape up, he won't play. At the moment it's a comfort zone for them because they don't have competition for places.'

Hah, always nice to get an individual mention. I'd only been whacked in the game before and bits of me could hardly move. Scapegoat came to mind. Nice to beat Leeds 4-2 at Turf Moor in another pre-season friendly, although if memory serves 'friendly' was hardly the best description.

It was the end of August before there was a league win although there had been a League Cup win away at Chesterfield thanks to penalties. 'All the charm of an abattoir,' wrote one fan of the away end, in the London Clarets' magazine. But the Gillingham win down in Kent was an eye-opener. 'This was a magnificent display featuring swift, incisive and innovative passing, terrific movement, unrelenting competitiveness, robust defending and capable finishing.' At one end was an advertising hoarding for John Weir Funeral Directors. The form we were in, before the game, you could be forgiven for thinking this was not a good omen.

Fans certainly look for omens. One group had a fixation for nuns. If they saw a group of nuns, they expected a draw. If they were able to help them in any way, opening a door for example, it meant a win. Away games were dominated by the search for nuns. The fans were convinced it was working until the day came that they saw a huge group of them at Euston station on their way to the Watford cup game (the fans not the nuns). We all know only too well what happened at Watford on that dismal day. The 2-0 defeat blew their superstition out of the water and the search for nuns ended that day.

'Money, money, money, it's a rich man's world,' says the song. As true then in football as it is now. And Burnley had none. There was one player who came on trial but on realising how poor this club was, upped sticks and left, announcing 'this club has no money'. To help survive the season the begging buckets really were out. The 500 Mile Club was an invitation to supporters to donate £1,000 to ensure that wages would be paid and the club could survive. Each donor would have their names printed into a commemorative shirt and every donor would receive a shirt at the end of the season.

I volunteered, or was I coerced, it's hard to remember, to tramp the streets knocking on doors to try and sell claret and blue bonds. This was a club at that time living from hand to mouth. Fast forward to today and the Premier millions that nestle in the club's bank account, although much of it goes out as fast as it comes in. I'll say it again, the gaffer and his small squad worked miracles in 2003/04. I walked around the Stoops Estate, one of the poorest areas of Burnley, knocking on doors with one of the agents. Some of them hadn't got two pennies to rub together, yet here we were asking them to stump up a quid a time, or to become regular subscribers. They came to the door when we knocked because they could see the Sky cameras that followed us around, otherwise they'd have ignored us, probably thinking we were debt collectors. 'What am I doing here?' I thought, getting money from people who had none. I only did it the once: it was enough.

Chairman Barry Kilby, it was reported, had put £6m of his money in. He was probably on pins wondering if the Gareth Taylor sale would go through since Gareth had received a nasty poke in the eye during the Leeds friendly that put him out of action for weeks with fears that there was serious eye damage. You could imagine the chairman muttering a resounding 'phew' when he recovered and the sale went through.

Come December and there were wild reports that the gaffer had stormed off and handed in his resignation. Sky Sports announced that he had either resigned or been sacked after a ludicrous 5-3 defeat away at Preston. In the absence of derby games against Blackburn Rovers, Preston becomes the substitute game and this one was a horror. They had this player called Ricardo Fuller, a tall, Jamaican, gangling but skilful and powerful centre forward who always seemed to terrorise Burnley and inspire a degree of dislike amongst Burnley supporters that was far and away above any normal level of antagonism. His disciplinary record was far from perfect but that was down, I suppose, to the edge in his game. Horrible to play against, but you wouldn't mind him in your own side.

It was one of those daft games that you lose 5-3 but could easily have won 5-3. Glen missed a sitter, the Beast had a mare of a game, and Fuller was unplayable: he might even have scored three of the Preston goals. When last I heard he was still playing for Nantwich, nearly 20 years since he first played for Crystal Palace. Stan Ternent was incandescent in the dressing room. 'We should have scored ten,' he said. 'They should never have scored four of their goals.' Poor old Beast was singled out for public hanging and then Stan denied all stories that he was quitting, declaring he would never let the chairman down, never leave the club in the lurch. If the board wanted him to leave then he would do. That, alas, was prophetic enough. Karma came in the return drawn game at Turf Moor when Fuller was eventually sent off for one foul too many, at the end of an afternoon filled with them. It had to be him that fell in the box to earn Preston a penalty from which they duly scored, and then somehow proceeded to avoid red cards until at last in stoppage time out came the card, ironically for something that none of us saw.

To add to the gloom the club's chief exec announced that the club was running out of cash reserves and was allegedly losing £12,000 a week. The buckets were out again. The gaffer kept things going, juggling the players, getting us to play when not fully fit, papering over the cracks, geeing us up, flogging us publicly, tearing his hair out at some of the defeats, probably as surprised and relieved as us at some of the wins when they came.

There was no win at Millwall in the FA Cup. The chairman and bank manager were praying for a cup run but it ended at The Den and I was sent off for good measure. This was a horrible, ugly game in a horrible atmosphere filled with abuse and acrimony, 'a bare-knuckle encounter', wrote supporter Tim Quelch in the London Clarets diary. Dennis Wise, another loveable player who knew full well how to wind people up, provoked me into a stupid act of retaliation so that I was sent off. He did something that annoyed me, maybe it was a stamp, so I pushed him. That's all, just a little push in the chest, not even strong enough to push over a three-year-old. But down he went as if he'd been hit by a ten-ton truck. Fans suggested afterwards that if I was going to be sent off, I might as well have whacked him good and proper with a decent right-hander. The referee was close by and fell for it so off I went. The match report related that Wise did a bit of kicking and then concentrated on going to ground whenever a Burnley player went near him. 'For play-acting and gobbing he couldn't be beaten,' wrote Andrew Firmin. All's fair in love and war and on a football field, the latter as long as the referee doesn't see it. If he doesn't see it, it isn't a foul, is the maxim. But in this game, we decided that it was Dennis Wise doing most of the refereeing, which as he was player-manager, probably gave him more respectability in the real ref's eyes. The whole thing left a nasty taste though, especially the incessant booing of Mo Camara and you couldn't help wonder if there was something racist in this. The game was lost 1-0 and that was that for another year.

Despite all his antics and skill at winding people up, you couldn't dislike Dennis, unlike Robbie Savage. I couldn't stand him; he was gobby and annoying and had that hair that you just wanted to pull as hard as you could as you ran past him. Maybe the only other one was Andy Gray at Crystal Palace but that was because he put his studs right through my shin guard in one game. His name went into my memory bank with me thinking, right, I'll get you back the next game. I don't think I did.

The league game down there at Millwall was only two weeks later and this time the racism row really did blow up. 'An arrogant chairman, repulsive fans and an obnoxious manager,' one report began. It might have been something to do with us not being able to beat them and being knocked out of the cup by them. Apart from that they seemed OK …

The gaffer was adamant that Mo Camara was targeted again and this time there was mention of monkey chants. Millwall was infamous back then and racism was still rampant in football. Even today it has not gone away. The row grew and grew involving Alastair Campbell, who wrote a long piece in *The Times*, and both chairmen, Barry Kilby of Burnley and Theo Paphitis of Millwall, who denied the whole thing. Paphitis was outraged by the accusations and the article. Stan had said that the racists should be locked up, that Paphitis had his head in the sand, and that Millwall was a BNP area. Paphitis replied that the comments were beneath contempt and had a real go at Stan.

'What does he know? I doubt if he knows what BNP stands for. He probably read it on the back of a cornflakes packet.' Nor did Campbell escape the wrath of his pen, referring to his dodgy dossier in *The Times*. 'I think there is a village somewhere missing a fool and I know where he is.'

Eventually it all blew over with no real evidence or witnesses to say there had been clear racist monkey noises. We lost, by the way, 2-0.

Stan thought a break would do us good, take some of the pressure off, so what a rare treat Marbella was, but what a fuss it caused: a storm in a teacup. A few days in the sun, blue skies, recharge batteries. Marbella: whenever did we get taken to such a sunny place, a step up from the Isle of Man? The row escalated: who had paid for it, how could the club afford it, the club was skint, fans had been throwing their coins in collection buckets. It was a disgrace. 'Were the players taking wage cuts to help the club? No,' said the angry fans, they were swanning off to Marbella for a jolly. Fans' message boards were melting with indignation. The CEO told people it was a private donor, an anonymous benefactor but fans were sceptical and reminded him that only days earlier he had been expressing concern that the club would be unable to meet the March wage bill.

'But it will do them good,' was the other side of the argument. 'They're facing possible relegation, they can do with a break, they'll come back refreshed for the tough games coming up.' And we promptly lost 4-0 to Coventry with a performance so limp that it had fans calling for our heads. Stan had this expression 'throw one in', that he used for any weak capitulation, and this was just such a game.

'We are back to where we were six years ago and I feel sorry for the fans who paid to watch this.'

The rage flared up again about the trip to Marbella when club staff were invited to take voluntary redundancy because the finances were so bad. When Glen Little in the local press spilled the beans about our little break, the hackles rose again at the descriptions of running on the beach, relaxing by the pool in 75 degrees, a bit of golf and then a nice meal in the evening.

The gaffer explained that we the players had paid for it out of the players' cash pool that accumulates during a season from fines, and a mystery benefactor had helped us out. No one seemed to believe any of this.

The back end of March: ten games remained and there were real worries that relegation loomed. The gaffer announced we needed to win four games. One of them was away at Bradford, one of those brilliant, dramatic results that supporters remember for a long time. Bradford were in a worse state than us financially, with things so bad they could not afford to print advance tickets so it was a pay at the gate free-for-all. It was chaos at the gates with long queues and turnstiles without enough coins to give as change. Bradford is only a spit from Burnley so it was almost a derby and Burnley hadn't won away from home for six months. They might grumble but when the chips are down Burnley fans turn out in force to support the team when the occasion demands. They were there at Bradford in their thousands and one of them was Julian Booth. I've said before, this book is not just a collection of match reports, but this critical game merits coverage. For many people it was the result that started the collection of four crucial wins that saved the season.

> This was one of those occasions when the result was everything. The collecting of any points is all we should care about. At any other time of this campaign this performance itself would have been torn to shreds by the press, but now it is praised as a battling result against all the odds. It was a means to an end, the end being First Division safety. This was much more than the Clarets' first away win since September, it was a shot in the arm that helped us restore some belief and that clawed Burnley out of a perilous position in the relegation drop-zone. This is a start and with five out of the eight remaining games at Turf Moor, there has to be a chance that survival isn't the eighth wonder of the world.
>
> No wins in six games and a barren spell of six months without an away win did not inspire hope. Then from everywhere came the massed Clarets and roared their side to victory. But what an inept decision to make it a pay on the day policy, madness. At no time did the police take control of the situation as people struggled to get in. What would Justice Taylor have made of the debacle, only a miracle saved these stewards from causing a disaster. The inept stewarding continued inside when Burnley fans were ejected for reacting to taunting from Bradford fans. They paid again and came back in. Was this a cunning plan to swell the empty bank balance of this club?
>
> The game started at a pace and it was Bradford having most of the possession in this fiery War of the Roses clash. The ball found its way to Little on the right wing, his defence-splitting pass was received by Blake who drilled the ball into the top right-hand corner of the net. It was his

twentieth goal of the season and his third in three games against his former club. The finish was that of a man in form and it sent the Burnley fans crazy.

Was this the day that our luck would change, the day we were the team with all the good fortune? That rosy picture was shattered when ten minutes later Cadamarteri ghosted past West and side-footed the ball past Jensen. Bradford started the second half like a bear with a sore head, the half-time talk by Bryan Robson still ringing in their ears. His rallying cry of four home wins out of four offered Bradford a slim chance of survival. But this was the game when Brian Jensen showed us that he is not a bad goalkeeper when he wants to be.

[Julian describes three wonderful saves in great detail; suffice it to say they were match-winning stunning saves. Strikers get the glory for their goals and we forgive them their misses. We expect goalkeepers to make saves but their clangers are remembered. In this game, Jensen was a giant.]

Just when you feared the worst Burnley came back into the match. It seemed only the ineptitude of the officials could rob us of three points. David May, unmarked, slammed the ball into the back of the net to put us ahead. His run seemed to be timed to perfection but he was adjudged offside. Passions were high and May couldn't leave it alone and was booked for dissent.

And so, the game seemed to be heading for a draw, and then it happened. We had just entered stoppage time when a hopeful ball into the box by Grant found its way to Little. He returned it back into the middle where a mass of players waited. Little Ian Moore jumped above the admiring

> defence to loop his header slowly towards the far corner. It all happened so fast but then the ball took an eternity to drop into the back of the net. Frankly I have no idea what happened in the last three minutes, there was so much pandemonium as the travelling Burnley fans celebrated this goal with uncontrolled rapture. All I do know is that I floated out of the ground in a wave of disbelief.
>
> A lot more work has to be done and let's just hope we can get the points in the bag and breathe a sigh of relief in the summer.

It's a game I remember well; I only played the last 20 minutes but this was a result you could never have envisaged with just a couple of minutes to go. Of course, there is always the chance of a nicked goal and with Brian Jensen making such saves, world-class said manager Robson, you dig in and keep going.

The three points lifted Burnley to 19th place, but with Bradford in danger of liquidation we could easily have seen the six points we had taken off them wiped off the records and that would have put us well back into the bottom three. At least 3,500 Burnley fans swelled their bank account and Bradford stayed in business. Surprise, surprise, the next game, at home was lost, another of those silly games with a daft scoreline of 5-3. We were good at letting fives in.

It was against Norwich and reporter Tony Francis was there. He mentioned that we were just two points above Derby and the red relegation line. After the game, standing in a crowded shelter on the station platform with rain dripping down their necks, waiting for his train to Preston, he had met supporter Douglas Alderson who informed him that the game was now all about money and Burnley just couldn't compete. He'd been watching Burnley for 73 years but he only looked about 55, wrote Francis. Douglas explained that his fine complexion was down to ginseng tablets and romantic sex. Football provides such lovely stories.

'We used to play total football,' he went on. 'Now it's total bollocks,' said another ageing supporter next to them.

A mention on *Coronation Street* was always a possibility at this time. The scriptwriter was a guy called Peter Whalley, a season ticket holder, maybe he still is, who had fun naming some of the characters in the street after his favourite Burnley players. His favourite player was Robbie Blake and apparently, he used a few names for some of the minor characters who appeared briefly, like police officers or shop customers. He could definitely have used Paul Cook's name for a bookie maybe. That's what we called him, Cookie the bookie. Maybe I'm in some long-forgotten episode from 20 years ago: Mr Weller, the lollipop man. When he was stuck for a name, he just thought of our previous game and who had played.

Another win lifted the gloom, another defeat and the gloom returned. The latter was a home game with hopes if not expectations of a win that would maybe make Burnley safe for another season. Another injury for me, this time, hamstring. Now there were just five games left and two wins were essential, and the club was running out of players. The squad was as threadbare as it had ever been. The lumbering, half-fit Adebola was by now drafted in along with the old warrior Lenny Johnrose into a situation that was both precarious and desperate. Other teams around us were winning.

But cometh the hour cometh the man, in this case Graham Branch, a tall handsome Mr D'Arcy lookalike, frequent butt of the supporters' displeasure in days gone by; now Mr Utility, Mr Dependable, Mr Play Anywhere You Need Me, centre-half, midfield, left-back, and now dashing centre-forward. This has not been a book where I have incessantly recorded that I did this and did that, I haven't filled it with mentions of crosses or passes I made that resulted in goals; it isn't filled with descriptions of any mazy runs, or twisting dribbles I made. But as we tried to ensure safety from relegation I can say that I made the cross that Glen Little knocked down for Branchy to score the all-important first goal against Wimbledon.

What mammoth results these were, the wins against Wimbledon and Derby in the space of just four days with Branchy scoring two of the three goals. The day of the Derby game was gloriously warm, a rare treat for a match at Turf Moor, it's more often horizontal rain or sleet. A crowd of 16,000 turned up for the game that could ensure safety. It was reminiscent of the Plymouth game of '98, one of those last-ditch occasions when the result is everything. It was furious and end to end, a real relegation scrap with all the trimmings. I don't think I ever ran in a game as much as this one, made as many tackles, the classic do-or-die six-pointer. It had been as long ago as August since we had won two in a row but the Branch goal was a classic. He picked up a pass on the left wing and then ran and cut inside, passing the defender as if he wasn't there. He unleashed a shot that curled into the far corner. The crowd went berserk with jubilation and relief. And so did we. Then it was backs to the wall; Jensen made saves, Chaplow cleared off the line, Camara made a last-ditch challenge, the whistle went, we weren't mathematically safe, but relegation was now unlikely.

I would be out of contract in the summer and the gaffer had not had his contract renewed as yet. There was no reason for me to think that huge upheavals and changes were imminent. There was no way that Stan had any intimation of what was to come. In my head there was no reason to think that both of us were now on borrowed time. I was due to be married in the summer, it was reasonable to expect that Stan and I would sit down and talk about a new contract. The bombshell would come after the Rotherham game.

It was a game that was a disaster, a 3-0 defeat, with bickering amongst the players and soft goals, and it is thought now that this was the game when the chairman realised that new management was needed. The gaffer blasted us after the game; maybe we deserved it but the rant may well have been the deciding moment in the chairman's deliberations as to what to do. The end of the line for Stan left several of us needing new contracts. Uncertainty descended like a black cloud. Myself, Dean West, Mark McGregor and David May were in limbo having featured throughout the season.

Football is cruel. Pundits are merciless. Words on a page are heartless as these written about me at the time demonstrated. If I'd read them then, I'd have been hurt, angry even, muttering what do they know? Now, all these years later with the benefit of hindsight and realism, they are true enough I suppose. It takes someone on the outside to see the slowing up, and the diminished sharpness. Fitness is just that bit less, recovery rates are slower, injuries are more frequent. The London Clarets' magazine said of me:

> A good club servant who is now past his best and would benefit from a change or move. It would be interesting to see if he did leave what division his next club would be in. I think it might mean a step down. The days of his pomp backing up Little at wing-back and helping to tear into teams down the right are long gone. He was a particular crowd target and visibly lacking in confidence as a result. In forward positions he often seemed to lack the conviction to attack and tended to hesitate. He clearly has great reserves of tenacity to have returned to playing professional football after a horrendous illness, which I admire, but being dispassionate I think we've got what we can out of him.

It reminds me of when Brian Clough said that if Eddie Gray, ruined by injuries, was a horse, he'd have been shot.

Lacking in confidence? No, I never lacked that. Lacking in conviction? No, I never lacked conviction; so, this critic got those wrong. But yep, along with Glen and Dean West, our best days were over, I guess. That threesome of ours down the right was a treat to watch at its best, we had such a good understanding. Stepping down a level? I didn't yet know it, but that's exactly what happened.

The tears flowed down the gaffer's cheeks at the final game of the season at home to Sunderland, as he paraded around the ground after the 2-1 defeat. But they didn't hide the acrimony at the end of the season between him and the chief exec. Or between him and us. He publicly blasted us after the Rotherham game. The decision not to renew his contract came as a bombshell; despite the struggles and the poor displays and results, nevertheless on a shoestring he had kept the club in the Championship. A cup defeat away at Cheltenham had been critical though. The chairman had made a note of the Cheltenham manager's name, Steve Cotterill.

The Player of the Year Evening was cancelled at short notice. Supporters had been fed up for some time about the poor quality of these events with players almost glued to their tables, and hardly allowed to move around the room and mingle with fans. They sat at a couple of tables and then most left as quickly as they could after the event. The whole evening was embarrassing. As a result, the chief exec Dave Edmundson cancelled the event and promised better in future. It was clear that there was real division between him and the gaffer. The letter that Edmundson sent to supporters' clubs suggested the rift between them. For good measure (or retaliation) Stan then forbade players to present their shirts to kit sponsors and their families.

The news regarding Stan was released before the final Sunderland game and he promised a statement after the game. We all expected it to rip club, board and chairman to shreds. In fact, it didn't. As he progressed around the perimeter, he received wonderful applause and tributes from the crowd. His heart was claret. His life had been Burnley since the day he arrived in the town. The sun shone, 18,000 were there. The result was irrelevant with another season in the division in prospect, but with who in charge? We remembered the good times, the nearness to a top six place, not once but twice, Gazza and Ian Wright, and some wonderful cup wins. Stan had been in charge for six years and none had been dull.

Perhaps it was the warmth of the farewell he received that mellowed any intent on his part to leave with an explosion of anger. When he did speak, he did say it had been a rocky ride but one thing he said was abundantly true; he was leaving the club in a better state than he found it. He found just a little bit of humour as well. 'I'm really pleased we stayed up because, on a lighter note, for staying up if you get the bullet, then for going down there could have been a public execution.'

Speculation about who would replace him moved up several levels. Speculation in my own head about what would happen to me went into overdrive. Any expectation of a new contract, a summer getting ready for a new Championship season and getting really fit, all the anticipation of a couple more years at Turf Moor, went out the window.

And, I was due to get married.

Chapter 18

LIMBO LAND

WE'D SEEN the story in the press of the young Chelsea starlet, one of the youth squad. Out with his girlfriend he'd been robbed of an £8,000 watch. £8,000! The madness of football today. Just 18 years old and buying £8,000 watches. We could only shake our heads. In the language of my era, just an apprentice. I didn't get that in a year at his age.

Life goes on but for some players better than others. For some it is a disaster with emptiness, divorce, loss of investments, addictions, be it gambling or alcohol. Loss of self-esteem is huge, kudos is now just a five-letter word, now you are just an ordinary Joe Soap, suddenly having to stand on your own two feet, trying to settle into a normal life; all take their toll. That time was approaching for me with a grim inevitability.

The gaffer had been dismissed; all we could do was wait to find out what would happen to us when the chairman announced that in view of a new manager's appointment, he could not be offering new contracts. It would be up to the new manager.

Stan's dismissal was a shock. At the end of April, newspaper reports were clearly saying that the chairman was desperate to offer Stan an extension to his contract. And Stan wanted to stay, saying that he would sort things out, including players' contracts which was good news for us, especially me. I expected to be retained with a new contract. All this was just prior to the result at Rotherham. There it was in black and white, with the chairman saying, it was no secret he wanted Stan to remain in charge and they had already held various meetings.

'In my view he is one of the greatest managers this club has ever had,' he said. Just days later he was yesterday's man. So, what happened?

Who knows? Only the chairman and the directors I suppose. Maybe the antipathy between Stan and the CEO Dave Edmundson, nibbling away in the background, played its part. It was no secret they didn't get on and the cancellation of the Awards Night was the symbol of that. When a manager is leaving you might expect some kind of mention; but Edmundson's programme notes for the gaffer's final game against Sunderland contained no mention of Stan. There was no acknowledgement of what he had done for the club during his time. There was no tribute to his feat of achieving a promotion and keeping the club in the Championship. There was just a huge picture of a beaming Edmundson and a few brief words about 'here's to next season'. It was pretty much a waste of a page.

Tony Livesey on the other hand was hugely grateful. He thought it was a hoax when he heard the news. Before Stan arrived, this was a club in chaos, he wrote. And then Stan arrived, 'a whirlwind in white pumps, cajoling, ordering, persuading, begging and demanding performances on the pitch that brought professionalism back to the club. Turf Moor is his spiritual home.'

The gaffer's final programme message was moving. 'I can't quite believe I'm about to take my last walk out of the tunnel as Burnley manager today. I will take a last look at a few familiar places. I will try to take in the amazing atmosphere generated by you the fantastic fans. I will fight, but I can't promise, to keep my emotions in check.

As a kid I dreamed of playing for Burnley in the big league. Lately I felt I could take us there as manager. You know how close we came; two points away in 2001. One goal away in 2002. Now, for me, it's over.' There was more, and all of it came from the heart. Without any doubt, but for the money fiasco caused by the ITV pull-out, he would have done it. Before that, he was the first ever Burnley manager to shell out £1m on a player.

With the Sunderland game out of the way and all of the tears, the dust settled in and around the town. Who would get the job? The names were bandied about; Ronnie Moore, Steve McMahon, Steve Cotterill, Peter Reid, Adrian Heath, Sammy McIlroy, but Brian Flynn was the favourite. Some of these names were just speculation, ways of filling in spaces on a newspaper back page, but Adrian Heath would have suited me fine.

The penultimate game had been at Rotherham and it was a God-awful performance; a chaotic display at that ramshackle ground, with players bickering and squabbling on the pitch. The courses of lives are changed by football results; it changed mine, that's for sure. If the club had already decided to dismiss Stan, this was a result that cemented their decision. Stan was furious with the players after the game but the rant was just another day at the office for us; we were used to them. Of all the results during his six years in charge, and there had been some grim ones, for the gaffer, the Rotherham result was one of the worst. Thankfully we were safe in the division. Against all the odds he had worked his miracle. The Rotherham result was in fact irrelevant.

But as for me, there's a page in the scrapbook with the header 'Claret star feels let down'. Common sense told me that it was over for me but you hang on to the hope that the new manager will keep you on. Dean West was on the way to Lincoln City so he was OK. I was in limbo. I'd given years to the club and battled back from that damned illness. The club was in a tricky position, I knew that, but players just can't sit around waiting. Until the chairman confirmed that it was up to the new manager to sort things out, I thought we might have been given a short-term deal. But no. Without any kind of offer you are out of it, it's over and you have to reach that common-sense but hard decision to move on. There is no part for you, no place, disposable, dispensable; to put it crudely, it's on yer bike. I was just 29 and had to sort myself out. Nobody else does it, it's down to you. At Burnley Football Club my time was up.

The mechanics are simple enough; you return your forms to the PFA saying you have not been offered a new contract and your name is then circulated to other clubs. You have no idea what the response will be, you have no idea if any other club might be interested. Something will turn up, you think; and then you remember you are just one of hundreds up and down the land in the same boat. That's when the doubts begin, that's when the uncertainty hits home; that's when you feel angry and even bitter that your club hasn't stood by you and offered even a three-month contract so that the new manager can assess you properly.

We went through the rest of May and then into June, more limbo, more uncertainty, and don't forget I was getting married in June. I still wasn't fixed up at another club. At a time like this, previous achievements count for nothing. Things go through your head, the times you've played injured or just half fit, and what you see as the ingratitude of others. Do supporters really give a damn? In my case probably not. Glen Little was leaving and fans were truly sad to see him go. But me? Never a fans' favourite, I doubt anyone gave me a second thought. Weller, West, McGregor, May, we were throwaways, our sell-by date had arrived.

Fans have no idea of players' problems, worries, mental states. I loved every minute of it, every minute training, every minute playing, but for some it is torture, some are physically sick. I'm saying this because if supporters knew that some players go through hell, they might be more sympathetic, might be a bit kinder when we depart, might be less abusive when we fluff a pass or miss an open goal. I can tell you the story of a player that didn't achieve much at Burnley but is remembered for one thing, a dreadful miss in a cup game that his side were losing 1-0. In the dying minutes there was the glorious chance of a headed equaliser. The goal gaped. The cross was inch perfect. All he had to do was head it. Just get his head in the way, nothing more needed. And he froze. Chance of a goal gone. Chance of glory gone. Chance of a replay gone. Sadly, it is the one thing he is remembered for at Burnley.

But did fans know of his coping problems? For some players going out on to that pitch, there is real torment. They've lost the will, the confidence and the inclination. This player's career had been ruined by injuries; he'd had a succession of operations over a five-year period. Even in his early twenties breakfast was Ibuprofen and a can of Red Bull. At the age of 26 he could barely get out of bed; it took him ten minutes to get mobile. The grind of football, operations and rehab had taken its toll. But the game was all he knew so he signed for Burnley, and struggled. By the end of his time at Turf Moor the game was a chore, he just wanted to go home, so he went back to Ireland. Psychologically he was wrecked. But not a single supporter would have known this. Imagine being in that state and you go out knowing that there might be 14,000 people watching you, but out he went on to the pitch on the occasions he was selected. And froze when that headed chance arrived.

There's a salutary lesson for all supporters in that little story. Think twice before you give someone hell. Don't forget I was subjected to it several times, on one occasion quite mercilessly, during the Adrian Heath days. Fans can be an unforgiving lot but whereas some players would buckle, that was never in my nature. I just went out there and got on with it. Barracking, abuse and insults you could argue are part of a footballer's lot, but on the occasions that they go way over the top, it is hurtful. More often than not you don't hear them out on the pitch when you are caught up in the game and focussed on one thing only. But suppose you are on the touchline taking a throw-in and the abuse is right behind you and personal.

You could say that back then I was just learning my trade, just 22; you either cope with it or you don't, there's no halfway. There's a bloody-minded streak in me. I coped. And the best way to do that? In one of the next games score the winner in a 1-0 win. Millwall I think that was. 'Paul Beats Boo Boys', was the headline. Those were the days when we played the likes of Stockport County, with no love lost between the two sets of fans. Today Burnley play the likes of Arsenal and Chelsea and Stockport are non-league. How times change.

I doubt tears were shed at my exit, but I'd given everything, never shirked, come back from that horrible time of illness and long recovery; a temporary three-month contract did not seem an unreasonable thing to hope for.

On 1 June the name of the new guy was released. Not Brian Flynn, not Adrian Heath, but Steve Cotterill. We knew nothing about him. Apparently, he was soon to be christened BTMOTP. Best Young Manager Outside the Premiership. By the time his own end came, it hung like an albatross around his neck. We'd wondered and waited for weeks, reports said he was chosen from a final list of nine. He'd done well at Cheltenham but then he'd had something of a chequered time in brief spells at Stoke and Sunderland. But here he was with my career and future in his hands.

He rang me, in early June, on the night before my wedding to say I was not needed. The night before my wedding. It was half-expected but numbing just the same. And the timing – words fail me.

In the media I was described as a free agent. It's a bit more respectable than saying an unemployed, unwanted footballer, a cast-off, a player the club doesn't want. A club or manager needs to gloss things over. He announced he would not stand in the way of the group that was out of contract. Well of course he bloody wouldn't, he didn't want us. It threw the ball back in our court and made it sound that it was he that was in the difficult position. It made it sound as if it was our choice, did we stay or leave. But there was no choice. It was a masterpiece of managerial speak. If we received offers from any other clubs, he would understand if we upped sticks and left. Brilliant: he surely knew full well we wanted to stay and we had been on pins all summer. He announced that out of courtesy he'd spoken to the players affected and called us all. He said he'd told us that if something happened somewhere else and we could get fixed up, we should look after ourselves. It made it sound so reasonable, civilised and humane.

The phone call I got from him simply said: 'Paul, I don't need you here.'

But that's football. It happens to hundreds of us. Except the difference in my case was that it was on the eve of my wedding. Is there any kind way to end a player's time at a club? Not really.

Wedding over and I was still looking for a new contract somewhere. By now there were several options and possibilities but still nothing definite. Chris Brass, former team-mate and same age as me, was astonishingly manager at York City. He'd got Steve Davis there in a player-coach capacity and Chris offered to sign me on at York. Lovely place York but a bit of a drive over from Burnley. Any wages would have gone on buying petrol. Nevertheless, I took up his invitation to train and look after my fitness.

Hindsight, a wonderful thing. There were things I should have done differently. In January of that final season I should have done the sensible thing and had the knee operation that I badly needed. But I didn't. The club on its beam ends, the squad wafer thin, all hands to the pumps; so I decide I'll have the operation in the summer, delay it when I really should have had it done, help the club out, play with a crocked knee, have it drained of fluid before a game, have the cortisone injections. Fans don't know this, do they; they see a player struggling half fit, and don't know why. The condition of the knee is out of sight to them. There was the doc before a game with a big syringe just inside the doorway. Glen used to walk in, look, shake his head and look away.

What an idiot I was, not to have the op when I needed it. That decision, made for the good of the club, as good as ruined my career, playing on when I shouldn't have. It was life-changing, the worst decision I ever made. Back to the idea of an agent. An agent might have said, 'Don't be so stupid, get the operation, the club won't thank you for delaying it.' So, I had a fourth operation on my knee at the end of the season then, and another mistake. I should have insisted on the club assisting me with rehab but I didn't. I did it on my own and at York where the facilities were not good.

'The club won't thank you, this is misplaced loyalty,' an agent might have said; neither chairman nor CEO will show any loyalty to you. And so it proved. Stan knew what I'd done but he was on his way out and hadn't got round to offering me that new contract. He'd already told me the £5,000 I was on would be reduced to £2,000, but I'd have taken it. The club had stayed up by the skin of its teeth, so success for them. But what success for me? None. What thanks for me? None. What recognition? None. Football isn't glamorous for everyone.

There were a few offers to look at but they were teams that wanted to take me on trial. Hang on a minute, I thought, a trial, but they surely know about the number of games I've played, the experience I've got, and I'm not even 30. It came as quite a surprise. Any thoughts of walking straight into another Championship side went out of the window.

The trouble is, if you are released by a club, other clubs are suspicious. They wonder why. Is he crocked? Is he past it? Is he damaged goods? Exactly why has he been released at the grand old age of 29? There must be something wrong with him. So, they offer a trial to suss you out. In the meantime, I was watching those who were still at Turf Moor with just a little envy. Even at this stage I was still so disappointed that Cotterill hadn't offered a contract, since he had taken over the club with just eight professionals. But he intended to bring his own choices in, a manager's prerogative.

It turned out to be Rochdale I joined. They were Fourth Division and perpetual strugglers and had been in the bottom division for as long as anyone could remember. Funnily enough they had a history of hating Burnley with a vengeance dating back to a time when Burnley were one of the top teams and Rochdale fans perceived them as looking down their nose at little Rochdale in their tiny stadium. When both clubs were in the old Fourth Division, Dale fans were over the moon and quite beside themselves on the occasions that they actually beat Burnley. The only good thing about me joining them was it was near to home.

But joining them was only on a trial basis and daft as this sounds, the games I played for them I played for free. This was a club not just skint, but desperately skint. At first over there I trained with the youths to get up to some kind of speed. There was no mention of money until I actually said to them, 'You have no money, do you?' There was a nod and an agreement that they had no money. There was no mention of a contract.

'Well how about I play a game for nothing and you can get a proper look at me?' My proposal was accepted.

One game stretched to something like five games and at the end of that we talked money. 'We can offer you £180 a week.'

£180 a week! It was less than the first ever deals I had had at Burnley ten years earlier. I said nothing, turned and walked out. My heart just wasn't in it.

Perhaps I shouldn't have. In hindsight I could have taken the £180 a week, swallowed my pride, got really fit, got my game back and put myself in the market. But I didn't and even today I regret not doing that. Instead, I was as good as out of the game: my own choice, my own fault, but that didn't stop me from feeling angry and bitter. Annoyed with Kilby and Edmundson at Burnley, annoyed with Cotterill, disappointed with myself. I was not even 30 and could still have had three or four more years in the game.

I say as good as out of the game because I dropped into non-league football, and there followed two games at Leek Town. Just a few hundred spectators and some of them even brought their dog along.

Then there were two games at Stalybridge Celtic. Just what the hell am I doing here, I thought. This was still 2004, only six months earlier I'd been in the Championship at Burnley playing in meaningful games, the last one, the emotional one, in front of 18,000 people. At this point I just felt let down, my football career was over. And it was all I knew. One of hundreds over the years that had been in the same situation, nothing to move straight into, no qualifications, no certificates and at that point no prospects. And newly married.

Being a footballer is not a qualification. It doesn't prepare you for anything else that is 'normal'. Teacher, plumber, electrician, plasterer, doctor, all skills that allow you to move around and get more work, slide into another job somewhere else, the money doesn't suddenly stop: but not the footballer. In no way is being a footballer a proper day's work.

I'm Pisces. 'Meek, mild, timid and placid, not a harmful bone in their body. A tendency to daydream and not face reality. They excel at art, literature, acting or music. They need to toughen up and not dream their lives away. Shy, kind and mysterious.' What a load of rubbish, forgive me for not believing in the stars and horoscopes. Although funnily enough there was one that said I should protect my feet. It didn't mention hamstrings and knees, or bowels.

Next, there came six months doing nothing. Identity gone, I wasn't a footballer anymore, so what was I? At that point nothing. There is a certain image when you can say I am a professional footballer and I play for Burnley. In the Premier League, even more so. Back then the Championship, respectable, impressive even. You are doing what hundreds of other blokes would love to do. People recognise you, at an airport going off on your holidays they'll point to you, even me, not a star, not that well known, but Burnley fans are everywhere.

'Hi Paul, what you doing here?' 'I'm on holiday mate, how you doin'?'

In the supermarket, 'Hey look that's Paul Weller doing his shopping.' They stop for a chat. Jimmy McIlroy always used to say it took him three hours to get around Tesco, he was stopped so often.

Daily routine goes out the window. The anticipation of a new day, the drive to Gawthorpe, changing, out on to the training pitches. The sheer pleasure and joy of doing something you love and actually getting paid for it. Pals and mates at the ground, banter, 'Jesus Glen, where'd you get that shirt?' 'Andy, when you gonna get a decent car?' Jokes, the simple act of getting a shower after training, get all the mud off, warm glow, satisfaction. Somebody's birthday. Cakes. This isn't work. It's a hobby for which you get paid. All I ever wanted to do. Didn't know anything else.

It was my 'happy place'. Jordan North, Radio One DJ, Burnley fan, locked in a box of snakes on *I'm a Celebrity Get Me Out of Here.* Screaming in there, nearly dying, but determined to get the stars that ensured a meal for the group. The lad was terrified. 'Happy place, happy place,' he muttered to get him through the ordeal. 'Turf Moor, Turf Moor … happy place, happy place.' It hit the headlines. Twitter and Facebook went wild. TV crews hit the street outside Turf Moor to ask people what was their happy place. Turf Moor was mine.

A matchday, breakfast, anticipation, the drive into Burnley, arriving at the ground, threading through the small crowd of fans looking for autographs, pictures thrust at you to sign, the same regular faces, the greetings and smiles. 'We gonna win today Paul?'

Down the long corridor to the tiny dressing room. Above our heads the fans in the Cricket Field Stand, we're bang underneath them, we can feel them, sense them, hear them, the stamping feet. And it's the away fans too.

Some players are already in there, one or two just make it in time, the noisy ones, quiet ones, nervous ones, confident ones. On the pitch nerves get the better of some players like Jamie Hoyland and they are actually sick out there. Where's the glamour in that?

The kit hanging in your place, all laid out by the kit man, some of it folded on the chair. Coaching staff geeing us up. Kit on, clothes hanging on the pegs, stamping feet, the sound of studs, the smells of liniment, Vaseline, a last visit to the loo. Ritual backslaps, hugs, handshakes, Stan standing by the door as we file out of the dressing room, the sound of studs louder now, along the corridor, and then a sharp turn down the slope and out on to the turf; we emerge with the away fans directly behind us and can hear the abuse and ribaldry. The home side being spat at. Nice. They've changed it now so that you come out at the corner between two of the stands, home fans on either side.

Run on to the green turf, comrades, all for one and one for all, the roar of the crowd; at the far end facing us, the Bee Hole End with the home fans, to our left the James Hargreaves Stand and the corporate boxes. To the right, the Bob Lord Stand with the directors and the benches for the subs directly in front of it. If you are a sub or management you hear the wisecracks from the Bob Lord crystal clear. The sun in Brian Jensen's eyes.

'Give 'im a bloody cap Ternent.'

Cruel sometimes, personal, insulting, vulgar, crude. Fans can do better than us, they can be a better manager, they know all the answers, they've paid their money, entitled to shout and scream, is what they say.

Let battle commence. The buzz of football, the adrenalin rush, in your bubble, in the zone, nothing else matters for that magic 90 minutes. Even the communal bath that we all crowded into after a game. What a leveller that was. And sometimes you didn't want to know what was in it. Health and Safety would have had a field day. But it was part of the life and now it was over, although I didn't know it at that exact moment.

Now you've to learn a new lifestyle. No need to get up in the morning, no need to watch what you eat, no need to go to bed early, no need to stay in shape. You can get short-tempered, frustrated, you can only read a newspaper once, the TV becomes your friend. If the wife goes out to work, you're on your own, solitary, where's the noise, joking, wisecracks and the busy days you once had? Silence can be deafening. Bills to pay, the mortgage, you've never earned megabucks, there's not much in the bank. Never got my coaching badges, never thought about it, if you're not yet 30, you don't. A father- and mother-in-law wondering how you are going to take care of their daughter.

Luckily, I wasn't a big drinker. Thank goodness I wasn't. That way damnation lies but I can see and understand how so many players spiral downwards when they have finished. Time on their hands and a beer in the fridge, then another and a few weeks later a beer in your hand is the comfort that gets you through a long day. From beer it's on to the real stuff.

Luckily, I wasn't susceptible to depression. At the end of the day I was a 'doer'. I always believed and still do that you get on with things and sort things out. Just do it. I would do, but not yet.

Dean West played nearly 400 league games, including over 100 at Burnley, and then more at non-league level. He was an integral part of the West, Little and Weller right-wing triangle that at its best was a joy to watch. Never one of the highest earners at the club, nevertheless like many players of the era, he earned a tidy wage, £2,000 a week; enough as a Yorkshireman to think he was a millionaire, but nothing like the high wages paid to Glen Little and Robbie Blake. Nor was it enough to live off for the rest of his days. But, with a philosophy of 'every pound's a prisoner' his money did not go to waste.

He is today a good example of a player who managed the transition to a post-football life with some skill. He did this by continuing to play at non-league level for as long as he could until the age of 38, at which point his body told him it was time to stop. That transition he describes today as a kind of slow drip-feed. There was never a time when the football suddenly stopped overnight. There was never a time when the finish resembled the kind of chasm that some players fall into and with nothing to do, lose their money, through failed businesses, or hooked on gambling or drink. It helped him that he was always of the persuasion that money is not there to be squandered. That some do squander it, is a life choice, he feels. It was never his.

His choice, with his wife, a trained nurse who is now a health visitor team leader, was to invest in a children's nursery that they ran for several years. Today he is now a scout for Blackburn Rovers, is paid a retainer and expenses, nothing like enough to live on, but the football connection remains. With that and his wife's salary he has a comfortable life and a place in Spain. Not all footballers fall by the wayside when they finish, and he is a good example although he did find the first two years of not playing tough.

Gareth Taylor became coach of the Under-18s at Manchester City and is now manager of their women's team. He puts his smooth transition down to luck. 'It was difficult initially but I was fortunate to move quickly from playing to coaching, which is probably the next best thing. The major thing I struggled with was feeling low from not exercising but once I started to get back in the gym, I felt much better. I applied for coaching jobs at Manchester City but had some connections there who got me in front of the right people so I was lucky.'

Today bankruptcy and divorce rates are staggering. Studies claim that 33 per cent of footballers are divorced within a year of finishing playing and 40 per cent of players are declared bankrupt within five years of ending their careers. Some of them are big names who have lost phenomenal amounts.

The public might not feel inclined to be sympathetic with footballers who lose their money, gamble, drink, or whose marriages fail. But there is one area that is so often under the radar as far as supporters are concerned and that is the price footballers pay in terms of physical health. It is thought that something like 80 per cent of retired players will suffer from osteoarthritis, a degenerative joint disease. Simply put, it means that thousands of former players will suffer from a crippling condition that will affect their daily lives. Football has brought this affliction on them yet it is not seen as an industrial disability so there are no benefits available.

Currently the focus is on footballers and dementia, the degenerative brain disease linked with repeated heading of a football. There is no agreement on the link between the two; you can suffer from dementia and not be a footballer. But brain surgeons who have undertaken research will say that an affected brain shows the same injuries as those received by a boxer, repeated minor traumas. Over a period of ten years and more the accumulation of all these blows can be catastrophic. Six of the great Burnley team of 1959/60 that won the title ended their days with dementia.

In a feature about Gazza in *The Athletic,* this was written. How many ex-players might identify with it?

'I miss football badly. It was my life. I miss every game. I miss every Saturday. Come 3 o'clock now, I switch off. Because from three o'clock to quarter to five, that was my life you know. I loved it so much.'

The *Daily Mirror,* 20 January 2020, and a big feature about Gazza. I'd seen him up close at Burnley, trained with him, saw his troubles at first hand. Now it was saying he was the new Gazza, happy at last. If he really is, it's taken him a long time. His £20m fortune was gone it said, he wasn't a wine connoisseur, he was a connoisseur of rehabs. Pellets implanted in his stomach made him feel sick if he had more than one glass of wine or beer. But he was finally at peace and loving life again. He'd had so many low spots he'd lost track but the most recent was the accusation of sexually assaulting a woman on a train. He had been cleared but went through hell in the meantime. He'd just had his first holiday in 15 years, in Tenerife. Today he can deal with the intrusions of press and photographers. His behaviour is still obsessive, he says, but the cocaine is done, the drink under control. His humour is intact. He says he calls Harry Redknapp (who he still sees) Gregg the Baker, because he has a finger in so many pies. For ten years he has lived in Bournemouth where he can sit in a seafront café and enjoy a coffee.

My old team-mate Andy Payton was another who suffered badly when his career ended. He has said himself that he struggled and found it so difficult to come to terms with his career being over. He felt he had no future and no identity, felt worthless and depressed, felt he was a has-been and of no value. A recent interview with Andy Jones was telling. You stop being a footballer and some of your friends stop being friends. You realise they were just hangers-on. Everybody is looking and waiting to see what you will do now, without football. The routine you have had for 20 years is over. He'd won the Golden Boot and now it counted for nothing. He'd been with his mates every day and then it all stops. The buzz, the banter is over. You don't keep fit, there's no need. You feel down all the time. There is no point to the day. The abiding emotion is self-pity. Days can be long and empty with nothing to do.

'I'd wander into town and head for a pub. Finished, no good to anyone and I'd drown my sorrows.'

The drinking problems doubled up with gambling. It was a good way to fill the time. As a player, gambling was so easy as another of the players took the bets. It was too easy. There were cards and gambling on the bus and you weren't just putting fivers on. A win at the bookies becomes as good as scoring a goal.

Andy Payton went through some tough times, well documented in and around the Burnley area. He himself asked the graphic question: who wants to know a drunken former footballer? But since then he has dramatically turned his life around and quit the drink and has been teetotal for several years. Plus, he has his coaching badges and works at Burnley College Sports Centre. Somewhere in Burnley there is a green bench in a park that Andy will say was the key to his turnaround. At his lowest point that must have been something like eight years ago, he sat on that bench and thought 'What am I doing here?' It's a familiar question. The realisation hit him that he had to change, had to straighten out his life. Having daughters to care for was a major spur as well. Now, one of them is on the verge of making the breakthrough into professional football.

Peter Swan was another team-mate at Burnley. His book *Confessions of a Lower League Footballer* is a good read. 'Is there life after football,' he asks? He writes about walking away from his last club, York, a man with a past but no idea about his future. He'd played for the last two years in agony most games but kept going as long as he could. His body said, 'no more'. 'But,' he asked, 'if I stop, how do I support my family?'

As a player you kid yourself, he says, that it is never going to end and when you retire there will always be something on the coaching side. You expect the phone will ring with job offers from people you know. The phone doesn't ring. It took a while, but to cut a long story short, Peter is well set up now with media work.

But for many: 'Now those days are gone. It's empty, I'm nothing.' Boxer Mike Tyson said that recently and broke down into tears. The same could be said by many a footballer when the golden age has passed. Arsene Wenger summed it up: 'They lose passion, fame and income at a very young age. To replace that is nearly impossible.' The next time you watch Match of the Day on a Saturday night, statistics indicate that nine of the 22 players you see in any game will be bankrupt and facing financial ruin within five years of retiring.

Where does pride and self-respect go? I was proud to be a footballer. What did I have to be proud of when I finished? Finishing my career in front of a few hundred people at Leek Town. No disrespect to Leek Town and the dedicated people who keep it going, but it was not for me. The oldest cliché in the book, from hero to zero in the space of a few months. One week, people are asking for autographs and now you are yesterday's man. Great times, great experiences, all the good things, the exhilaration of a win, the joy of a dressing room, that sense of purpose and belonging, being valued, wanted, all gone. Psychologists write whole books about all this. And from the club itself, absolutely no aftercare whatsoever. Disposed of like an old settee. But then that's what happens at most clubs. Everton might be the exception.

My old team-mate Graham Branch did not find it easy. 'Tough, like getting out of prison, learning new routines and your friends soon went. Not having any regular income was hard, starting all over again at 36 is just not easy. The banter, the big matches were all gone. I just knew I'd be released by Steve Cotterill as soon as he could when my contract ended. I didn't like him and he knew it. I hated that Cotterill era, he brought players in who changed the whole Burnley dynamic. There was no team like the one we had with Stan; we would have gone to war for each other. Today I run my Football First Academy, coaching kids, loving every minute of it and life is settled and good.'

'Like getting out of prison' might be an odd thing to say, but I think I know what he means. You've had a life where decisions are made for you, organised, regimented, do this, do that, toe the line, do as I say, that kind of thing. Institutionalised almost. But you come out and it can be bewildering unless you have support. And football is infamous for having no support for the leavers.

Luke Chadwick was only at Burnley for one season, on loan from Manchester United. A product of the Manchester United production line under Sir Alex Ferguson, he loved his brief time at Burnley. But like many others, he found it difficult adjusting to not being a player any more.

'I found it massively difficult on leaving. I always thought I'd be fine and as a player gave it little thought. I just assumed I'd stay in the game. But I never had a plan. The loss of identity was hugely difficult, the loss of feeling important. I no longer knew quite where I fitted into life. I did some coaching at Cambridge United with the Under-8s and then the Under-13s but when I moved to the Under-18s I just didn't enjoy it. Fortunately, I had looked after my money and I was in the group that were the last to get a pension at age 35. It was a pension based on what I had paid in as a player, and on good wages at Manchester United, I was able to put quite a lot in. If I had any issues, they were mental, not financial. At the end of the week there was no game, so there was no target to work to. On top of that I lived in a small village where I was known as Luke Chadwick footballer. That recognition was over.

'What happened to me was being able to come to the realisation that I was no longer a professional footballer, and just had to step away from that and accept reality. There comes a time when you just have to be brave enough to step away. So, I'm now involved in the Football Fun Factory. It delivers football fun for boys and girls of all ages and abilities. We have fun camps, inflatables, work at birthday parties and in schools, offer coaching, training, matches, but above all, fun. It's football without pressure. We have all ages, even groups from age two to five, on a soft, friendly, inflatable pitch. It's great and I've found something I love doing.'

Maybe Steven Caldwell, an ex-Burnley player and a key member of the promotion side of 2008/09 can sum it up:

'There will be times when I will be watching a game and I could cry such is the urge to be back out there on the park. I miss the feeling of doubt, the butterflies in the stomach and the elation and comfort of all that going away as the match kicks off. I miss sitting by my locker after a win feeling so satisfied as if nothing else in life matters for that small length of time.'

Chapter 19

LIGHT AT THE END OF THE TUNNEL

WHAT LIFE SKILLS did I have? Football was all I knew and that was the problem. It's a rare footballer that very early on in his career thinks about what to do when he finishes. In fact, there was a time when established players were not encouraged to do this since it took their concentration away from the job in hand, and that was playing football for the club that paid their wages.

To his credit, Stan had taken me aside as early as January in the final season and explained the situation. What you got from Stan was honesty. He told me there would be wage reductions because the finances were so poor, but at least I knew I was in his plans. With that in mind and because we would be getting married in June, the house was put up for sale so that we could downsize to something more affordable.

A new season, but Burnley was over. After the drudgery of Rochdale there was still that glimmer of intent inside me that said I could get fit and try again. Port Vale and from there to Leek Town. But it was hopeless. Gordon Armstrong, who I had played with at Burnley, suggested Stalybridge Celtic. Again, that glimmer of purpose, but it soon evaporated.

Paul Simpson invited me up to Carlisle. The head that said enough is enough, over-ruled by the heart that wanted one last try. How many footballers do the same? A boxer keeps getting knocked down and gets up again. He wants one last fight, convinced he still has the capability. A footballer does the same. I even played a couple of pre-season games and scored in one. But I knew I couldn't do it, couldn't last the distance, couldn't get fit. That last few months, York to Rochdale to Port Vale, Leek Town, Stalybridge and then Carlisle. There's no damned glamour in any of those. It was over.

From a decent final wage to nothing at all coming in. Weeks followed of sitting around thinking what do I do, I need a job. I have to do something. But what? Gizza job Mister. The first-born had arrived, Flynn, and with that the responsibility of needing to do something.

In the big wide world outside nobody would be interested one jot, and why should they? Does anyone give a damn about an unemployed footballer? Footballers don't have the best image. The image is one of overpaid, aloof prima donnas, but that is thanks to just a few of the ones at the top end who flaunt their wealth and live in their big gated mansions. A small number are arrogant, egotistical; sadly, the public makes its opinions based on these few. Unfair. The majority of footballers are at the lower end with a lifestyle simpler than you might think. For some it was a real struggle if they had a family.

The knees were bad. The body said that's enough. Crocked, and not even 30. Osteoarthritis was setting in. Oh, the price you pay for such a fleeting career. If you drive a car into the ground it won't last long. Footballers are the same. I have a knee that today needs replacing but I can't get it done until I'm 50. Osteoarthritis, the curse of the footballer. Cartilage gone, bone scraping on bone. How many of us are there, footballers who walk with difficulty, footballers who in later life need walking aids? Footballers retire sure in the knowledge that injuries will come back to haunt them in later life. Peter Swan has just had a knee replacement operation having reached the age we need to get to. I have to wait.

Many a player will receive a warning in his 30s that he could be in a wheelchair by the time he is 50 if he doesn't stop playing. I am one of hundreds of footballers that today pay the price for that short career. Some can't handle it. I'm one of the lucky ones. Yes, I have osteoarthritis but I can cope and deal with it. Research shows that footballers suffer from this up to 15 years before the average male. It isn't recognised as an industrial illness or disability. But footballers console themselves with the view that it was all worth it for the career while it lasted. We think, well it's just the price we pay for living the life we loved. The games, the goals, the crowds, the acclaim, the fame (for some). We played through injury for managers who simply expected us to play through the pain. At some clubs, players didn't dare admit to anything in case they lost their place in the side. I played at a time when long-term effects were pushed to one side. Osteoarthritis, you never thought it could happen to you and in your early 40s you'd need a new knee. Thirty years ago, the well-being of players was secondary to the needs of the club. Stan Ternent was better than most in that respect, however.

A year ago, the PFA paid for me to have knee examinations, it was clear I'd need a new knee at some stage. They sent me for a consultation and paid the £500 for an MRI scan. The consultant was another £250. He advised me to wear a brace, but it's a half an hour job to get it on. I don't wear it, but there's another five years before I can get the operation so maybe I will need to use it by then. For now, I can still play football once a week with some friends and put up with the soreness afterwards. I can't say it often enough; footballers pay a price.

It's estimated that up to a third of players have undergone surgery since retiring, the vast majority of these for hip and knee replacements. At least a third are on medication to relieve pain that has come from old injuries. Possibly ten per cent are registered disabled. At Burnley as we write this, two players seem bedevilled by injuries, Robbie Brady and Johan Gudmundsson. Supporters lose patience, players even become a figure of fun, the nickname 'sicknote' is attached. End of season and 'sell them' becomes the comment on message boards. But get treatment wrong, bring them back too soon, play with an unhealed injury (how many times did I do that) and a player risks irreparable damage and long-term consequences. Who wants to be disabled at the age of 40? Nobody.

What did I do for the six months that I did nothing? How did I spend those days and hours? Sitting on the sofa watching TV basically. But Zoe was at home and there were two young children to help with. So, there was no moping, no depression, that's just not in my nature. Zoe and the in-laws were always supportive and encouraging. And something to do was just around the corner. I never worried.

The best man at my wedding had been Dean Ramsdale and he knew I was kicking my heels. He was head of the Community arm of the club and told me to come on down and get involved and help out. I did and as far as I remember that must have been in 2006. It was coaching in schools mainly, not five days a week but enough to get me busy again. Vince Overson was head of the Centre of Excellence and got me into that. Suddenly I was working full time, partly for Community and partly for the Centre of Excellence.

My skills outside of football were non-existent and I needed to do something about that. There was the realisation that I needed to learn about how things worked in the real world. I started a computer course one night a week at Burnley College. I did a leadership course one night a week. Completed them both over a year. Local Radio, 2BR, got me involved in Saturday afternoon commentary. I've always had opinions and still do, and never been afraid to express them. From kicking my heels for six months, life had now become busy.

Sunday mornings were games with the Under-9s, Under-10s and Under-11s at Gawthorpe. Nobody really watched you or your progress at that level but as I moved up the age groups, the attention became more focussed with meetings on this kid and that. Opinions became important. And internal politics. People were watching me and my performance as much as the kids. Is he any good? Can he actually coach? And sadly, is he a threat to my job?

I got as far as the Under-15s working with John Francis. He'd been a hero of the promotion era of Jimmy Mullen and a bit of a cult hero at that time. I left after differences with him, and the politics of the situation decreed that it was me that needed to leave. But on the day that I left, I simply moved upwards to another job at Bury.

There is so much that a football club can do for its community. Today at Burnley it is a massive concern with 130 staff and 50 ongoing projects from schools to pensioners, from refugees to the disabled, from young offenders to forces veterans. The Leisure Box is a converted mill that is now a £4m leisure facility. The Whitehough Outdoor Residential Centre is flourishing. The Community Kitchen in the town centre provides meals, courses and foodbank support.

I spent something like three years at Burnley in the Community and the Academy, and then joined Bury in either 2009 or 2010. Through working with Burnley's Community group I'd got to know the Football League Trust area manager, Dean Grice. He made me aware that the post of head of the Community group at Bury was becoming vacant. Get an application form in, he advised. Life skills. When had I ever had to fill a job application form in during my previous life? Success: I was invited for an interview. Life skills. When had I ever had to attend an interview in my previous life? This was new territory, the comfort zone a distant memory.

At Bury, I sat with the Board of Trustees and did a PowerPoint presentation. There were three of them interviewing me in a small pokey room with barely space to swing a cat. Dean Grice had prepped me and advised me what things to present to them. 'Just tell them what you did at Burnley, they'll love it,' he said. 'Just present yourself properly and you have a great chance.' Presenting myself smartly and well has never been a problem. As a youth it might have been called cockiness. Now, it was called self-assured confidence.

It all came across extremely well. There were some ground-breaking things going on at Burnley that I had contributed to. As well as the football coaching there was dance, cheerleading, fitness, gymnastics, rugby and cricket. All things that I could talk about.

Bingo: the job was mine, thanks to the year I'd spent on the computer course; the year at college had paid off. It showed them all the things I'd done in Burnley schools, many of them new, fresh and innovative. I must have impressed. I was head of Community at Bury Football Club.

There was a lot to get stuck into. The big thing we did, though, was to bring Community and Academy under the same umbrella after a year, so that it was now Community and me running the Academy. In just a few words, the Academy was in a mess: facilities were poor, badly run and with too many young kids just not good enough. A re-structuring programme was implemented. I brought in ex-Burnley men Alan Moore and Vince Overson to work with the players. The pruning that took place was severe, but slowly we raised standards to the extent that we produced players good enough to be sold. And that was the eventual problem once new owners arrived. Me running the Academy worked well.

But it was whilst at Bury that Crohn's reared its ugly head. What's the difference between Crohn's and Colitis? Crohn's can be anywhere in the digestive system from mouth to anus. Colitis is the large intestine; when Colitis knocked me out, the large intestine was eventually removed. So, it wasn't there that I was suffering this time; it was the small intestine. A couple of years into the Bury job and this happens. Now it was my small intestine that was causing me agony.

It wiped me out, left me bedridden, in and out of hospital again, losing three stones in weight as doctors figured out what was going on. They found that the pouch inside me that had been made back in the Colitis days was now riddled with ulcers.

It was back to the diarrhoea, stomach aches and cramps, and irritation. It was back to the unpredictability of the bowel system and being taken short but nothing like as bad as before in that respect. It can be brought on by stress and my job at Bury was most definitely stressful. Board meetings that were tiresome and annoying, club politics, slackness in the club and poor organisation behind the scenes. Finances that were getting worse and worse. It was easy to feel angry at some of the things going on. The Community chairman was supportive and sympathetic as by and large all the work carried on during any absences I had, and these were not as lengthy as previously. Yes, there were hospital stays but there were no operations. The job now was to get food passing through my stomach. With Colitis it had been blood but no pain. Now it was no blood, but just dreadful pain.

It was back to being on steroids and a case of keeping off solid food, and drinking special milkshakes. Ironically a full English is fine, nice and fatty to get through the system. But healthy fruit and veg, nuts and grains were a no. The impact was and is nowhere near as bad as the Colitis I experienced. Today, it affects diet and lifestyle. It's been a couple of years since the last period in hospital but it has put me in the Covid at-risk category.

When the new owner came in, Stewart Day with his business partner Glen Thomas, the academy was seen as a cash cow to help pay off the club's debts. It was getting to the point of daily meetings with all and sundry. Day decided that the Academy should once again be separate from Community so that I was no longer in charge of it. The good work we had done was being undermined. I'm condensing a four-year story into a few brief words but it left me disillusioned and irate.

Day had arrived with a reputation as a property developer from Huddersfield and became chairman in the summer of 2013 after the previous board of directors had resigned following a cash crisis; say what you like about them, they were genuine Shakers to a man. Day maintained that he was only interested in the club. They swept in and took down all the old pictures of Bury heroes and club history and replaced them. History was airbrushed off the walls. With the changes they made and the money they spent it was as if they were saying 'everything so far has been rubbish, but here we are to sort it out'. It wasn't a perfect club, some things were in a mess, but there was a clear bond between club and fans that was now being damaged.

They weren't asset-strippers by any means and there was, maybe – does anyone really know – an intention to boost the club and be a good chairman. But it all went wrong, with reckless spending, high wages and irresponsible financing. Money was spent on huge contracts. After I had gone, for example, Jermaine Pennant arrived. At Bury. As one fan said, fancy Dans in a huge Mercedes, were not what fans wanted, or the club needed.

Anyway, there we were producing good saleable players but it came to the point when Day and Thomas decided that it was time for me to go. I didn't see an awful lot of Day but there were daily meetings with Glen Thomas who was also one of the Trustees of the Community section. I appreciate people who do their job well, and who know what they are doing. Glen Thomas would argue he knew what he was doing. I would disagree. When they took over the Academy bank account it crossed my mind to involve the legal people. As far as I could tell they were then using Academy money to pay higher wages to players. It was simply unsustainable.

He asked to have a one-to-one meeting with me and it was at this meeting that he simply said it was time for me to go. Constructive dismissal went through my mind, but I let it go.

'Go now and we'll pay you for the remaining months of your contract,' he said. Well, that was fair enough by me, and that was the end of Bury Academy, Community and me. A lot of work, a lot of improvements and progress; and then just thanks very much, we don't need you. There was a sense of relief to be rid of the stress and the politics. To this day I never got the money I was owed.

What happened after that was simple enough. The debts were enormous and Day, according to fans, didn't want to be seen as the man that killed Bury Football Club. He eventually sold the club to new owner Steve Dale for £1. Bury Football Club was on the way to going out of business; a sad and sorry tale of football financial mismanagement leaving fans angry and broken-hearted. Ironically, they had won promotion back to Division One in April 2019. It was all for nothing when in August they were expelled from the EFL.

My club car was taken away, of course, when I left, but where one door closes another one opens. My friend who ran a car business helped me out with a motor and asked me why not come into the business with him. After all, I had a lot of contacts and an interest in cars. That was 2014 and it's what I've done ever since, running W18 Cars from our Colne Showrooms with Gary Hunt and Tim Entwistle.

The phone call from Radio 2BR came out of the blue while I was still at Bury. It was a local radio station based in Nelson just along the road from Burnley. 'Come and do some co-commentating and summary work for us.' They covered all the Burnley games and had the rights to them all. Steve Cotterill was Burnley manager and we met many times. The manager I really liked was Owen Coyle, a good man, who would do anything to help you. When he left, he got so much flak for leaving the club in mid-season. 'No loyalty,' said fans. I'm in the group that says loyalty doesn't pay the mortgage and all the other bills. Brian Laws was another one I met. Robbie Blake was scathing about him and his management. Just out of his depth, he described him.

The highlight of working at 2BR was the Wembley day when Burnley beat Sheffield United to win promotion to the Premier League. It will live long in the memories of all Burnley fans, and for sure the directors of the club. Without that win the club faced real financial problems if not administration. Then there was the first home game back in the Premier League. An evening game and what a glorious night. No one could have written a better script. Blakey scored that wonderful goal with a volley from the corner of the box. The goal was sensational; he has scored some stunning goals over the years but this was probably the best. If there's a top ten best ever Burnley goals this is one of them. But when asked what was his best moment, he'll say not this goal, but his first goal for Darlington. Robbie was a wonderful player. He'll confess himself that with more application and dedication he would have played in the highest league all of his career and achieved a lot more. David May once said to him at Burnley, 'What on earth are you doing here? You're better than this.'

I liked it at 2BR but being local radio, their budget was small and they lost the right to cover every Burnley game because they couldn't match the fee the club were now asking; it was one of the reasons they went out of business.

Radio Lancashire got in touch; to say it's more professional does 2BR a disservice because we had some good times there. But Radio Lancashire is the BBC and as soon as you walk into the offices in Blackburn you know it's the BBC. It became too much, though, doing every away game; they were long days from seven in the morning to 11 at night on many occasions. I had a family and a business so now I pick and choose games, getting Glen Little to do some of the away stuff when it's down his end of the country.

And there was another memorable game, the League Cup win away at Chelsea during the Coyle promotion season. The atmosphere, the equalising Akinbiyi goal, the tension in extra time, the penalties, the Jensen saves, he had a season to remember, but above all the 6,000 Burnley fans in the away end. They roared and supported all night, and the scenes at the end were just unforgettable. This was a Championship side beating the megastars at their own ground, totally unexpected. Euphoria, cloud nine all the way home in the early hours of the morning. There was a West End show that was stopped so that the announcement could be made that Burnley had beaten Chelsea.

The 2-0 win over Wigan under Sean Dyche was another great day. It was the home game that sealed promotion again to the Premier League. It was an absolutely glorious game. The football that day has rarely been bettered since.

I still see many of the lads and Stan Ternent. Finalising this book coincided with the 20th anniversary of the promotion game at Scunthorpe in May 2020. Thanks to coronavirus, a big reunion was cancelled. I still listed my best team drawn from all the players I had played with. I played with so many players over the years, or as a 16-year-old was able to watch and learn from senior players up close. My mind still goes back to the 91/92 season when I was there as a 16-year-old and the great thing was it was such an open dressing room, you could be in there with the senior players as you collected boots or cleaned up and they were so good with us. Big John Pender for example, scary bloke, sat there silently, legs crossed, and he'd look at you. You thought 'oh my God' but then he'd give you a little nod of the head to acknowledge you, and you thought this is great. You'd be with John Deary and you'd just want to be in the same midfield. Then there were people like Roger Eli. Great times, loved it.

So, of all the ones to choose from, who were the best, the team players, the influential; which ones would make a final best eleven?

Gareth Taylor: centre forward, Shaggy after the Scooby-Doo character, under-rated, great in the air, big presence, a real moaner if he didn't get the right ball, moaned because he cared, team man, no one to replace him when he was sold. Now on the Manchester City coaching staff responsible for the women's team.

Andy Payton: Payts, striker, poacher, the worst trainer ever, the last pick in any five-a-side, last in and first out, but magic, just the knack of being in the right place at the right time, a winner and so alert to the chances. Bit of a loner. Scoring record speaks for itself. Today private coaching, coach at Burnley College, and all his troubles behind him; a Facebook advocate of the good life and that everyone can, if they really want to, conquer their demons. Andy had a Burnley twang so strong you could set it to brass band music. He lived for scoring goals wherever he was, be it Burnley, Hull City or Celtic, or any of the others he played at. He was one of the reasons we rescued the Waddle season. He had some bad times, did some daft things, and at one point not that long ago, it looked like he was heading just one way, down, one of the many footballers that found life after football too hard to handle. But he stopped drinking and turned his life around. Now, he encourages others to do the same. On Facebook he doesn't miss a chance to remind us all of the goals he scored. And why not? Strikers, like goalkeepers, are a breed apart, living for goals and saves.

David Eyres: wide midfield, didn't play that much with him, but such skill, such a left foot, a winner, hard worker, came to the game late so appreciated everything, give him the ball right, or you got a shouting. Today, an agent.

Kevin Ball: midfield, Bally, the Rottweiler, carried a presence and an aura, respected for everything. Hard as nails. Shake his hand it was like a vice he squeezed so hard. Studs like rugby studs, you heard him coming down the corridor, as hard in training as he was on the field. 'You can't train like a fairy' was his mantra, 'and then go and be hard on the field.' Who will forget his tackle that sent David Dunn six feet up in the air and he just walked straight off? Has held a number of positions at Sunderland including twice caretaker manager, now a club ambassador and legend.

Robbie Blake: midfield, Blakey, a magical player, best player with his back to goal I knew, or free kicks within shooting range, twist and turn like an electric eel, the nearest thing to the great Jimmy McIlroy. Give him the ball and he made things happen. Great favourite with fans, drove Stan Ternent mad. Google *Under the Cosh* on YouTube for some great stories from him. Today coach at Bognor Regis.

Glen Little: wide midfield, another Blakey, but in his case because he resembled Blakey from *On the Buses.* Devoted a whole chapter to him such was his importance and place. Another poor trainer, another victim of Stan's wrath, but another that made things happen. Some wonderful individual goals. Today does some commentary and after-dinner work.

Mitchell Thomas: defender, Bruno, don't ask me why, maybe a resemblance to Frank Bruno in physique and power. Quiet, never said much off the pitch, but so good at talking you through the game. Calm and composed. Such a high-level player that Stan persuaded to sign, when he did speak you listened. Could play anywhere along the back four. When last I heard, he was an agent.

Steve Davis: defender, Skip, such a good player but as much a captain off the field as on it. A good go-between between us and Stan. Led by example on the pitch, so powerful, so good at coming up into the box, scored so many goals, so strong in the air. We had several captains on the pitch so he didn't need to be vocal. Today a scout for Everton.

Jamie Hoyland: defender, just Jamie, I leaned such a lot from him. A Prem player with Sheffield United so great experience, solid and dependable. Today chief scout at Everton. Loves his dogs.

Gary Parkinson: defender, Tight Arse we called him, great for banter, could give it and take it, great for a dressing room, never a hoofer, always cultured. A winning goal at Wembley in a Burnley play-off final against Stockport. Today, sadly, suffering from locked-in syndrome.

Marlon Beresford: goalkeeper, Mungo, don't ask me why. Just a good keeper, great shot-stopper, we made fun of his kicking but he commanded his area. Last heard of in Abu Dhabi coaching.

Special mentions for Andy Cooke, always gave 100 per cent, we were such good pals and still are; Chris Brass and John Mullin because we were young lads together and had such good times from the age of just 16. Great memories and I sometimes think those very early apprentice years were the best times I had.

Manager: Stan of course. He took a club that was in a dire state both on and off the field and got to grips with it. You either shaped up or shipped out. He got together a team of winners and leaders, so the dressing room sorted itself out. He inspired a real sense of togetherness.

Plenty of stories in the book about his 'mad' side when fists would swing. But he had your back, and if you needed it you got the right medical treatment. Today retired and part of a group in Burnley that consists of other ex-players and managers in the town: Colin Waldron, Paul Fletcher, Jim Thomson, Frank Casper, Brian Flynn. All of them prime contenders for lead roles in any remake of *Last of the Summer Wine.* When I was playing, he pushed my buttons, we had face-to-face rows, we went nose-to-nose once, but he knew I wouldn't sulk and would try to prove him wrong.

I look back and when he was telling me I wasn't mentally or physically right, and I thought he was an idiot, he was right and I was the idiot.

I'll think about things sometimes. Lenny Johnrose finished his book about his career and his battles with Motor Neurone. I've ordered one. He was the first person I came across who told Stan Ternent to fuck off. He was frightened of no one. Astonishingly it was during a game. Stan was on the touchline bellowing at Lenny, do this, do that, and Lenny was either ignoring him or just not hearing him. More likely just ignoring him. Stan was going spare and collared me. Tell Lenny, tell Lenny, do this do that. I passed the messages on. Lenny looked at me.

'Tell 'im to fuck off, tell 'im to fuck off.'

I looked at him. 'Yer what, tell 'im what?'

'Yeh tell 'im. Tell 'im to fuck off.'

Next chance I got by the touchline I relayed the message. 'Lenny says you can fuck off.'

Stan stared at me then stared over at Lenny, some distance away. And that was the end of that. Lenny carried on playing his game. Stan gave up bellowing at him.

He used to wear an earring, Lenny that is, not Stan, and Stan had a thing about footballers with earrings. He used to come in it to training.

'Take that earring out,' said Stan in the changing rooms. Lenny told him no so Stan told him to take it out or leave. Lenny walked out and left. We watched all of this and decided that maybe we too should all wear an earring. Then we could walk out and have a day off.

But that was Lenny. If you wanted to take someone out of a game, you asked Lenny to do it. Stood up to anybody and anything and that's how he tackled Motor Neurone, head on. 'Tell it to fuck off.' That's how he dealt with it.

As we complete things, the club was embroiled in take-over bids. Americans versus Egyptians. Nobody really knew what was going on outside the boardroom. Chairman Mike Garlick was tight-lipped; it was Operation Rhubarb. Keep fans in the dark. Suddenly there was a rush of information in the media when things began to come to light. ALK was the American group. Mohamed el Kashashy fronted the Egyptian offer that was allegedly for £200m. Nobody knew what to believe. Fans were divided; did they really want outside investors in this little town club that so far had been run by local men? How would it change things? Were they genuine football people? The Americans seemed genuine but there was real suspicion about the Egyptian and his UK lawyer. People thought back to the Shackleton saga over 20 years earlier. Who was this Egyptian, based in Dubai; where would this £200m come from? Did it really exist? A Sunday newspaper piece said he was worth over £9bn. Eyes popped wide open. And then all went quiet again.

When it re-appeared, the American group said that talks were in a 'happy place'. They must have been watching Jordan North.

The old Burnley chairman of the 60s and 70s, Bob Lord, would be turning in his grave at the thought. A recent biography of him tells his story and one of the stands at Burnley is named after him. Old Bob thought the world ended at Padiham just outside Burnley. An Egyptian owning Burnley; his chin would hit the floor. Cantankerous he may have been but he predicted so much of what is going on in football today; European competitions, professional referees, dominant city clubs, TV ruling the game.

My Crohn's is still there. It's not going to go away, but you learn to manage it with medication and knowing what is right for your body. I still have occasional days in hospital. My immune system puts me at risk, so when coronvirus struck in 2020, that was me out of action for the required 12 weeks in isolation at home. Don't leave the house, the golden rule. We set up a gym in the garage; stuck at home I might have been, but no reason why I shouldn't try to keep fit. The car dealership in Colne was on hold. Click and collect became the new slogan. As we finish off the book, it is now open again. W18 we called it: W for Weller of course and 18 because that was my number.

I had great times playing, loved the life, got over Colitis, missed out on a move to West Ham but have never dwelt too much on that. What would be the point? You deal with life; you take what comes and get round it. Life was good as a footballer and despite the Crohn's that still puts me in hospital from time to time, I just get on with it.

As a footballer, along with the illness and the bad times, I had the best of times; so not such a bad life, was it? What more can you ask?